# THE LIVES OF THE GREEK POETS

# THE LIVES
# OF THE
# GREEK POETS

## Mary R. Lefkowitz

The Johns Hopkins University Press

Baltimore, Maryland

© 1981 by Mary R. Lefkowitz

First published in Great Britain in 1981 by
Gerald Duckworth & Co. Ltd.

First published in the United States of America in 1981 by
The Johns Hopkins University Press
Baltimore, Maryland 21218.

ISBN 0–8018–2748–5
LC 81–83450

Filmset in Monophoto Baskerville by
Latimer Trend & Company Ltd, Plymouth
Printed in Great Britain by
Redwood Burn Ltd,
Trowbridge, Wiltshire

# Contents

For
Hugh Lloyd-Jones

# Introduction

If Greek historical writing were as much like ours as we sometimes think, it would be possible to write for Greek poets the
careful explanatory biographies that are now being written for
nineteenth-century authors. We would know what the poets
read and studied, and how they learned to compose verse; what
their families were like, where they travelled and when. We
would be able to judge with some accuracy why they wrote
what they did, and to account for many idiosyncrasies of style.
But the uncomfortable truth is that virtually nothing of the
sort can be known about the lives of the Greek poets. There are
no diaries to read, no caches of letters to discover in hidden
attics; no contemporary newspapers; or registers of births and
deaths. Not only were there no such records; no one thought it
worthwhile to keep them. A general like Alexander might
attract a Callisthenes, but no ancient poet had a Boswell.

Not that all the information in the Lives seems implausible;
many details sound as if they had some historical value, for
example, that Aeschylus fought at Marathon, or that Sophocles was one of the ten elected generals. Occasionally a contemporary independent source will offer confirmation at least of
probability: an inscription records that Sophocles of Colonus
served as Hellenotamias in 443/2; according to Herodotus,
Aeschylus' brother Cynegirus was killed at Marathon. It is
another question how to use such information: should we
deduce, along with ancient biographers, that Sophocles'
*Antigone* was written immediately after his service as general,
or that Aeschylus fought at Salamis as well because he describes the battle in the *Persae*? If we had the poet's own mem-
oirs or correspondence we could perhaps establish some direct
connection; without them, we must inevitably rely upon hypothesis.

Far more numerous are details that seem valuable but cannot be confirmed by any contemporary sources: thus Philochorus said that Euripides wrote his dramas in a cave near the sea at Salamis. Aulus Gellius, centuries later, saw the cave, but no fifth-century writer says anything about it. The story seems to fit in with Aristophanes' characterisation of Euripides as an anti-social and abstracted philosopher who prays to his own gods (*Ran.* 892f.), but how reliable a source is Aristophanes, who was not a historian but a comic poet?

Other anecdotes have seemed convincing because they bear a close relation to what a poet says about himself. Until very recently no one questioned statements in the ancient commentaries that Pindar was misunderstood by his audiences and had problems with rival poets, because the 'I' in the odes speaks of problems of composing his songs and insists on his superiority to others. Instead of noting that archaic poets regularly make such claims to establish their authority, ancient scholars imagined circumstances that would have occasioned the poets' assertions and complaints. The notion of the isolated poet has had a lingering appeal, not least because many people imagine themselves to be dishonoured prophets; even Hitler claimed early in his career that his true excellence would be appreciated only by succeeding generations.

Recent work has shown that most of the material in the lives of some poets, or some of the material in the lives of all poets, is basically fictional. But no one has yet tried to discuss the lives of all the important poets, or to distinguish differences in the biographer's purposes and the interests of their audiences. In making this first attempt, I hope to show that virtually all the material in all the lives is fiction, and that only certain factual information is likely to have survived, and then usually because the poet himself provided it for a different purpose. If I have sometimes been too sceptical, it is in the hope of offering a corrective to the too eager credulity of the past.

I will contend that ancient biographers took most of their information about poets from the poets' own works. Their starting premise was not dissimilar from that of some contemporary psychologists: that every creative act must have grounding in a particular experience. But where psychologists would rely on interviews or diaries, ancient biographers turned directly to the poems themselves; even the chorus of a drama, speaking generally, rather than in their dramatic persona, might seem to represent the poet; the smallest hints of personality in conventional statements could be developed into character traits. The process of 'recovery' of biographical information thus required imagination, but within the limitations set by their audiences' expectations: poets (partly because they themselves claim superiority) should have lives like those of heroes, involving confrontations, requiring isolation and, often, violent deaths; but unlike heroes, poets could be portrayed as ordinary or even as foolish men, so that their creativity would not seem mysterious or even particularly difficult.

I hope that by presenting for the first time some of the more influential lives in English, readers will get an immediate impression of their quality. In contrast to modern practice, ancient biographers rarely indicate their sources in direct quotation. Occasionally we can see a direct relation between what a poet has written and an event in his Life: Euripides, for example, is said to have complained of his wife's unfaithfulness in a verse that paraphrases a line in his *Electra*. But in most cases the process of transformation is more elaborate. More often than might be imagined, the biographers drew on caricatures of poets in comedy; the comic poets in turn started from the premise that the man was his work, that is, if Euripides wrote the *Hippolytus*, he approved of women like Phaedra, and that women hated him because he had revealed their secrets in his dramas. Removed from their context and phrased in colourless language, summaries of comic verse and plot come to resemble information obtained from more factual sources, especially if the anecdotes are arranged together by topic, and no reference is made to their original provenience.

How seriously the Lives were meant to be taken is another question; in the absence of statements of intent, it is usually impossible to distinguish between the results of naïveté and deceit. If biographies were meant to be representational, rather than historical in our sense of the word, it would suffice to present any material so long as it seemed to express something characteristic. Comparison reveals certain general trends:

increasing maliciousness; a tendency to omit details rather than merely to summarise them. A biographer like Satyrus in the third century makes it clear that he realises that some of his biographical interpretations of Euripides' verse are purely entertaining; he indicates that some of his information comes from Aristophanes. But at other times he records without raising questions material obtained by identical means.

Much has been made in recent years of Sophocles' piety, Euripides' perversity, Callimachus' resentment of Apollonius. If this book can establish that these stories can be disregarded as popular fiction, some literary history will need to be re-written, so that it starts not with the poets' biographies, but with the poems themselves. Once studies are undertaken on these new premises, it may appear that of the three tragedians, Sophocles is the boldest innovator, both in technique and his vision of human experience, that Euripides is self-consciously archaic and that Callimachus and Apollonius had very similar aims, tastes and methods.

Rather than describe schematically the different ways in which biographers adapt their sources, I have discussed the biography of each author separately, in chronological order. This is the most convenient arrangement for readers who want to know about a particular author; it also helps to show how the character of each poet's works have made his Life develop differently. The Life will bear closer relation to the poetry if the poet has occasion to speak about himself or to describe poets in his narrative; the biography will sound proportionately more like caricature if the biographers have had access to characterisations of the poet in comedy. In some cases, such as Euripides' Life, it is possible to trace how fifth-century verse is transformed into anecdotes over the centuries; in other cases, where more original source material is lost, one can trace the transformation only partially, and by analogy.

Ancient biographies preserve no records of working arrangements. They mention only obvious correspondences and debts, but not what a poet heard or read. Poems are composed instantaneously or are recited when already completed; if a poet is seen in the process of working, it is in isolation, like Euripides in his cave by the sea. An ancient biographer might judge from this book that I had studied with Wilamowitz, even though he died four years before I was born, or with Jacoby, whom I never met. He would not see that I first became interested in the biographical tradition when I was working on the poetry of Pindar and knew how his original intentions, more than that of any poet, had been misunderstood because scholars had based their interpretations on ancient information about his life.

Most particularly ancient biographers would find no visible record in this book of help from friends, especially Sir Ronald Syme, for consistent encouragement over many years, and Colin Macleod, who urged me to write the book, provided much of the information in it, and made improvements throughout; or Frederick Williams, for raising the standard of verbal accuracy throughout. Nor would biographers have any means of discovering how much I am indebted to the generosity and support of several institutions: Wellesley College, The National Endowment for the Humanities and St. Hilda's College, Oxford.

# CHAPTER ONE

# Hesiod

Homer says nothing in his poems about his family or his background, but Hesiod tells us about his father, his brother, and his own credentials as a poet. The information emerges in context, not as autobiography (in the contemporary sense) but as documentation of the major themes of his poems. The *Works and Days* is addressed to his brother Perses, who he says has cheated the poet of his property (37ff.); as such Perses is an ideal person to whom to address an epic about the need for justice and hard work in human life. The information about his father is presented as an example of how men earn a living by merchant shipping: Hesiod and Perses' father came by ship to Ascra near Mt. Helicon in Boeotia from Cyme in Aeolia (633–40). Hesiod gives the story dramatic emphasis: his father did not flee 'luxury, wealth, and happiness, but evil poverty, which Zeus gives to men'; Ascra is 'bad in winter, harsh in summer, no good at any time'. The details about climate sound authentic, but may be exaggerated: Plutarch confirms that Ascra gets winter winds and no summer breezes, but still in his day he thought the town had a climate relatively pleasant for that part of the world (fr. 82 Sandbach).[1]

A few lines later (646ff.) Hesiod tells us that he won a prize for his song in Euboea. Again he provides this information about himself to support a claim: he knows about the sea, seafaring and ships, even though he himself has never made a voyage longer than across the narrow strait between Aulis and Chalcis in Euboea. The reason he can make such a claim is that he is a prize-winning poet, to whom the Muses have taught a song

---

[1] West 1980, 317; cf. Archilochus' unkind remarks about Thasos, fr. 22 W. Richardson 1979, 171 suggests that the lines reflect, 'with an exile's typical nostalgia', Hesiod's *father's* opinion of his new home.

'too vast to be described' (*athesphaton hymnon*, 662). Details
about the contest provide validation; 'contests in honour of
warlike Amphidamas, many contests planned and set up by
his sons, where I boast that I won by my song and brought home
a tripod with handles' (654–7). He does not offer more information about himself, such as his parents' names, or how
old he was when he won the contest, because that would not
help explain to Perses (or the rest of his audience) why they
ought to trust his advice about seafaring.

Hesiod also describes his professional credentials at the beginning of the *Theogony* (22ff.), but here, since his poem is about
the gods, he does not talk about prizes awarded in a contest
judged by men, but about a visitation from the Muses. The
Muses came to him while he was pasturing his sheep and spoke
to him 'first of all'; they gave him a laurel branch and a 'sacred
voice' (*thespin audēn*) (31) to 'sing what will be and what was
before, and the race of the gods, and first and last of themselves'
(33–4). The goddesses point out how their knowledge and
power of speech set them apart from the 'shepherds of the
wilderness, evil disgraces, mere bellies' (26);[2] their gift to
Hesiod of laurel (30) marks him also as speaker and singer,
distinct from the rest.[3] Unlike the other shepherds who live in
the wilderness and think only of eating, the poet will not deal
with present concerns but with the future, the past and the
race of the gods. He lends excitement to his account by quoting
the words the Muses spoke to him; he offers no specific information about time or his reaction to what the Muses told
him, because he does not wish to talk about himself so much
as to establish his poetic authority.

Because Hesiod offers in his first-person statements only a
professional autobiography, his biographers were compelled
to seek elsewhere the kind of information that they needed for

---

[2] On the significance of *gasteres*, see Svenbro 1976, 50–9; Kambylis 1965,
62. According to Timaeus (*FGrHist* 566F4/D.L. 1 114), Epimenides himself
was never seen to eat because he had received special food from the Muses
(*FGrHist* 457T1); Jacoby compares Pythagoras' diet.

[3] On Hesiod's encounter with the Muses, see West 1978, 163–4; Nagy 1979,
263–4; Vernant 1974, 1 85.

their Lives. The poems themselves provided clues. The Muses' visitation could have been seen as having conferred on him a hero's status; by the fifth century he was believed to have died in a manner divinely ordained, fulfilling the prediction of an oracle. Thucydides alludes to Hesiod's death, when describing a military expedition: the army camped in the sanctuary of Nemean Zeus, 'where Hesiod the poet is said to have died at the hands of local people, after he had received an oracle that he would die in Nemea' (3.95–3.96.1).[4] The story illustrates briefly the difficulty of interpreting oracles.[5] Homer also was said to have died because he could not answer a riddle; Heraclitus used the story to illustrate 'that men are deceived in respect to knowledge of the apparent, like Homer, who was the wisest of all Greeks' (22B56 DK). Such a death removes all possibility of envy, human or divine, incurred in life by the poet as the result of his superior knowledge.[6]

An epigram attributed to Pindar (*EG* 428ff.) implies that in the fifth century also there was a legend that Hesiod had lived a second life:[7] 'Hail, you who were twice a young man, and twice encountered a tomb, Hesiod, who set the standard among men for wisdom.' Aristotle (fr. 565 Rose) explained that Hesiod had bypassed old age; the proverb 'a Hesiodic old age' in the Suda is glossed as extraordinary longevity. Neither source says how he managed it, but Epimenides, who imitated Hesiod in proclaiming 'Cretans are always liars, foul beasts, idle bellies' (3B1 DK), fell asleep for fifty-seven years while pasturing his sheep, and returned to become a prophet (3A1 DK = *FGrHist*

---

[4] Cf. Friedel 1879, 236n.1. Farnell 1896, 1 170w lists cults of Zeus Nemeios also in Argos and Caria; the site of Oenoe has not been identified, Stillwell 1976, s.v. W. Locris.

[5] For the *topos* of mistaking the site of death, cf. Cambyses (Hdt. 3.64.3–5), Epaminondas (Suda, s.v.), Hannibal (Paus. 8.11.10–11), and Henry IV's Jerusalem chamber; Fontenrose 1978, 59–60.

[6] Lefkowitz 1979, 202; Chroust 1973, 178–81. The notion of illustrative death was established by the fourth century; cf. how at the end of Plato's *Phaedo* the manner of Socrates' death portrays his doctrine of the immortality of the soul, not the actual symptoms of hemlock poisoning; Gill 1973, 25–8.

[7] On the epigram, McKay 1959, 1–5; Brelich 1958, 321

457T1 = Theopompus *FGrHist* 115F67).[8] Epimenides also claimed to have 'come back to life many times'. A return from death, like an extraordinarily long life, is a sign of heroic status.[9] And either provides a convenient means of dealing with traditional chronologies that made Hesiod older than Homer.

A line in the *Works and Days* provided material for a legend about the circumstances of the poet's death; there the poet states: 'I would not be a just man (*dikaios*) among men, nor would my son, since an evil man is just, if the more unjust man can have a greater justice; but this I expect that wise Zeus will not bring to pass' (270–4). According to the fourth-century sophist Alcidamas, Hesiod was murdered by two brothers because he had seduced their sister; the poet's body was thrown in the sea, but brought back to land by dolphins during a local festival of Ariadne (*Cert.* 14).[10] This evidence of divine favour caused the Locrians to lament and bury Hesiod. The brothers fled by ship, only to be struck by Zeus' lightning bolt. The story neatly confirms Hesiod's prediction: he cannot be called a just man, and neither can his son, because he is by definition not *dikaios* since he is illegitimate;[11] Zeus' justice prevails in the end over the murderers. Aristotle (fr. 75 Rose) and Philochorus (*FGrHist* 328F213) record an elaboration of the story that explains the continuation of literary tradition: the son

[8] On Hesiod's longevity, Huxley 1974, 207. Cf. the prophet Tiresias, who according to Hesiod (fr. 276 MW) lived through seven generations. Wilamowitz 1916, 407n.2 suggests instead that the poet's second youth came through his son Stesichorus; but cf. the rationalisation in the epitaph in Ps.Plu., *Vit. Hom.* p. 23 Wil/p. 241 Allen, which gives Homer a second life through his poetry, *phthimenos d'eti pollon agēros*.

[9] See esp. Scodel 301–20. Cf. how Callimachus says he hopes to avoid old age by becoming a cricket (fr. 1.29ff.): Pfeiffer 1960, 116 26; cf. Anacreontea 34.15; Macleod 1976, 41 2.

[10] Cf. Plu., *Mor.* 162e. Nilsson 1906, 383–4 suggests that the story of Hesiod's death is an aetiological myth for the ritual, which may have involved mourning and a representation of hanging, like the festival of Ariadne at Crete; cf. Burkert 1972, 225–6.

[11] *dikaios* connotes legitimacy in Soph., *Ajax* 547; cf. Arist., *Hist. An.* 586a13; *Pol.* 1262a24.

born to the girl Hesiod raped was Stesichorus, the next important author of long poems about myth.[12]

Alcidamas also described the games at Chalcis as a contest specifically between Hesiod and *Homer* (*Cert.* 588). Hesiod himself had written about a contest between the prophets Calchas and Mopsus; Calchas lost and died soon afterwards of grief (*Melamp.* fr. 278, 279 MW).[13] In Alcidamas' story Hesiod wins as in the *Works and Days*, but because of what he says rather than how he says it. Homer's technical skill proves superior, because he can easily improvise verses in response to Hesiod's challenges; Alcidamas approved of improvisation in oratory.[14] But Hesiod wins because his poetry concerns the works of peacetime. The decision has an ethical purpose; in Aristophanes' *Peace* Trygaeus helps establish peace by rejecting the son of the general Lamachus who sings only of war in a contest with another boy (1288); Plato allows Homer's poetry no place in his rationally ordered Utopia (*Resp.* 606e–607a).[15] Regarding Hesiod as a competitor of Homer makes the two poets equal in importance,[16] though the nature of his victory indicates that his work is to be valued more for its content than its style.

The fourth-century historian Ephorus of Cyme expressed Hesiod's importance in a genealogy that made him Homer's

---

[12] By a similar process, Hesiod's description of the rulers of the *polis* (*Op.* 264) became the basis of Aristotle's anecdote about the Thespians disapproving of trades and agriculture; Huxley 1974, 208–9.

[13] See esp. Loeffler 1963, 48–9. Cf. also the contest between Lesches (*Little Iliad*) and Arctinus (*Sack of Troy*), according to Phanias (fr. 32, 33 Wehrli); Podlecki 1969, 120. Heraclitus thought of Homer and Hesiod as competing in contests (22B42 DK).

[14] On Alcidamas' rhetorical theory, see bibliography in Lefkowitz 1978, 468n.27; also West 1978, 319; Richardson 1981, 5–6. On improvisation in epic, see Willcock 1977, 53.

[15] Cf. also Anacreontic 2.22; Ar., *Ran.* 1032–6; Plu., *Mor.* 223a; Richardson 1981, 2–3; Wilamowitz 1916, 404.

[16] Making the two poets competitors required changing traditional chronology. Most authors made Homer older; Aristotle (fr. 565 Rose), for example, told how Homer won a contest not against Hesiod but Syagrus, author of another epic about the Trojan war; Huxley 1974, 208; Jacoby on Philochorus *FGrHist* 328F213. Hesiod is older according to the Parian Marble, *FGrHist* 239A28, 27; Homer, in (e.g.) Xenophanes 11B13 DK; Jacoby IIBD 667ff. Both traditions are reported in *Cert.* 4.

cousin (*FGrHist* 70F1, cf. *Cert.* 4). He found in the poetry also indication of names of the poet's parents: because he addresses Perses as 'of illustrious family' (*dion genos*, *Erg.* 299), his father's name is Dios; because he refers in both poems to his vast knowledge, his mother's name is Pycimede ('close intelligence').[17] That his father left Cyme 'not for merchant trade but because he killed a kinsman' (*FGrHist* F100) helps to account for the poet's interest in justice. It is impossible to tell from the excerpts in which Ephorus is quoted how he meant these anecdotes to be taken; like Alcidamas' story of his death, Ephorus appears to endow Hesiod with a hero's ambivalent status, combining indications of divine support with events of violence. Ephorus makes Hesiod's father a murderer (*Cert.* 14); Alcidamas makes the poet's murderers sons of Phegeus, whose two other sons murdered the hero Alcmeon, and were themselves killed by Alcmeon's two sons (Apollod. 3.7.4).

New details of Hesiod's biography were still being developed in the third century; as in the case of other myths, motivations and names could be changed, and new characters added, so long as the basic outline of the plot was preserved. The Alexandrian poet Eratosthenes wrote an epic about Hesiod (fr. 19 Powell) that vindicated the poet's honour.[18] In his poem the girl's seducer was not Hesiod but Demodes, a travelling companion of Hesiod; both men were killed by the girl's brothers.[19] The poet's murderers were recognised by his dog, and then sacrificed by Eurycles the seer to the god of hospitality.[20] Like his contemporaries Callimachus and Apollonius, Eratosthenes

---

[17] On Dios, West 1978, 232. Commentators on *Op.* 271 also suggested the appropriate names Mnasiepes and Archiepes for his son (p. 4 above); cf. the names of Homer's family (p. 13 below). Hermesianax, perhaps not seriously, says Eoie was Hesiod's beloved, and the model for others 'like her' (*ēoiē*; fr. 7.21 Powell); cf. Bell 1978, 60.

[18] Probably the *Anterinys*; Fraser 1972, II 902n.200. On its contents, see Hiller 1872, 80–93. Euphorion of Chalcis also wrote a poem on Hesiod, but we have no indication of its contents.

[19] Hiller 1872, 90–1; cf. Pollux 5.42; Plu., *Mor.* 949e, 162d–f.

[20] Since there is only one *theos xenios*, Zeus, were the plural 'gods of hospitality' in *Cert.* 14 incorrectly inferred from a Homeric allusion in Eratosthenes' text, like *Zeus kai athanatoi alloi* (*Il.* 13.818)? For cases where *theoi* means Zeus, see Fraenkel 1950, II 182; Nägelsbach 1884, 121–2.

wrote about events in a manner that emphasises their effect on the lives of all involved and limits the role of divine intervention.[21] A dog loyal to his master replaces the miraculous dolphins;[22] the seer is called by a proverbial name that connotes predicting trouble for oneself;[23] human sacrifice replaces Zeus' lightning bolt;[24] the sister hangs herself; her brothers are sons of Ganyctor, himself the son of the Amphidamas in whose honour the contest at Chalcis was held (fr. 21 Powell, *Cert.* 14).

By the second century A.D. the biographical traditions about Hesiod's life appear to have been established. The anonymous author of the treatise *On Homer and Hesiod, their origin and their contest*, had no new anecdotes to add.[25] Of the various accounts, he preferred a version of Hesiod's genealogy that stressed the poet's divine origin: he was descended on his father's side from Linos, son of Apollo, and from Orpheus; his mother Pycimede was Apollo's daughter (*Cert.* 4). He reports both Alcidamas' and Eratosthenes' versions of Hesiod's death (*Cert.* 14) without attempting to reconcile the contradictions.[26] In his treatise the contest is followed first by the death of Hesiod, then of Homer. He provides an epigram for the dedication of Hesiod's tripod, and an epitaph for Hesiod's death. But he leaves the impression that Hesiod is the lesser of the two poets because he gives pro-

---

[21] Cf. Callim., *Cer.* 94–110, esp. Erysichthon, who 'ate the mongoose (? *malouris*, Gow 1967, 195–7; cf. Benton 1969, 262) at which the little mice trembled'. In Ap. Rhod. 1 311–16, as Jason departs, the priestess Iphis 'is left there on the side of the road, as the old are by the young'.

[22] On the omission of the dolphins in Eratosthenes, Nilsson 1906, 383n. Plutarch combines both accounts, unrealistically, in *Mor.* 984d. Cf. Eratosthenes' story of Eupolis' loyal dog (p. 115 below); in his *Erigone* (fr. 22–7 Powell) Icarius' dog leads his daughter to her father's body, identifies his murderers, and the girl hangs herself; Hiller 1872, 95–7; Fraser 1972, II 903n.202; for the story, schol. *Il.* 10.29. The dog's name in Apollod. 3.14.7 is Maera; cf. Eratosthenes fr. 16.7 Powell. But according to Pollux 5.42, it is Sirius.

[23] Cf. schol. Pl., *Soph.* 252c, p. 44 Greene; cf. Wilamowitz 1916, 408n.2.

[24] Cf. Epimenides' sacrifice of two young men to remove blood guilt, 3A1.16–19 DK/Neanthes *FGrHist* 84F16. For other examples, Burkert 1972, 11n.10; also Leos' daughters, Paus. 1.5.2, Fontenrose 1978, L 44; Erechtheus' daughters, Philochorus *FGrHist* 328F85, Fontenrose 1978, L 32, Apollod. 3.15.4, Eur. fr. 50, 65.65–72 Austin.

[25] On sources, West 1967, 444–50; translation by Evelyn-White 1914.

[26] Cf. also Paus. 9.38.5.

portionately more space to Homer. At the beginning of his treatise he considers in detail the different traditions about Homer's genealogy; then after Hesiod's death he recounts at length where Homer went and what he wrote before he died. In the competition Homer easily deals with all challenges set by Hesiod.

The author of this treatise, and thus presumably his audience, appears to have been interested particularly in Hesiod's date, background, death and memorials.[27] He notes when Homer wrote the *Margites*, *Odyssey* and certain epigrams, but he makes no reference to Hesiod's encounter with the Muses. Perhaps he does not wish to refer to the occasion for the composition of the *Theogony*, because the authenticity of the *Theogony* had been questioned, at least by his contemporaries in Boeotia.[28] Pausanias records that natives of the region near Mt. Helicon claimed that Hesiod wrote only the *Works and Days*, starting with the passage about the Strifes (9.38.4). Plutarch, another native Boeotian, also seems to have excluded the first ten lines of the poem in his edition of the text (*Mor.* 736e).[29] Plutarch seems interested in emphasising the poet's moral purpose; he also omits other lines where Zeus is called into question as unworthy of Hesiod's views of justice (fr. 38 Sandbach).[30] The story of the poet's death had particular appeal for him, especially in versions that demonstrated the poet's innocence (*Mor.* 162e, 984d; fr. 82). Pausanias too devotes twice as much space to Hesiod's death as to his life and works.

Plutarch's views about Hesiod's date[31] caused him to remove from his text as 'nonsense' Hesiod's account of the contest at Chalcis and the dedication of his tripod (fr. 85 Sandbach). Again Plutarch seems to be commenting not so much on what

[27] It is misleading to think of him simply as a 'compiler'; cf. Wilamowitz 1916, 400; West 1961, 449. Cf. pp. 18–19 below.

[28] On Alexandrian criticism of Hesiod's text, West 1978, 65–6.

[29] See fr. 25 Sandbach. For Plutarch's knowledge of Boeotia, cf. also fr. 34, 71; West 1978, 67n.4. Cf. also Plutarch's account of the festival of Agrionia, *Mor.* 291a; Russell 1973, 42.

[30] Russell 1973, 50–1.

[31] Problems with chronology are emphasised by Tzetzes, who relied on Proclus, who in turn used Plutarch's commentary on Hesiod's text; West 1978, 68; Wilamowitz 1916, 405.

Hesiod himself says as on what ancient critics thought about the passage. The lines had long been regarded as evidence for the contest between Hesiod and Homer; if one did not think that the two poets were contemporaries, the notion of their contest and Hesiod's text along with it could be considered fictions dating from the fourth century B.C.[32] As a result, and most ironically, scholarship in later antiquity chose to exclude the poet's own testimony from his biography.

Scholarly doubts about the biography survive in the *Vita* which serves as a preface to John Tzetzes' twelfth-century edition of Hesiod.[33] He accepts as historical that Hesiod was the son of Dios and Pycimede and that he herded sheep on Mount Helicon, since many other ancient authors had practical professions. But he can understand only as allegory the story that nine women came and gave the poet laurel branches. The idea that the poet saw them in a vision at least had analogues in Callimachus' dream that he was taken from Cyrene to Mt. Helicon for instruction (*Aet.* 2) and in Ennius' story of how he was taught by Homer's shade (*Ann.* fr. 6 Vahlen).[34] Tzetzes puts the encounter with the Muses early in his *Vita*; Hesiod himself did not say how old he was, but Callimachus says that he had his dream about the Muses when he was first getting a beard (schol. fr. 2.18 p. 11 Pf).[35] Then, like Plutarch, Tzetzes questions the authenticity of the contest, because he thinks Homer older than Hesiod, and rejects narrative fictions invented to resolve it, such as the notion of a second, younger Homer.[36]

Tzetzes follows Aristotle's account of Hesiod's death, which makes the poet father of Stesichorus (fr. 75 Rose; pp. 4–5 above),

---

[32] Cf. also *Mor.* 153f.; West 1978, 68, 319.

[33] On Tzetzes, West 1978, 69–70.

[34] Fronto, writing to M. Aurelius in the second century A.D., speaks of Hesiod's being asleep; see schol. Callim., *Aet.* 1.2 Pf; Kambylis 1965, 55–60.

[35] Cf. Quint. Smyrn. 12.309. Also the boy Archilochus' encounter with the Muses: Lefkowitz 1976, 183–4; the boy Pindar falling asleep and awakening with his mouth full of honey: Lefkowitz 1975, 73–4 and p. 59 below; Kambylis 1965, 94–103.

[36] Doppelgänger also provided a convenient means of solving textual problems; Lefkowitz 1976, 180. Epimenides' longevity (pp. 3–4 n.8 above) helped reconcile discrepant dates assigned to him.

but makes no mention of traditions that exonerate the poet
(p. 6 above). Like Pausanias and the author of the treatise
about the contest, he concludes his biography by citing an
anonymous epigram about the places where he was born and
died which mentions his poetic wisdom. To this he adds a
second epitaph, the elegiac couplet attributed to Pindar
(*EG* 428, p. 3 above), which claims that the poet was young
twice and buried twice. Tzetzes does not comment on the
implication in the couplet that Hesiod had a second life; in the
tradition he was following, as in epigrams and in Diogenes
Laertius' biographies, death assumes a curious priority in
representing the significance of a man's life and works.[37] In an
epigram by the third-century poet Alcaeus of Messene (*EG*
3230ff.), the sweetness of Hesiod's song is represented in the
circumstances of his burial: the Muses wash his corpse and
shepherds sprinkle it with milk and honey.[38] Like the bones of
the heroes Orestes and Theseus, Hesiod's remains were believed to have beneficial powers.[39] The Delphic oracle ordered
that his bones be brought from Locris to Orchomenus in
Boeotia in order to cure a plague; the bones were still being
shown to visitors in the second century A.D. (Plu., fr. 82 Sand-
bach/*Mor.* 162c).[40]

In its final form Hesiod's biography seems curiously remote
from the confident autobiographical statements in his poems,
with their emphasis on his professional skill and knowledge.
In the *Theogony* he speaks about what the Muses said to him,
but in his biographies contact with divinity is represented by
physical means, divine recognition, the magical powers of his
remains. Increasing importance is attached to what he does not

[37] On the Hellenistic practice of writing fictitious epigrams about particularly appropriate deaths (e.g. Leonidas *EG* 2424ff., 2430ff.), Wehrli 1973,
194; Wehrli 1974, 105–6. On Diogenes' interest in death scenes, esp. in
epigrams, Mejer 1978, 32, 37, 49–50; Momigliano 1971, 72.

[38] Gabathuler 1937, 91–2; cf. 73 GP.

[39] On the heroes, Hdt. 1.67.2–4; Fontenrose 1978, 74–5, Q 89, 80, 164,
and cf. Rhesus' bones, Q 188.

[40] According to Paus. 9.83.3, the oracle said a crow would lead them to the
site where the bones were hidden; Fontenrose 1978, L 42. In myth the bird
represents Apollo; ibid. Q 191. Cf. also the story of Archilochus' death;
Lefkowitz 1976, 184; Nagy 1979, 301–2; p. 29 below.

mention, the names of his father and of his mother, the identity
of his son, his dog, and the violent manner of his death; his
encounter with the Muses is transmuted into a dream; his
victory in the contest is regarded as an interpolation. The
events of Hesiod's 'life' are related to his poetry only in distant
and general ways. By representing him, at least in death, as a
hero, they suggest his importance; but they make no attempt
directly to interpret the meaning of his poetry or even to record
an impression of its contents.

# CHAPTER TWO

# Homer

Nothing specific is said either in the *Iliad* or the *Odyssey* about the name and background of the poet who composed them. Yet what is said about poetry in the two epics led to a tradition that they are the work of the same man. He emerges in the biographical tradition as a humble itinerant, like the bards Phemius and Demodocus in the *Odyssey*, dependent on others for support. Although his poetry is acclaimed by ordinary people, he wins no contests. Hesiod said in the *Works and Days* that he could speak of seafaring although he had never been on a boat because the Muses had taught him (661–2). But the poet of the *Iliad* sets his ignorance and weakness against the goddesses' knowledge: 'we hear only report and do not know anything; I couldn't tell or name the multitude, not if I had ten voices, or ten mouths, or had an unbreakable voice, or a bronze heart within me' (487–90). The story he then tells about Thamyris reinforces the value of humility: Thamyris boasted that he could beat the Muses in a singing contest, but they made him lame and took away his song and made him forget how to play the lyre (*Il.* 2.599).[1]

Other biographical data about Homer also derived from his poetry. As in Hesiod's case, some 'facts' were produced by inference: Demodocus was taught either by a Muse or by Apollo himself; Homer is the son of a Muse and of Apollo (Suda, p. 33 Wil) or a direct descendant of Apollo through Orpheus (*Cert.* 4) or Musaeus (Gorgias 82B25 DK) in genealogies known to writers like Hellanicus (*FGrHist* 4F5) and Pherecydes (3F161) in the fifth century.[2] Other attempts to

---

[1] According to other traditions, Thamyris was blind, perhaps on the analogy of Demodocus and Homer; Lesky 1966, 169–75.

[2] More poets are added as time goes on; Jacoby on Hellanicus *FGrHist* 5F11.

show that the poet's work in direct ways reflected his life
experience give Thamyris or Telemachus as Homer's father
(*Cert.* 3); Penelope as his beloved (Hermesianax fr. 7.29–30
Powell).[3] According to Ephorus in the fourth century (*FGrHist*
70F1), Homer studied poetry with a school-teacher called
Phemius (the bard in *Od.* 1.153–5). Other characters from the
*Iliad* and the *Odyssey* make their way into his life (*Vit. Hdt.* 6, 7)
Mentes (*Od.* 1.105), who takes him to his homeland Ithaca,
where Homer stays with Mentor (*Od.* 1.180–1); Homer sings
for Tychius the shield-maker (*Il.* 7.218–21).

Having Telemachus as father or Mentes as friend helps
account for Homer's detailed knowledge of the remote island
Ithaca. In the biographies the site of Homer's birthplace also
provides some explanation of geographical and linguistic
diversity in the poems. Writers who believed the prominent
dialect of the poem to be Aeolic set his birthplace in Smyrna
(e.g. *Vit. Hdt.* 37); the singer of the *Hymn to Delian Apollo* claims
that he comes from rocky Chios (*HHom* 3.172). These are the
birthplaces mentioned by writers in the fifth century (Stesimbrotus *FGrHist* 107F22, Pindar fr. 264, Simonides fr. 652
P = fr. 8 W). That Pindar is alleged to have said that Homer
came from both Chios and Smyrna (Ps. Plu., *Vit. Hom.* p. 23
Wil) suggests that attribution of homeland was meant as
aetiology rather than as literal fact. Philochorus in the fourth
century suggested Argos, because of the importance of Mycenae
in the *Iliad* (*FGrHist* 328F209); later Pylos and Athens were
suggested, to account for complimentary references in the poems
(e.g. *Vit. Hdt.* 28).

But other aspects of the poet's life have only an indirect
relation to the *Iliad* and the *Odyssey*. Accounts of Homer's
parentage acknowledged the importance of the poems by
giving him the uncertain origins of a mythological hero.
According to Aristotle (fr. 76 Rose), his mother Critheis, a
girl from Ios, was made pregnant by 'some divinity' among the
dancers in a festival of the Muses. She went and hid in a place
called Aegina, but was stolen from there by pirates and brought
to Smyrna, which was under Lydian rule. There the king

---

[3] Cf. Hesiod's *Eoie*, p. 6 n.17 above.

Maion fell in love with her because of her beauty. She gave
birth to Homer near the Meles river but died in childbirth.
Her son, called Melesigenes after the river, was raised by
Maion as his own. Later when the Aeolians captured Smyrna
he offered himself as a hostage (*homēros*) and afterwards was
addressed by that name. The story, with its Euripidean pace,
reversals and ultimate success of its hero, could serve as the
outline for the opening book of a Hellenistic romance. But in
the course of the action, scholarly questions are addressed:
although his mother comes from Ios, his birthplace is Smyrna,
and an explanation is offered for his two names.

However, where Aristotle enhances the poet's stature by
making him the son of a god in disguise, in Ephorus (*FGrHist*
70F1) his father is his mother's uncle, who raped her in Cyme
while she was entrusted to his care and then married her off
to a school-teacher Phemius in the neighbouring town of
Smyrna. The child was born while she was doing her laundry
by the river Meles. Her son, Melesigenes, was called Homer,
not because he courageously offered himself as a hostage, but
because the Cymaeans and Ionians called blind people
*homēroi*. Ephorus' story, like Aristotle's, gives Homer's birthplace as Smyrna and accounts for Homer's names. But Ephorus' Homer is blind from the start, and by background is in no
way superior to other people. Where Aristotle's geneaology
suggests that Homer is extraordinary, like his poetry, Ephorus'
account makes him no better (if not worse) than an ordinary
member of his audience.

Places not mentioned in the *Iliad* and *Odyssey* assume a prominent place in these biographies: the home of Homer's
mother is Ios or Cyme. Patriotic motives may have led Ephorus
to pick his hometown; Antimachus, a contemporary of Plato,
had claimed that Homer came from his hometown Colophon
(fr. 130a Wyss).[4] Ios figures in the oracle about Homer's
parents and origin: 'there is an island Ios, your mother's
fatherland, which will receive you when you are dead' (*AP*
14.65); there is no disagreement in the *Lives* that Ios is the site
of the poet's grave. To some extent the story of Homer's travels

---

[4] Also Wyss 1936, xxx–xxxi.

to these places accommodates strong local tradition: a group of rhapsodes recited the Homeric poems on Chios (schol. *Nem.* 2.1); in Smyrna Pausanias saw at the source of the river Meles the cave where Homer wrote his poetry (7.5.1). According to one tradition the river Meles himself was Homer's father (*EG* 3305/146 GP).

By the fifth century, a reference to 'the man from Chios' could be understood to mean Homer (Simonides fr. 8 W/*PMG* 652), just as 'the man from Boeotia' meant Hesiod (Bacchyl. 5.191ff., cf. Hesiod fr. 359 MW).[5] Thucydides took the end of the *Hymn to Delian Apollo* as a reference to Homer (*HHom.* 3.165ff). There the singer does not give his name, but provides obvious clues to his identity: he is the sweetest singer, in whose songs men most delight; he is a blind man who lives in rocky Chios (3.104.5). By implication, he is a travelling singer, who is competing at Delos (*HHom.* 3.150). A fragment of a poem attributed to Hesiod says that Homer and Hesiod first sang as bards in Delos, and composed new hymns for Apollo (fr. 357 MW). Retrospect provided the epic poets with the characteristics of their successors: like the rhapsodes, Homer and Hesiod travelled and sang in contests at religious festivals.

In other cases Homer's presence in a place explains why he should have written particular poems or verses. Visits to Athens and Argos (like being born in either city) explain the presence in the poems of complimentary lines (*Cert.* 16, 17); a trip to Delos verifies that he wrote the *Homeric Hymn to Apollo* (*Cert.* 18/fr. 357 MW), which was also attributed to 'one of the Homeridae' (Ath. i.22). By being on Samos he can have reason to compose several poems associated with that island: the *Sack of Oechalia*, also attributed to Creophylus (Allen p. 145, Strabo 14.638): the *Eiresione*; and the *Kiln Song*, also attributed to Hesiod (fr. 302 MW)—'Samian' in Roman times was a synonym for 'clay'.[6] In the third century Salamis in Cyprus was suggested as Homer's birthplace (Callicles 758F13/*EG* 3305), perhaps in order to address the question of whether or

---

[5] Burkert 1979, 57; West 1974, 180; cf. Lefkowitz 1976, 73.
[6] Burkert 1972b, 79. On the Kiln song, Noble 1965, 103; Detienne and Vernant 1978, 194–5; Herter 1975, 45–7.

not Homer wrote the Cypria, an issue that had been disputed since the fifth century (cf. Hdt. 2.116).[7]

'Family' became another means of accounting for problems of transmission and authorship. Pindar in the fifth century wrote of 'bards . . . sons of Homer (Homeridae)' (*Nem.* 2.1–2); he also told the story of how Homer, at a loss for what to give his daughter as a dowry, gave her the Cypria (Ael. *VH* ix. 15/ Pind. fr. 265, also attributed to Stasinos). Creophylus, according to some the author of Homer's *Sack of Oechalia*, was said to be either Homer's friend (Pl., *Resp.* 600b) or his son-in-law (Suda, s.v.). Such a relationship was an efficient way of begging the question of authenticity that was still unresolved in Callimachus' day (Ep. 6 Pf/ 55 GP). In the third century the Sicilian historian Hippostratus (*FGrHist* 568F5/ schol. *Nem.* 2.1) spoke of Homeridae descended from Homer who sang his poetry by right of succession (*ek diadochēs*) and rhapsodes called Homeridae who no longer claimed descent, among them a Cynaethus of Chios who both interpolated lines into Homer's poetry and wrote the *Hymn to Apollo* (p. 15 above) and attributed it to Homer. An inscription seems to confirm that Cynaethus, as Hippostratus says, recited the Homeric poems in Sicily at the end of the sixth century; stating that he was not descended from Homer is a biographer's means of indicating that his work was not genuine.[8]

Many stories about Homer tell of inhospitality or rejection in the course of his travels. In epigrams quoted in the biographies the poet asks for support in Cyme (*Epigr.* 1,2), but his request is turned down and he travels elsewhere (4). He complains to a Thestorides of the unpredictability of human behaviour (5); he asks for revenge on a man who has deceived him and angered Zeus, god of strangers (8); he curses a pine tree (9), an old woman (12), and low-born boys (12). The world he describes is hostile: the earth is angry at some cities (7); dogs bark and must be fed because they protect the house (11); a

[7] Since Homer's father could not very well be the river Meles (p. 15 above) if his birthplace were Salamis, the name Dmesagoras was substituted (Callicles *FGrHist*. 758H13/ *Cert.* 3/ Alcaeus *EG* 3306/ 147 GP); cf. the names invented for Hesiod's son (p. 6 n.17 above).

[8] Burkert 1979, 56; Fehling 1979, 193–4.

home wins praise for having a fire in it (13). With prose glosses that attach them to specific situations and cities, the epigrams tell of the life of a lonely wanderer, compelled to struggle against the world. A third-century inscription preserves De-meas' biography of the poet Archilochus, written in prose with long quotations in verse from Archilochus' poetry, in-cluding a description of a battle in which the poet participated (5 Tarditi). Homer's conflicts are of a different nature, in keeping with the humble character of his first-person statements and the portraits of the bards in the *Odyssey*; in Cyme his re-quest for public support is rejected, like the poet Xenophanes' (21B2.11–12 DK) or the philosopher Socrates'. Plato contrasts his bad treatment by Creophylus to the heroisation of Pythag-oras by his followers (*Resp.* 600b).

The notion of rejection is inherent in the professional stance adopted by archaic poets; it is the natural response to the poet's statement of his superiority to 'shepherds of the wilder-ness, mere bellies' (Hes. *Th.* 26; p. 2 above). So it is possible that the epigrams about Homer's life that complain of hostile treatment date back at least to the fifth century B.C. Heraclitus, at the beginning of the century, gives a version of one of the epigrams, the riddle asked of Homer by fisher boys. Heraclitus cites the riddle to show how Homer knew less than people think he did: 'men are deceived in respect to knowledge of the apparent, like Homer, who was the wisest of all the Greeks': Boys killing lice deceived him when they said 'what we saw and caught we left behind, what we didn't see and didn't catch we bring'. Heraclitus' version of the riddle is in prose, because of the special emphasis he wants to put on 'seeing'. Alcidamas,' a century later, apparently linked the riddle to the oracle about Homer's origins (cf. *Cert.* 18) itself another epigram (16), that the poet would die on Ios where his mother was born (*PMich*, 2754.9).[9]

In Alcidamas' account prose explanations precede and follow citations of poetry, as if to place them in appropriate settings: 'seeing him the boys improvised this verse (1–2): what we caught we left behind, what we caught we didn't

[9] On Alcidamas, pp. 4–5 above; text in Renehan 1975, 85–6; cf. Fontenrose 1978, L 80.

bring (17). When Homer couldn't find the solution he asked them what they meant and they said that they had gone off to fish but didn't catch anything so they sat down to pick lice. Of the lice the ones they caught they left behind, but the ones they didn't catch they brought with them in their clothing' (3–9); 'after he recalled the oracle that the end of his life had come, Homer composed the following epigram for himself: "here the earth covers the sacred head of the poet who gave heroes glory, divine Homer."' In Alcidamas the pattern of Homer's death resembles Hesiod's, an oracle not followed, a degrading death away from his homeland: 'and when he went away from there, since there was mud, he slipped and fell on his side, and thus they say, he died' (13–14). 'They say' shows that Alcidamas is following an older tradition, which he does not necessarily regard as accurate. But the form of Alcidamas' 'On Homer' suggests that the biographical tradition about Homer in its earliest form contained explanations and quotations from his poetry.

In the Hellenistic age and after, conscious attempts were made to bring order to the chaos of the variant traditions, and to restore some of the honour the great poet seemed to deserve. Epigrams listed the names of all the cities that claimed Homer as their son, and concluded that he belonged to no one city but to all of Greece.[10] Instead of making Homer an illegitimate child, an epigram (*AP* 14.102) from the Roman period suggested that Telemachus and Polycaste, Nestor's daughter, were his parents; the same genealogy was sent by the Delphic oracle in reply to an inquiry by the emperor Hadrian (*Cert.* 3).[11] Other Hellenistic epigrams concerned the contest at Aulis, and the occasion of his death; but none related the stories of inhospitality recorded in the older epigrams attributed to Homer himself. The treatise *The Contest between Homer and Hesiod* prefers Telemachus as Homer's father, and records the honours paid to Homer by various cities he visited after the contest, before he came to Ios, where he died.

The author of the treatise *The Contest between Homer and Hesiod* reports events without editorial comment, and without

---

[10] Skiadas 1965, 17–32.        [11] Ibid., 32–7.

seeming to distinguish among the relative historical merits of his sources. But to regard his work as naïve is to misunderstand his purpose.[12] He did not see himself as a historian in the modern sense of the word, but as a recorder of myth, at liberty to present his material in ways that would impart a general truth about his subject. His narrative emphasises divine recognition in the form of oracles about Homer's parents and his death, and mentions the sacrifices offered to him in Argos (17). His narrative accounts (in that order) for the composition of several minor epics (15), the *Odyssey*, the *Iliad* (16) and a few epigrams. But at the same time he makes it clear that although Homer is undoubtedly a more facile and popular artist, he loses the contest because the ethical quality of his poetry is inferior to Hesiod's, and like the sophist Alcidamas, he has Homer die after failing to answer a riddle, by slipping in the mud. The ambivalence of his narrative, with its alternating successes and failures, balances fourth-century concern about the content of poetry against the poems' continued popularity and cultural importance; in that sense (though certainly not in ours) the *Contest* offers a valid impression of the significance of Homer's poetry in the second century A.D.

The author of the *Contest* indicates clearly to his readers that he is writing for them as their contemporary; he cites many of his sources by name; he mentions the oracle that 'we have heard to have been spoken to the most sacred Emperor Hadrian' (3). But the author of the longest surviving biography of Homer[13] pretends that he is the famous fifth-century historian: 'Herodotus of Halicarnassus wrote the following history of Homer's background, upbringing, and life, and sought to make his account complete and absolutely reliable.' This opening, with its claim of accuracy, bears some resemblance to the forged history of Dictys of Crete: 'when by chance some books had come into our hands, the desire for true history came over us to put them into Latin' (*Ep.* 1.14 Eisenhut).[14] Unlike the author of the *Contest*, 'Herodotus' cites no sources or conflicting opin-

---

[12] P. 8 n.27 above.     [13] See Appendix 1.
[14] On fraudulent history, Syme 1968, 118–25. Cf. Lucian, who writes his preposterous *True History* 'honestly'; or Dares, who according to Cornelius Nepos wrote *vere et simpliciter*, Syme 1971, 266.

ions about Homer's ancestry or adventures but offers instead a straight narrative account of Homer's life. 'Herodotus'' or Dictys' audiences may not have been deceived by these protestations of veracity; fanciful 'correspondence' between persons long dead, like Stesichorus and Phalaris, had appeal in late antiquity. Alciphron in the fourth century A.D. composed a book of letters between the third-century B.C. comic poet Menander and his *hetaira* Glycera, who bore the name of the heroines of several of his plays.[15] But the existence and apparent success of the *Historia Augusta* indicates that an audience for learned fraud existed and might be exploited.[16]

'Herodotus' does even more than the author of the treatise on the *Contest* to improve the poet's stature. In the *Contest*, Homer dies when he cannot answer the fisherboys' riddle about the lice (*Cert.* 18); in 'Herodotus'' life the poet dies of weakness, not after being found ignorant (36). In fact the boys' taunt gives Homer an opportunity to compose an insulting epigram about their low descent (35; *Epigr.* 18). 'Herodotus' explains the epigram that complains to a Thestorides of the incomprehensibility of the human mind (*Epigr.* 5), by telling how Thestorides mistreated Homer and stole his poetry (16). Later it was discovered that Homer is the true author of the lines, and Thestorides goes into exile (24). From the beginning of his life Homer's talent wins recognition. Where Ephorus said (*FGrHist* 70F1) that Homer was the product of an incestuous union, and that his uncle married off his mother to the local school-teacher, 'Herodotus' leaves the identity of Homer's father a mystery, and has the school-master marry her because he likes her work and admires her son. Homer takes over the school, is taken by a merchant friend to Ithaca, and later made tutor to the children of a wealthy Chian, who gives him a new start in life.

In 'Herodotus'' account, Homer's difficulties derive not from defects of character but from his physical dependence on others. 'Herodotus' constantly reminds his audience of the problems caused by blindness: Homer must be led from place to place, addressed slowly and with consideration (13), not

---

[15] Cf. p. 114 below.     [16] Syme 1972, 13–17.

only greeted, but embraced (18, 19), and reassured (24). But even so, blindness gives Homer a seer's status and divine protection: fishermen who refuse to take him on board are driven back by adverse winds (19); he arrives without a guide at Pityos in the centre of the island of Chios (21). A crowd of people gather round him as he lies dying on the beach at Ios, and bury him (36).

'Herodotus' also tries to show how and where Homer could have written most of the poetry attributed to him. He gains some credibility by not trying to claim everything: Alcidamas has Homer write his own epitaph,[17] but 'Herodotus' says explicitly that the verses are not Homer's, but composed, long after his death, by the people of Ios. 'Herodotus' never states explicitly that he is dealing with questions of authenticity throughout his history, but anyone familiar with the Hellenistic commentaries on Homer would have understood why he takes proportionately so much space to explain why the *Iliad* and the *Odyssey* contain special verses in praise of Athens (28). Three of the passages he cites were questioned by the Alexandrian scholars Zenodotus, Aristophanes, and Chaeris.[18] 'Herodotus' has Homer compose these verses on Chios, in anticipation of a trip to mainland Greece. He prefaces his story by citing two lines about Athens whose authenticity was never questioned; after this the three questionable passages, cited out of context, appear as appropriate as the first.

Since the authorship of the *Iliad* and the *Odyssey* was not disputed in antiquity, 'Herodotus' notes only in passing that Homer wrote them while he was on Chios; he ignores the tradition recorded in the *Contest* that Homer wrote them in mainland Greece after a visit to the Delphic oracle (*Cert.* 16) But he makes his narrative take account of Homer's minor works.[19] He says that Homer wrote the *Cercopes, Battle of the*

[17] P. 17 above.
[18] Schol. *Il.* 2.452–4, 557–8; *Od.* 7.80–1; cf. *Il.* 2.547. Callimachus in his poetry frequently alludes to controversial readings in the Homeric text; Williams 1978, 5.
[19] On the development of fictional narrative to 'satisfy interest in juvenilia', Syme 1972, 9. The discrepancy in style between major and minor works was noted in antiquity, e.g. Stat., *Silv.* 1 prooem./ T5 Allen p. 163. The

*Frogs and Mice*, and other minor poems for the Chian's children, thus explaining their comic subject matter and low quality (24); Vergil's biographers explained the *Culex* and *Ciris* by making them creations of the poet's early manhood (*Vit. Donat.* 17). 'Herodotus' painstakingly accounts for all the epigrams attributed to Homer. Homer spends the winter on Samos, composing two short epigrams (12, 13), the *Kiln Song*, and the *Eiresione* song; 'Herodotus' makes no reference to the Samian Creophylus, credited elsewhere with the authorship of the *Sack of Oechalia*, but Homer's presence on the island gives him opportunity to have written this work as well.[20] 'Herodotus' has Thestorides steal Homer's poetry; other authorities credit him with the authorship of the *Little Iliad*.

'Herodotus' further enhances Homer's stature by making no reference to the famous contest at Chalcis that Hesiod won. In his biography Homer is never defeated, and no one is given opportunity to criticise the content of his poetry. His international reputation and connection with mainland cities are explained in other ways. In part his associations with mainland Greece can be accounted for by his ancestry: his grandparents come from Magnesia, his mother's first guardian from Argos, her second from Boeotia; he travelled to Ithaca as a young man, before his sight failed. Wilamowitz suggested that 'Herodotus'' account of Homer's genealogy preserved traces of folk epic;[21] but since local historians tended to account for the past in terms of their understanding of the present,[22] 'Herodotus'' version of Homer's background may simply help represent in narrative form how a man who was primarily associated with Ionia and the eastern islands came to know so much about the rest of Greece. 'Herodotus' has Homer write an epigram for Midas' tomb (3) early in his career (11), not after the contest (cf. *Cert.* 15), because Homer's talent, in his account, was recognised from the start.

---

Batrachomyomachia and *Margites* were also attributed to Pigres (Suda, s.v./ T4 Allen); Aristotle explains the *Margites* (to which 'Herodotus' does not refer) as a model of comedy (*Poet.* 1448b38ff.).

[20] Cf. p. 15 above. Allen 1924, 145; Burkert 1972b, 79.

[21] Wilamowitz 1916, 413; nor does it depict for an illiterate audience 'the lowest sphere of life', as Parnell 1715, 25 thought.

But 'Herodotus' does not try to explain in any serious way how the blind poet was able to compose so great an oeuvre, given the deprivations of his life. Neither he nor his sources seem to have been interested in trying to understand the mechanics of Homer's art or to suggest how an itinerant poet could commit so much to memory and easily revise it, or how he was able to learn so much without the guidance of another poet or tradition. 'Herodotus' accepts Homer's achievement as anomalous. He is concerned rather with showing how Homer's talent was immediately apparent to everyone he encountered in his lifetime, by educated men like the school-teacher Phemius and the rich Chian, and by ordinary townspeople and working men throughout Ionia. It is in this respect that his biography is in fact 'complete and absolutely reliable'. Surviving papyri testify that even in late antiquity Homer remained the most popular author in the Greek-speaking world.[23] Quintus of Smyrna's epic tells 'What happened after Homer'. 'Herodotus'' short history documents in narrative form the continuing appeal of Homer's poetry.[24]

Yet for all his efforts, 'Herodotus'' Homer seems inadequately equipped for the magnitude of his achievement. In this respect he is no different from the Hesiod of the biographies, though the contrast between expectation and portrait is greater because of the relative importance of Homer's work. One may well compare the ambivalent characterisation of Heracles:[25] for all his accomplishments, including victories over death in three different forms, Heracles is portrayed as a glutton and a buffoon; he spends longer in slavery than any other god or hero. Because the greatest hero was capable also of such extraordinary failings, ordinary men are able more readily to tolerate his success. Instead of dying in battle, Heracles is poisoned by a woman; Homer too dies as a consequence of being unable to exercise the powers that had served him well previously in his life.[26]

[22] Jacoby 1949, 133.
[23] Winter 1933, 194.
[24] On the date of the Herodotean Life, Wilamowitz 1916, 416.
[25] Kirk 1973, 289–90.
[26] Wehrli 1973, 194; cf. p. 10 n.37 above.

Perhaps the best illustration of how Homer's achievement is reduced to the comprehensible may be found in his portrayal in works of art. In the Homereion created by Ptolemy IV in the late third century, a seated statue of Homer was surrounded by statues of the cities that claimed him; a painting by Galaton showed poets collecting water that spewed from the poet's mouth (Ael., *VH* 3.22). The painting offered a visual representation of the Hellenistic notion that Homer was like Oceanus the source of all rivers and springs (Callim., *H.* 2.105–13; *Lyr. Adesp.* 10.14–16 Powell).[27] A second-century relief shows him seated with symbolic representations of his works around him, Ptolemy and Arsinoe and personifications of the types of poetry and learning are in attendance.[28] A sixth-century A.D. poet describes a late Hellenistic statue that shows a bee bringing a honeycomb out of Homer's mouth (*AP* 2.342–3).[29] In their final tangible form the traditional attributes of poetic achievement become trivial and ludicrous.

[27] Webster 1964, 114–15; Williams 1978, 88–9.
[28] Webster 1964, Pl. iv.
[29] Cf. p. 59 below.

# CHAPTER THREE

# Archaic Lyric Poets

What Homer can say about himself in the *Iliad* and the *Odyssey* is determined by the nature of epic poetry; only the most functional and modest statements are appropriate. Even Hesiod, in an instructional epic addressed to his brother, says only as much as he needs to establish his credentials. Their biographies accordingly concentrate on events in their professional lives, and give them the place in society that they give to themselves or to other poets in their poems. But the lives of writers of elegiac and lyric poetry involve a greater variety of experience, because the first-person statements in the poems express opinions about subjects other than poetry.

Archilochus appears to be the first real person among Greek poets because he wrote about ordinary events of life, love affairs, campaigns, civil strife. The characteristic passion with which he describes feelings, with emphatic repetition and vivid metaphors, gives the impression that he is personally involved in the events he describes in his poem.[1] Archaeological evidence confirms that Thasos was settled around the time he is said to have gone there;[2] an epitaph of the seventh century (T1 T) commemorates his friend Glaucus. But significantly only the most destructive aspects of his poetry survive in his biographies; there is no trace in the Lives or anecdotes of the Archilochus who consoles his friend Pericles (fr. 13 W = 10 T), disdains riches (fr. 19 W = 22 T), or reveres the gods (fr. 26, 30 W = 30, 94 T).

In the fifth century Socrates' pupil Critias claimed that

---

[1] On historical elements in the poems, cf. esp. Rankin 1978, 9ff.; Rankin 1977, 129–32.
[2] Graham 1978, 84–93.

Archilochus had a bad reputation in Greece because of his own statements: 'If he had not published this view of himself in Greece, we should not have known that he was the son of Enipo, a slave woman, nor that he left Paros because of poverty and destitution and went to Thasos, nor that when he was there he was on bad terms with the inhabitants, nor that he vilified friends and enemies equally. Moreover, we would not have known that he was an adulterer, nor lustful and violent, if we had not learnt it from him, and—most disgraceful of all—that he threw away his shield' (295 W = 88B44 DK).[3] Enough of Archilochus' poetry survives to confirm that the source of much of this information is, as Critias says, Archilochus' own poetry:[4] he left Paros (116 W); he attacks enemies like Lycambes (30–87, 172–84, 234, 96, 167); he describes how he makes love to a young girl in a meadow (*PCol* 7511) and other sexual encounters (e.g. 118, 119, 191); we have the famous epigram about how he threw away his shield and saved himself (5).[5] If Archilochus said in a poem (now lost) that he was 'the child of abuse' (*enipē*), a biographer could easily have deduced that his mother's name was Enipo, the way the name of Hesiod's father Dios was derived from Perses' epithet *dion genos*.[6]

Like the anecdotes about Homer and the riddle of the lice or Alcidamas' story about the murder of Hesiod, Critias' assessment of Archilochus describes the more negative and degrading aspects of his life. Because he wrote invective, Archilochus could be represented as 'blameful, fattening himself on heavy-spoken hatred', and as the antithesis of a poet like Pindar who wrote songs of praise (*Pyth.* 2.54–5 = T133, 161 T).[7] Aristotle accepted the principle that a man wrote the kind of poetry determined by his character: 'the more solemn among them would represent noble actions and the deeds of noble persons, the cheaper among them the deeds of insignificant men'

[3] Tr. Freeman 1957.

[4] Lefkowitz 1976b, 182.

[5] On the exaggerated importance given to the shield epigram by biographers, Lloyd-Jones 1971, 39.

[6] See p. 6 above. Cf. 'child of woe' (Men., *Dysc.* 88, with Handley's note); 'child of bad luck' (*PMG* 929f.), Kassel 1979, 19, perhaps originally from an insult, like Alcaeus fr. 72.8–9 or Homer, *Epigr.* 18. Cf. Nagy 1979, 247.

[7] On the dramatic fictions of blame poetry, Nagy 1979, ch. 13.

(*Poet.* 1448b25).[8] Later tradition accused Archilochus of causing the deaths of Lycambes and his wife and daughter (T155–9 T). Perhaps stories of their suicides were suggested by threats in his poetry; Hipponax, who compared himself to Archilochus, is said to have caused the deaths of the sculptors Bupalos and Athenis (schol. Hor., *Epod.* 6.11ff., p. 110 W).[9]

But in the fourth century Alcidamas said that Archilochus was honoured by the Parians 'although he was a slanderer', and Homer was honoured by the Chians although he was not a native of Chios (Ar. *Rhet.* 1398b/T6 T). In the third century a hero shrine was built to Archilochus on Paros.[10] A long inscription recording how the shrine was set up in response to an oracle was put up by Mnesiepes, who says he was instructed to 'honour Archilochus the poet' (T4 T).[11] Mnesiepes' name ('recollector of epic poetry') suggests that by profession he was a rhapsode.[12] His sources, he says, are legends and his own 'research': 'about what we wanted to write down; this was transmitted to us by men of old and we ourselves have worked on it.' But the story he tells in the part of his inscription that is preserved, because of its detailed description of the narrator's reactions, appears to be a summary of a poem about how Archilochus as a young man learned that he would be a poet:

> They say that when Archilochus was still a young boy he was sent by his father Telesicles to the country, to the district called Meadows, in order to bring back a cow to market. He got up early in the night, with the moon shining, to bring the cow to the city. But when he came to the place called Lissides, he thought he saw a crowd of women. He assumed that they were leaving the fields and going to the town and he approached them and scolded them for doing so. But they welcomed him playfully and with humour, and asked him if he were taking the cow in order to sell it. And when he said yes, they said that they would give him a good price. As soon as the words were spoken neither they

[8] Cf. Satyrus' Life of Euripides fr. 39.ix, quoting Aristophanes apropos of Euripides, 'he is like what he makes his characters say'; p. 166 n.7 below.

[9] Lefkowitz 1976b, 184–5; cf. the story that Shakespeare attacked two brothers, Schoenbaum 1970, 79–82. Callimachus' *Ibis* was understood as an attack on Apollonius of Rhodes, pp. 117, 128 below.

[10] Cook 1951, 249; for bibliography, Rankin 1977, 107nn.9, 10.

[11] On the oracle, Fontenrose 1978, H 74; Rankin 1977, 110n.48.

[12] Cf. Nagy 1979, ch. 18 §4 n.4.

nor the cow were visible, but before his feet he saw a lyre, and was overcome. Some time later, when he had recovered his senses, he realised that the women who appeared were the Muses and that they had made him a gift of the lyre. He took the lyre and went to the town and showed his father what had happened (T4.22–40 T).

This matter-of-fact narrative resembles Tzetzes' version of Hesiod's encounter with the Muses (*Th.* 31ff.):[13] 'They say that some nine women came up, who had been gathering branches of Heliconian laurel, and fed him and thus he acquired his learning and poetic art.' The Muses become nine women gathering laurel branches; instead of giving him a laurel branch and a 'sacred voice', they simply feed him; there is no trace of the Muses' dramatic speech that sets Hesiod apart from his peers and suggests the great power of poetry to tell the truth or the lies that resemble it. Behind Mnesiepes' bland account also lies a poem that describes how Archilochus became a poet;[14] typically for Archilochus, the setting is unglamorous, and the result of his excursion different from what he had expected—he is the poet who says he left his shield behind and who approves of little generals. The Muses make fun of him; he is overcome when they replace the cow with the lyre.

An equally amusing poem may lie behind the next section of Mnesiepes' account:[15] Telesicles, Archilochus' father, has a search made for the missing cow, and when he can't find it, the city sends him and Lycambes to Delphi to ask the oracle. He receives an answer (in verse)[16] that whichever of his children greets him first on his return will be 'immortal and famous in song'. The father returns late in the day during the festival of Artemisia and asks if there is enough to eat in the house (fr. 299 W). The inscription breaks off without record of Archilochus' response, but again what in an epic account might be a

[13] West 1964, 141–2; p. 9 above.

[14] Momigliano 1971, 27–8 suggests that Archilochus' story was invented in the fifth century, citing a possible portrayal of Archilochus' encounter with the Muses on a vase painting dated to 450 B.C.; cf. the portrayal of Anacreon in vase painting in the first half of the fifth century, pp. 52–3 below.

[15] Fr. 251 W apparently cites verses, perhaps improvised by the poet; West 1974, 24–5.

[16] On the form of the oracle, Fontenrose 1978, Q 58.

grand mission, with a dramatic revelation, is set in an ordinary ambience, where people behave in a normally trivial fashion.

Despite the apparent nature of his source material,[17] Mnesiepes means to honour the poet, and his narrative stresses that the poet's calling was recognised early, not only once, but twice. He refers to the sanction of the oracle during Archilochus' lifetime, and its repeated authorisation to him for the present inscription and the rituals at Archilochus' shrine. The Life of Archilochus in the Suda records yet another statement by the oracle on behalf of the poet (T170 T): Calondas Corax ('the Crow') who killed Archilochus in battle is told first that he deserved the god's hatred, and ought to have been killed instead; but then he is told to go to Taenarus, where the hero Tettix ('the cricket') was buried and to give offerings to the soul of Telesicles' son.[18] 'Crow' and 'cricket' sound like metaphorical terms from a verse oracle.[19] The crow is Apollo's bird. Archilochus refers to himself as a cricket (fr. 223 W); they were thought sacred to the Muses and to live without growing old.[20] Even in this excerpted form the story shows that Archilochus' death, like Homer's and Hesiod's, is caused and avenged by the gods.[21]

Archilochus' hero shrine also contains a long inscription of the early first century with an account of 'what Archilochus did and wrote in chronological order' (*FGrHist* 502F1 = fr. 5A 1 7–9 T = 192.7ff. W). The portions of the inscription that survive describe a battle between the Parians and the Thracians, and cite portions of Archilochus' poem about it. Such evidence of 'piety and [zeal] for his fatherland' (5A 1 4–5 T) counteracts the emphasis in fifth-century tradition of his self-indulgence and his cowardice in throwing away his shield.[22] The inscription was put up by Sosthenes, a member of a prominent Parian family, from 'the writings of Demeas'. Sosthenes

---

[17] There were other Hellenistic treatises on Archilochus' poetry, esp. his shield; cf. Tarditi 17*, Ar. Byz. T24.

[18] On the oracle, Fontenrose 1978, Q 58; cf. T141 T.

[19] Cf. Fontenrose 1978, L 42, Q 191.

[20] P. 4 n.9 above.

[21] Nagy 1979, ch. 18 §1.

[22] Graham 1978, 83–4.

states his purpose in an epigram at the close of his inscription that represents Archilochus as saying: 'Sostheus (i.e., Sosthenes) son of Prosthenes honoured my highly praised song and gave me the legacy of eternal honours' (5A IV B T).

Whether Demeas (Sosthenes' source) wrote a biography of the poet or simply about Archilochus within the context of a general chronicle about Paros is not clear.[23] Writing his account in chronological order ('under each archon') replicates the structure of an annalistic history; but the form of his narrative, quotations from poetry with prose aetiologies, resembles the biographies of Homer by Alcidamas and pseudo-Herodotus. His main source material appears to be Archilochus' verse, which he sometimes summarises, and at other times cites directly as confirmation of important 'facts'. Demeas shows that the cave near the Syrian harbour is called after Coeranus, and is a shrine of Poseidon Hippios 'as the poet wrote, putting a memorial of him in verse as follows, "Of fifty men Coeranus . . . Poseidon Hippios" ' (fr. 192 W = 211 T). The Parians got all their gold back from the Thracians; 'the poet clearly states this in verses, "A man brought a flute and lyre to Thasos and had a gift of pure gold for Thracian dogs; but for private gain they worked trouble for the state" (fr. 93a W = 120 T), because they [the Sapaeans who brought the gifts] killed the Thracians and were themselves killed by the Parians'; 'after this Amphitimus became archon, and in these lines the poet states clearly that they conquered the Naxians as decisively, in verses as follows, "in their battle Athena stood propitiously, daughter of Zeus Thunderer, and roused the courage of the mournful populace . . ." ' (fr. 194 W = 121 T). Other statements, now lost, were documented by Archilochus' verses throughout the rest of the inscription ('the poet clearly states'; '. . . that he speaks the truth . . .;' 'here again Demeas made a memorial to his country and to Archilochus').[24] The citations of poetry are so loosely connected to the context that only an audience which knew Archilochus' poetry could readily understand his narrative.

---

[23] Jacoby, comm. to *FGrHist* IIB pp. 421–2; Graham 1978, 84.
[24] Tarditi 1968, 131–2.

That a shrine to Archilochus was built in the third century, with a detailed account of his life, and yet another was added in the first century, testifies to the poet's continued importance to the people of Paros, who would visit the shrine and read the inscriptions. It is significant that what interested them about Archilochus was not so much his poetry as the relation of his poetry to his life; the Archilocheion does not contain copies of his poems but excerpts of his poetry set into prose biographies. He is given heroic status by the Delphic oracle, which first declares that he will be famous and immortal (Q 56),[25] and then commands his killer to honour him and offer sacrifices to him, as it commanded the Astypaleans to worship the murderous Cleomedes (Q 167) or the Locrians to honour the athlete Euthycles (Q 168), or the Thasians Theagenes (Q 170–1).[26] Like the heroes who won their fame through achievements in games or in war, Archilochus' life appears to have been extraordinarily violent, noteworthy for his combativeness and sexual appetite. Only after his death can he be worshipped for his patriotism and courage, when his powers, like those of the heroes of myth, are attenuated and generalised. In the end he is not so much a poet as a fighter, a hero whose achievement can be readily evaluated within the context of ordinary human achievement.

We now know enough about Stesichorus' poetry to understand why we have so little information about his life. Long fragments of his poetry on papyrus do not contain the professional first-person statements from which significant portions of Hesiod's and Archilochus' biographies are derived. Thus many 'facts' about Stesichorus' life are as uncertain as Homer's (Suda, s.v.). His father was Euphemus or Euclides or Hyetes or, of course, Hesiod; he was born in Himera or Mataura in Sicily.[27] Like Homer, he was buried away from his home(s) in Catana. His dates are disputed. Like Homer, he acquired a second, descriptive name, Stesichorus, 'because he first set up choruses of singing to the lyre' (*choron kitharoidias estēsen*); his original name was Tisias. Before the new poems had been

---

[25] References are to Fontenrose 1978.
[26] Brelich 1958, 319–20; Nagy 1979, ch. 18 §8.
[27] West 1971, 302–3.

recovered (e.g. *SLG* schol. 11, 15), the aetiology of Stesichorus'
name seemed reasonable; now his poetic stance appears to
have been similar to Homer's, although his recitation may have
been accompanied by dancing.[28] 'Stesichorus' could denote
organising choruses;[29] but it may also simply be a non-descrip-
tive proper name, like Stesilaus or Stesandrus or Stesimbrotus.
The similarities in their lives and in the subject matter of their
poetry was strong enough to suggest in later tradition that
Stesichorus was Homer's reincarnation (Antipater Thess. *AP*
7.75 = *Garl. Phil.* 485ff. GP).[30]

The one first-person statement of Stesichorus which has
survived is the source of the most famous anecdote about the
poet. Plato in the *Phaedrus* tells the story of how Stesichorus had
been struck blind for slandering Helen, but recognised his
mistake and wrote a recantation or Palinode, after which he
regained his sight (243a–b): 'This story isn't true; you [Helen]
never went in the well-benched ships, you never came to the
citadel of Troy' (*PMG* 192).[31] Since Stesichorus mentioned
Helen's adultery in at least one poem (*PMG* 223), at first sight
the verses of recantation seem to provide credible documentation of the anecdote. But Plato quotes the lines out of context,
in order to document his own narrative; elsewhere he can be a
perverse interpreter of poetry.[32] He has Protagoras, Prodicus
and Socrates cite Simonides (*PMG* 542) out of order and out of
context in order to make false distinctions and to suggest that
Simonides was either confused or meant more than he actually
said. Socrates states that Simonides was often forced to write
poems of praise against his will (*Protag.* 346b); but when the
poem is read without Plato's commentary, it can be found to
contain ideas customarily found in odes of praise.[33]

What was the original context of Stesichorus' lines about
Helen? In later lyric, first-person disclaimers call attention to

[28] Haslam 1978a, 29–30.
[29] Calame 1977, I 88–9.
[30] Gow-Page 1968, on Antipater 485; Nisbet-Hubbard 1978, 336.
[31] Cf. also Isoc. x.94; all ancient testimony about the Palinode is collected
and translated by Davison 1968, 202ff.
[32] Cf. pp. 38 n.59, 47, 123 below.
[33] Dickie 1978, 1–33.

the poet's virtuosity. Pindar in *Ol.* 1 does not tell the usual tale about how Pelops was cut up and served to the gods at a banquet. Instead, he suggests, the banquet story was made up by envious neighbours, and Pelops was stolen away by Poseidon, who had fallen in love with him; Pelops' ivory shoulder, contrary to the standard myth, was a mark of distinction: 'It is impossible for me to call a god a glutton. I stand in revolt. Abundant losses are the lot of slanderers' (52–3).[34] Stesichorus also may have meant his lines as an indication that he would tell a story different from Homer's, i.e. honouring Helen; like Pindar, he could have backed up his disclaimer by a description of what happens to people who criticise the gods (Helen was worshipped as a goddess in Sparta).[35] In the anecdote about the Palinode, Stesichorus suffers the fate of Thamyris, who boasted that he could defeat the Muses at singing (*Il.* 2.597ff.), but they became angry and made him blind.[36] Pindar speaks of the great crowd of men who have 'blind hearts' (*Nem.* 7.23–4) and are deceived by the seductive skill of poets who do not speak the truth.[37] The anecdote about Stesichorus makes a physical reality of what Pindar suggests metaphorically in his statements about himself and his art. In the Euripides *Vita*, two lines from the *Melanippe* are cited as 'proof' of the story that Euripides apologised to the women of Athens for his attacks on them. The *Melanippe* is lost, so that we cannot know who said 'Women are better than men' (fr. 499 N), but the story about the women attacking Euripides comes straight from Aristo-

---

[34] In *Nem.* 7.102–3 a more defensive statement about choice of myth was understood by ancient scholars as a political apology; Lefkowitz 1980a, 39ff.

[35] The fourth-century biographer Chamaeleon (fr. 28–9 Wehrli) says that Stesichorus criticised Homer in one palinode for putting Helen and not her wraith in Troy, and criticised Hesiod in another (*PMG* 193)—he doesn't say for what, but Hesiod said Helen 'disgraced Menelaus' bed' (fr. 176, cf. 196 MW); cf. Davison 1968, 222; Podlecki 1969, 121. Chamaeleon also interpreted Pindar's encomium for Xenophon (fr. 122) as an apology to the Corinthians (fr. 31 Wehrli), p. 58 below. Cf. the biographer Hieronymus' account of Pythagoras' visit to Hades, where he saw the souls of Hesiod and Homer tormented because of what they had said about the gods (fr. 42 Wehrli = D.L. 8.21, cf. Heraclitus 22B42 and Xenophanes 21B11 DK).

[36] Cf. p. 12 n.1 above.

[37] Lloyd-Jones 1973b, 130.

phanes.[38] The story of Stesichorus' Palinode could easily be a similarly fanciful reconstruction.

Stories were also told in the fourth century about Stesichorus' relations with the tyrant Phalaris. Aristotle summarises a fable Stesichorus is said to have told about him (*Rhet.* 2.1393 = *PMG* 281), but mistakenly he locates Phalaris in Stesichorus' Himera and not in Acragas.[39] Like other writers of biography in the fourth century, Aristotle tends to particularise what in his sources had been allusive or general. It seems unlikely that Stesichorus in his narratives told fables with political significance; any poems he addressed to the tyrant would have been composed for symposia, like Alcaeus' about Pittacus, and would not have the extensive triadic structure of the *Oresteia* or the *Geryonis*. Anecdotes about confrontations tend to survive in the biographical tradition, because archaic poets often present themselves as adversaries in their first-person statements. Their enemies are never named, but their audiences (or readers), particularly after the fifth century, preferred to think of the poets as civic heroes, like Archilochus.[40] Stesichorus too had a substantial tomb and a gate named after him at Catana (Suda, s.v.).[41] Long after his lifetime, and as his poetry became increasingly obscure, stories that he was blinded because of what he said about Helen and accounts of his observations about tyranny gave him a hero's status.

Stesichorus' palinode is not the only illustration of how biographers reconstruct their original poetic source material. Aristotle, on the basis of some lines from one of the Spartan poet Alcman's maiden songs, deduced that the poet came from Lydia: 'You weren't a country fellow or clumsy [lit., left-handed] . . . or a Thessalian by birth, nor an Erysichaean nor a shepherd, but from lofty Sardis' (*PMG* 16). The context of the quotation is lost; but other ancient scholars disagreed with

[38] Cf. p. 90 below.

[39] According to Conon (*FGrHist* 26F1.42), Stesichorus' opponent was Gelon of Syracuse. Cf. also *Rhet.* 2.1395a = *PMG* 281b. These stories inspired the fraudulent 'Letters of Phalaris' (text in Hercher 1873).

[40] Cf. pp. 29, 31 above.

[41] The innovative design of the tomb, which was 'eightfold in every respect' (Pollux 9.100) sounds Hellenistic; Kurtz-Boardman 1971, 302.

Aristotle because the dialect and ambience of the poems was clearly Spartan.[42] One ancient commentator saw that Aristotle and another biographer (perhaps Crates; the text is fragmentary) were 'deceived by [the words] "country fellow" into supposing him a Lydian' (*POxy* 2389F9).[43] Aristotle may have supposed that Alcman's lines were addressed by the chorus to the poet. But since in no other surviving choral poem does the chorus speak directly to the poet who composed their song, it is more likely that they are complimenting a musician or someone assisting at the performance, the way the chorus of Alcman's *partheneion* praise their leaders for their beauty (*PMG* 1.50–9). The idea that Alcman came from Lydia may have appealed to Aristotle (or his sources) because there had been no Spartan poetry or art since the sixth century; fourth-century Athenians like Plato and Philochorus believed that the Spartan poet Tyrtaeus was an Athenian from Aphidna.[44] But the reference to lofty Sardis may simply have been intended to suggest the song's musical home; Pindar, in a characteristically elaborate metaphor, speaks of a song as a 'tuneful embroidered Lydian headband' (*Nem.* 8.15).[45]

When first-person statements refer to the poet himself, as in the case of Archilochus, the biographies preserve a general impression of the subject matter of his work. Ibycus is said to have been 'particularly in love with youths' and Anacreon's 'life was devoted to love affairs with boys and women and with song' (Suda, s.vv.) because they wrote love poetry. The biographies also emphasise politics: Ibycus wrote a poem addressed to Polycrates of Samos (*PMG* 282.47); Ibycus' biography, while omitting much else, mentions specifically that he went to Samos while Polycrates was tyrant. Alcaeus criticises Pittacus and Myrsilus in his poems (e.g., fr. 112, 70, 332, 348) and speaks about living in exile (348); Aristotle, in the lost third book of the *Poetics* (fr. 75 Rose) spoke of Alcaeus

---

[42] Huxley 1974, 209–10; cf. the discussion in *POxy* 2506 fr. 1.

[43] Cf. Suda, s.v. Alcman: 'according to Crates (mistakenly) a Lydian from Sardis'. On the passage, see esp. Lobel ad loc.

[44] Cf. p. 38 below; Philochorus said that Homer came from Argos, p. 13 above.

[45] Cf. also *Nem.* 4.45, *Ol.* 5.19.

quarrelling with Pittacus (Alcaeus fr. 471); in the *Politics* he says the tyrants beat the people of Mytilene with clubs (1113b26 = Alcaeus fr. 472), and he cites Alcaeus as evidence (1285a33 = Alcaeus fr. 348; fr. 470) that the Mytileneans made Pittacus tyrant.[46] Commentators made the emphasis on politics seem representative of Alcaeus' work by citing appropriate excerpts from his poetry, as Demeas picks the lines that best document his account of Archilochus' role in the battle between the Parians and the Thracians. Strabo tells us that in the Augustan age Alcaeus' poems about the tyrants were known specifically as his 'political poems' (Alcaeus fr. 468).[47] But where papyrus discoveries have revealed the larger context of a political allusion, Alcaeus seems to be as much concerned with his own feelings as with matters of state (e.g. 130b), and the setting for his recitation appears to be the symposium rather than the forum (fr. 70).[48]

Politics and conflict are missing entirely from Sappho's biography; instead we find fuller details about members of her family, friends and pupils than about any other archaic poet. This phenomenon suggests that her poetry included more references to her own life than Alcaeus' or Ibycus' or even than Archilochus'. If a fragment of her long narrative poem about Hector and Andromache did not survive, it might be possible to say that for once the biographical tradition did not distort the evidence. But her Life does not describe her poetic talent but instead emphasises her conformity (or non-conformity) to expected patterns of female behaviour. No reference is made in the two surviving biographies (fr. 252–3) of her going into exile in Sicily, though the chronicler of the Parian marble records it (fr. 251 = *FGrHist* 239F36). Instead we learn that she had pupils and therefore a school, according to one commentary, of the noblest girls from Ionia as well as Lesbos (*SLG* 261A).[49] Did she refer to herself in a lost poem the way the

---

[46] Since Alcaeus' poetry may be the source of Hellanicus *FGrHist* 4F93 (= Alcaeus fr. 439) and Herodotus 5.94ff. (= fr. 467), putting him into the context of Lesbian history is a circular argument. Cf. Page 1955, 159ff.

[47] Cf. also D.H. 5.421.

[48] Horace provides a more balanced assessment, e.g. *Carm.* 1.32.3ff. (= Alcaeus fr. 430).

[49] Dover 1978, 174–5.

chorus in Alcman's partheneion speak of their trainer Aenesim-
brota (*PMG* 1.73ff.)? Her brother Charaxus is said to have
spent a large amount of money on Doricha, a woman in Egypt
(fr. 15, 213a, 252); she herself to have married a very rich man
(253). Like Ibycus and Anacreon she is alleged to have indulged
in the homosexual love that she describes in her poetry (fr. 252,
262).[50] She is said to have been ugly, perhaps because she was
supposed not to be interested in men, and to have died by
throwing herself off a cliff because of unrequited love for a
ferryman. The story of her death may derive from a myth about
Leucas, the 'white rock' the souls of Penelope's suitors pass on
their way to Hades, that Sappho told about in one of her poems
(fr. 211).[51] In her biography her death, like Hesiod's, serves as
a negation in practice of what she professed in her poetry.

According to at least one tradition, Alcaeus died in battle
(*POxy* 2506F98).[52] Ibycus' death, like Hesiod's, shows the gods'
recognition of his talent: as he was being killed by pirates he
predicted that cranes would avenge him. Later one of the pirates
called some cranes flying overhead 'the avengers of Ibycus' and
was apprehended by bystanders (Suda);[53] in Eratosthenes'
*Anterinys* Hesiod's body was discovered by his dog. Stesichorus
and the flute player Aeschylus were also said to have been killed
by robbers (Suda, s.v. *epitēdeos*). The anecdotes suggest that
poetry was a profit-making business at least at the time the
stories were told: according to Herodotus pirates made the
poet Arion jump into the sea, but he was rescued and brought
ashore by a dolphin, and so was able to identify his assailants
(Hdt. 1.23). The idea of avenging cranes, like the story of
Sappho's Phaon, may ultimately derive from a fable or myth in

[50] Ibid., 174.

[51] Cf. Menander's *Leucadia* fr. 258 K-Th; Lefkowitz 1973, 116; Nagy 1973,
141–3, 172–7.

[52] Perhaps the story derives from a suggestion in a poem that he might die
in battle; see Page's note ad loc.

[53] The Suda gives no indication of the site of the poet's death, but Antipater
of Sidon, perhaps on the analogy of the story of Arion and the dolphin, places
it in Corinth and has the cranes themselves avenge the murder by their cries
(*EG* 3448ff.).

Ibycus' poetry:[54] Pentheus' being torn to pieces in the *Bacchae* inspired the story that Euripides was eaten by dogs.[55]

Tyrtaeus' biography says that he wrote elegies on government, exhortations for the Spartans, and war songs (Suda, T1 GPr); one of the elegies (perhaps 'Government') was given the title 'Order' (*eunomia*, T7) in the fourth century. Surviving fragments confirm that he was concerned primarily with public ethics, especially in wartime: 'It is good for a brave man to fall in the front lines and die fighting for his country' (fr. 10. 1–2 W = 6.1–2 GPr). The first-person statements in the poems give no information about the poet himself: 'Let us fight' (fr. 10.13 W = 6.13 GPr), 'I wouldn't recall or make a speech about an athlete' (12.1–2 W = 9.1–2 GPr). But their hortatory stance suggests that their speaker is in a position of authority and their subject matter denotes a military character. So in the biographical tradition he was said to have been an Athenian summoned to Sparta in response to an oracle, and to have been an adviser or even a general during the war against the Messenians (T11, 52, 60 GPr).[56]

The story of Tyrtaeus' role in the Messenian war is not told before the fourth century. Like the story of Alcman's Lydian origins, it shows how incredible the idea of a native Spartan poet seemed to Athenians familiar with the military regime of fifth-century Sparta.[57] The poets Terpander and Thaletas are also said to have been brought to Sparta in the seventh century by command of the oracle, again because of civic need.[58] That Tyrtaeus in the stories is not merely a foreigner, but Athenian and lame, shows that even though Sparta was the greatest military power in Greece, her most important cultural legacy, the elegies of Tyrtaeus, were the result of *Athenian* talent and training.[59] Though they might originally have been intended

---

[54] In Homer the cry of the cranes is a warning to the Pygmies of impending slaughter (*Il.* 3.3ff.); their queen Gerana had been turned into a crane (*geranos*) and rejected by them (Ath. ix.393e).

[55] P. 90 below.　　　　[56] Cf. Fontenrose 1978, Q 18.

[57] P. 35 above.　　　　[58] Fontenrose 1978, Q 53–4.

[59] Cf. stories of lame or maimed saviour-kings, ibid., 121. Plato in the same context says Theognis came from Sicilian Megara, because it better suits his purpose to have him be a foreigner (schol. *Legg.* 630a, p. 301 Greene).

for performance at a symposium, like Archilochus' elegiacs,
Tyrtaeus' poems were variously said to have been sung in battle,
or as inspiration for the young, or in contests after dinner (T11, 5,
6 GPr). Continuing uncertainty about how they were used seems
to indicate that no precise information was in fact available.[60]
The stories may not represent historical practice so much as
idealistic Athenian notions of Spartan ethics and discipline in the
aftermath of the Peloponnesian war.[61] By the Hellenistic age, the
Spartan ethic had come to represent the struggle for Greek
independence: a third-century epitaph in Acarnania in north-
west Greece says that the dead man, who died fighting for his
country, 'did not conceal his education, but observed the Spartan
saying of Tyrtaeus and chose virtue before life' (T4 GPr).[62]

---

[60] Jacoby on Philochorus *FGrHist* 328F216.
[61] Jaeger 1965, 1 96.
[62] Friedländer 1969, 237–41 attributes the poem to Demagetus of Sparta,
cf. *EG* 2674ff.; Gow-Page 1965, 223; Jaeger 1965, 1 116ff.

# CHAPTER FOUR

# Solon

The development of Tyrtaeus' biography suggests that much specific information about the poet Solon's life is also the product of later invention. Indications are that his poetry dealt with a variety of topics: ethics (fr. 1 GPr = 13 W) politics (fr. 4, 5, 7 GPr = 4a, 4, 5 W), the ages of man (fr. 23 GPr = 27 W), sex (fr. 16 = 25). But the biographical tradition known to Aristotle and to Plutarch represents him primarily as a statesman. The detailed description of events in his political career might at first suggest that biographers had access to sources other than his poetry. For example, it is repeatedly stated that he composed his poetry in response to particular political crises and that he recited it in public. But in at least one case it is clear that the circumstances of performance were inferred wrongly from his poetry. Solon wrote: 'I have come as a herald from lovely Salamis, placing an ornament of verse, a song instead of a speech' (agorēs, fr. 2 GPr = 1 W). In the fourth century, Solon's ant' agorēs was understood as 'before the marketplace', since the primary meaning of agora had become the setting for the speech rather than the speech itself;[1] the Salaminians set up a statue in the marketplace commemorating Solon's presence there (T35, 36 GPr). The phrase 'placing an ornament of words' also became difficult to interpret. Solon simply meant to say that he had written a poem,[2] but Diogenes Laertius (or his source) says that Solon hired a herald to read the poem, and Plutarch that he recited the lines 'from memory' himself.[3]

[1] See esp. Passow-Crönert 1912, s.v.

[2] Cf. Parmenides 28B8.22 DK, Pindar fr. 194.2–3, Orpheus 1B1 DK.

[3] Since both Diogenes Laertius and Plutarch say Solon was feigning madness, the Salamis poem may have contained a line like 'a little time will show my madness to the citizens' (fr. 14 GPr = 10 W).

There are other indications that a principal source of evidence for Solon's political accomplishments was in fact his own poetry. Aristotle frequently cites Solon's verse in his *Constitution of Athens* (fr. 4, 5, 7. 8 29b GPr = 4a, 4b, 4c, 5, 6, 34 W) and twice summarises what Solon says (T64, 65 GPr). Even when he does not say so explicitly he appears to be drawing directly on Solon: in the *Politics* (T56) he summarises the contents of fr. 7 GPr = 5 W without specifically mentioning it or quoting from it (cf. also T58). If he had not cited Solon's actual verses in the *Constitution of Athens* it might seem as if he were depending on an independent narrative, since only a few verbal parallels, and those of ordinary prose vocabulary, survive (fr. 7 GPr = 5 W, *dēmōi edōka dynamin*; cf. T56 GPr, *apodidonai tōi dēmōi dynamin*).

Aristotle's methodology suggests how other historians worked with their sources. Solon said he removed 'fixed boundaries' (fr. 30.6 GPr) and so made the earth 'free'; he brought back to Athens men who had been sold into slavery at home and abroad because of their poverty.[4] Uncertainty about the interpretation of these lines indicates that by the fourth century biographers did not have external evidence to guide them. Aristotle took the lines to refer to 'release from debt', but Androtion argued that Solon only reduced the interest payments.[5]

Biographers used quotations from Solon's poetry to document their portraits of Solon as lawgiver, emphasising his moderation and superiority to other men. In some cases the poetry they cite seems not to bear very close relation to the description it is meant to support. Proof of Solon's impartial personal ethics is provided by an epigram (fr. 18 GPr = 24 W) whose lines are so general in nature that they were also attributed to Theognis (719ff.). An epigram comparing the danger of great men to a thundercloud (fr. 12 GPr = 9 W) was inter-

[4] In this chapter I have not tried to draw a firm distinction between historian and biographer. Although the ancients recognised the different genres, in practice the two cannot always be separated, especially in the archaic period, when deeds were associated with particular men. Conversely, a historical account can be converted into biography by excerpting, e.g. Heraclides Lembos' version of Aristotle's account of Solon's reforms in the *Constitution of Athens*, ch. 9 §24. Cf. Momigliano 1971, 104.

[5] Jacoby on *FGrHist* 324F34 and 328F114.

preted as a prediction of Pisistratus' tyranny. The same sort of hindsight may have deduced from military metaphor (fr. 7.6 GPr = 5 W, fr. 31.8–9 GPr = 37 W) the idea that he served as leader of a campaign against Megara (Plu., *Sol.* 9); the authoritative stance of the speaker in Tyrtaeus' poems led fourth-century biographers to speak of Tyrtaeus as general.[6] Suggestions are understood as actualities; when Solon says that he kept his hands off violence and tyranny (fr. 32 GPr = 29 W) and pretends that people thought him a fool to have refused the opportunity to be tyrant (fr. 29 GPr = 33 W), commentators took him to mean that he turned down literal requests (Plu., *Sol.* 14 = T59 GPr).[7]

The biographers derived their estimate of Solon's importance first of all from Solon himself. Like other archaic poets he calls attention to the singularity of his achievement: 'If a man other than I had taken the goad, an envious or greedy man, he would not have held back the people' (fr. 30.2off. GPr = 36 W). He vividly portrays his isolation: 'By defending myself on all sides, I turned round like a wolf among dogs' (fr. 30.26 7 GPr = 36 W). Pindar, in comparing his art to the conduct of a just citizen, speaks of running at his enemies 'as an enemy like a wolf' (*Pyth.* 2.84).[8] He represents his enemies criticising him: 'Solon isn't a thinker or a counsellor; the god gave him good advice but he didn't take it' (fr. 29 GPr = 33 W). Use of dialogue vividly creates an atmosphere of dissent;[9] by calling on friends to witness wrongs and by insulting his enemies, Alcaeus also makes his listeners feel the immediacy of the political events he describes (e.g. fr. 129, 130, 348).

But Solon merits a major role in the *Atthides* and in Aristotle's account of the Athenian constitution because he was a lawgiver.

---

[6] P. 38 above.

[7] Cf. the anecdote about Empedocles reported by Aristotle: 'Aristotle (fr. 66 Rose) says that [Empedocles] was an independent, hostile to every form of government, and that he in fact turned down the kingship when it was offered to him, as Xanthus says in his work about him (*en tois peri autou*, *FGrHist* 765F32), since it was clear that he liked the simple life better' (D.L. 8.63 = A1, 1 p. 279 DK). On Xanthus (of Lydia, a contemporary of Herodotus?) see Momigliano 1971; 30–2.

[8] Lloyd-Jones 1973b, 125; Lefkowitz 1976, 29.

[9] The style anticipates drama; Fränkel 1975, 29.

He speaks of justice and law-and-order (*eunomiē*) in his poetry
in general terms and in Hesiodic language (esp. fr. 3.32, 1.37
GPr = 4.32, 13.7 W);[10] traditions about specific laws derived
from copies of the laws themselves, independently of his poetry.[11]
A few verbatim quotations from the laws are cited by biographers: like the civil laws of Gortyn in Crete, they deal with
theoretical situations and are expressed in conditional terms;[12]
nothing in his surviving poetry resembles them in subject or in
style. Historians in the fifth century could read the 'Laws of
Solon' inscribed on the *axones* (wooden blocks) or *kyrbeis*
(bronze tablets) displayed until 461 on the Acropolis and
thereafter in the Agora;[13] in 409 sections were later published
on stone.[14] The wording of the legislation had been modern-
ised, and some of the laws attributed to Solon clearly date from
later periods; his name gave them an authority they would not
otherwise have had.[15]

According to tradition Homer and Tyrtaeus left their home-
lands as young men and composed their poems in exile; but
Solon, as a lawgiver, goes into exile because of his laws, as an
older man, like the Spartan lawgiver Lycurgus.[16] Lycurgus
made the Spartans promise that they would not change his
laws until he came back, and so never returned; Solon goes
away for ten years and travels round the Mediterranean.[17]
According to Herodotus, he made the journey after his laws
were adopted so that he would not be compelled to repeal them;
Plutarch, who used fourth-century sources which retroactively
emphasised Solon's fear of tyranny and demagoguery,[18] suggests that he left in order to dissociate himself from his laws.
Plutarch cites a line from one of Solon's poems in 'support' of
Solon's decision: 'in great undertakings it is hard to please

[10] Ostwald 1969, 68ff.
[11] Cf. Andrewes 1938, 90.
[12] Fornara 1977, 88; Ruschenbusch 1966, fr. 1b, 30a.
[13] The earliest testimony is Cratinus fr. 274 = T13 Ruschenbusch 1966;
Stroud 1979, 3; cf. also Jacoby 1949, 14, Stroud 1979, 40–1.
[14] Fornara 1977, §15 = *GHI* 86.
[15] de Sanctis 1975, 256n.25; Finley 1975, 39.
[16] Szedegy-Maszak 1978, 202.
[17] Ibid., 208.
[18] Finley 1975, 55.

everyone, as he himself says' (fr. 9 GPr = 7 W). Plutarch (or his source) removed the line from its original context, but if it is like Solon's other references to dissent (e.g. 29b GPr = 34 W), his verses describe reactions to general policy, without the specifics of legislation and timing that biographers like Aristotle supply. The poetry cited by biographers describing Solon's visits to Egypt and to Cyprus likewise contains no specific reference to his political career or the timing of his journey; at least Alcaeus describes how he feels when he is banished from Mytilene (fr. 348).

In his voluntary exile, Solon is said first to have visited Egypt. Here, his purpose, like Lycurgus', was to learn about their laws.[19] Herodotus says he modelled his law requiring that every man report his income annually on a law established by Amasis (ii.177); according to Plutarch he spoke with priests, and learned the story of Atlantis, which he tried to bring back to Greece in poetry (*Sol.* 26). Plato (*Tim.* 20dff.) tells how he told the story to Critias, the great-grandfather of the orator Critias who was a contemporary of Socrates; the information was handed down along with Solon's poetry in the family.[20] The scholia on the passage cite two lines from a poem by Solon urging Critias to listen to his father (fr. 22 GPr = 22a W).[21] A line cited by Plutarch describing Egypt 'at the delta of the Nile near the shore of Canobus' (fr. 10 GPr = 28 W) may come from this poem. Even if the poem about Atlantis described his visit to Egypt and his meeting with priests, it need not mean that he actually went there;[22] Parmenides describes how he is taken by the daughters of the Sun along the resounding road of the goddess, 'which carries through every city the man who knows' (28B1 DK).[23] Parmenides speaks of his journey in the indicative mood, as if it had literally taken place.

Biographers inferred from verses about Soloi that Solon

[19] Szedegy-Maszak 1978, 202, 204.

[20] Schol. *Tim.* 20dff. = Martina 1968, §62 specifies that the elder Critias' father was Dropides, Solon's *brother*.

[21] The lines were used in oratory to exemplify how Critias' family was always disrespectful, T79 GPr.

[22] Cf. How and Wells 1912 on Hdt. 1.30.1.

[23] Tarán 1965, 8ff.

visited Cyprus: he bids farewell to the ruler and prays that
Cypris send him away in a ship, bring the city joy and fame and
himself a safe return (fr. 11 GPr = 19 W Plu., *Sol.* 26). The
purpose of the visit described in the verses, whether real or
imaginary, is to account for the city's name (*Vit.Arat.* p. 16.14ff.
Martin). Hecataeus in the fifth century knew this etymology
(T27 GPr = *FGrHist* 1F268). In the Hellenistic age, a tradition developed that Solon had visited Soloi in Cilicia, which
was by then a more impressive place than its namesake in
Cyprus. The origin of that story appears to have been a poem
of Euphorion, possibly mistakenly, since Euphorion (fr. 1
Powell) may have been referring to Solon of Lindos (*Vit.Arat.*
3, p. 14 Martin). A papyrus life of Solon (*POxy* 680) preserves
both versions, but Diogenes Laertius (1.50–51) says Solon
visited Cyprus but actually stayed at Soloi in Cilicia.[24]

Solon is also said to have met king Croesus of Lydia. The
story was questioned even in antiquity on chronological
grounds: Solon's archonship was dated to 594/3 and Croesus'
reign to a generation later.[25] But even if it can be presumed that
Solon enacted his laws after his archonship, as late as the 570s,
so that his voluntary exile from Athens could bring him to
Sardis at the beginning of Croesus' reign,[26] there is reason to
consider the meeting 'representative' rather than historical.[27]
Only one of the speeches Herodotus puts in Solon's mouth
refers to an extant poem, the verses that give the upper limit of
man's life as seventy (fr. 23.18 GPr = 27.18 W; cf. fr. 26
GPr = 20 W). Herodotus' Solon begins from there to calculate
the number of days in a man's life, and to deduce that the
chances are remote of having good fortune last through all of
them. In Herodotus the poet's general speculation has acquired
a specific ethical purpose. Solon's verses about the dangers of
wealth (fr. 18 GPr = 24 W) would make him an ideal adviser
for the wealthiest and therefore most vulnerable monarch of
his day.

[24] Gallo 1976, 29–36.
[25] Martina 1968, §26 = Plu., *Sol.* 27; the fluctuation in date is a sign of
mythology; Finley 1975, 15–26.
[26] Hignett 1952 316–21; Martina 1968, §261n. for literature.
[27] Wehrli 1973, 202.

A relatively elaborate tradition was preserved about Solon because Athens and her form of government had such great historical importance. If the achievements of a polis like Megara had attracted the interests of historians, an equally detailed biography of the poet Theognis might have been developed.[28] Verses attributed to Theognis describe his leading role in the politics of his country (39–52, 667–82), his views on government (847–50, 865–8, 891–4), his ethical advice (129–30, 197–208, 373–400), and his complaints about unfair distribution of wealth (831–2, 903–30). But the brief biography of Theognis in the Suda merely summarises the topics of Theognis' poetry, with specific complaints about 'the disgusting and pederastic love-poems scattered among them'. Solon too wrote about the pleasures of intercourse with young boys; Plutarch uses him as the exemplar of the *erōtikos anēr* (fr. 16 GPr = 25 W). But his biographers emphasise his political accomplishments.[29]

Comparison with Theognis also helps explain why Solon came to be considered one of the Seven Wise Men. Theognis complains about the political changes he is witnessing: 'who can bear looking at this?' (58, 1110); 'trample the mindless common people underfoot, strike them with a sharp goad' (847–8). But the 'I' in Solon's poetry says that he favours neither side and claims that he is uninfluenced by selfish motivations: 'if a man other than I had taken the goad, an envious or a greedy man, he would not have held back the people' (fr. 36.20ff. GPr = 30 W). The sayings of the Seven Wise Men emphasise restraint and moderation; according to Plato they were the authors of the famous warnings inscribed on the temple of Apollo at Delphi: 'Know Thyself' and 'Nothing to Excess'.[30] The sayings of Solon the Wise Man reflect in outline the balanced views expressed in his poetry, especially on law and government.[31] His apophthegm 'satisfaction is born from wealth and insolence from satisfaction' (D.L. 1.59 = M170) is a prose abstraction of Solon's verses 'satisfaction begets hybris, whenever great wealth follows men whose minds are not

---

[28] Cf. p. 38 n.59 above.
[29] Cf. p. 40 above.
[30] Cf. Snell 1938.
[31] Martina 1968, §§ 179, 180, 186; cf. fr. 29a GPr = 33 W, 7 GPr = 5 W.

sound' (fr. 8.3–4). But most proverbial wisdom attributed to him as a Wise Man has no direct relation to his surviving poetry, and some is even put by biographers into the mouth of one of the other Wise Men.[32] 'Never tell a lie'; 'Pursue worthy aims'; 'Make your mind your leader' (D.L. 1.59). If only the apophthegms of Solon had survived, and none of his poetry, Solon would not seem very different from Thales, or Pittacus, or Bias.[33]

Traditions about the Wise Men appear to have been formed in the fifth century.[34] Herodotus has Croesus invite Solon to his court, the way the fifth-century tyrant Hieron invited the poets Pindar, Aeschylus and Bacchylides. By the fourth century stories were told of a meeting which all seven of the Wise Men attended. The canon of the seven varies but Solon is always included.[35] Plato, as usual shaping the story to suit his purpose, includes Chilon of Sparta and says all approved and emulated Spartan culture (*Prot.* 343a).[36] Ephorus put them at Croesus' court in Sardis (*FGrHist* 70F181); Archetimus of Syracuse two generations earlier at the court of Cypselus of Corinth (*FHG* IV 318).[37] The ease with which fourth-century authors could vary participants and setting suggests that they regarded the meeting of the Seven Wise Men as a representative occasion like the contest between Hesiod and Homer or the debate between Aeschylus and Euripides in the lower world. A papyrus fragment preserves an account of the dinner composed in hexameters with prose interludes, like Alcidamas' fourth-century version of the death of Homer.[38] Perhaps this was the standard format for fourth-century and even fifth-century symposium entertainments about the lives of famous men.

If more of Solon's poetry survived we could distinguish with more confidence between the real events in his life and the

---

[32] E.g. Martina 1968, §§ 161–2, 165, 167, 174, 199.

[33] Wehrli 1973, 196.

[34] Momigliano 1971, 27.

[35] Martina 1968, §106; cf. Dem. Phal. fr. 114, with Wehrli's note.

[36] Page, *PMG* p. 514.

[37] An idiosyncratic interpretation of uncertain date; see Schwartz, *RE* 4.460.

[38] *PSI* 1093; Snell 1966, 115–17.

accretions of tradition. Several developments seem to be taking place simultaneously. Starting from the poet's own portrayal of himself as a heroic defender of his country and traditional religious ethics, biographers attributed to him specific legislative reforms and political actions particularly once the Athenian system of government had been altered in the aftermath of the Peloponnesian war. In fourth-century oratory Solon had become the archetypal ancestor of the Athenian constitution, a representative, like Abraham Lincoln, of the values that once made his country great. It is characteristic of such political traditions to endow one historical figure with the accomplishments of many.[39] In contrast with the political biographers' desire to credit Solon with specific facts, ethical popular mythology strives to make him fit a general pattern. Like other lawgivers he comes into prominence during a period of crisis, resolves it by his laws and leaves once his code is established.[40] His wisdom is made to seem proverbial, by stripping from it specific references to Athens and her land.

[39] Finley 1975, 44.
[40] Szedegy-Maszak 1978, 200.

# CHAPTER FIVE

# Simonides

Lest I seem unduly radical in suggesting that much of Solon's biography was created after the sixth century, we need only compare what happened to Simonides and Pindar. Although both poets wrote for the same sorts of occasions and even for some of the same patrons, tradition treats them quite differently. But once we have seen something of the biographers' methods it is possible to understand why. In the cases of these poets as well, traditions develop along two different lines apparently simultaneously: (1) a tendency to put general utterances of the poet into a specific historical setting; (2) a desire to remove distinctions so that events in the poet's life will conform to a recognised pattern of significant experience.

Enough of Solon's poetry survives to enable us to trace how biographers turned him from statesman into adviser and Wise Man. But so much of Simonides' work is lost that we can only conjecture on the basis of analogous oeuvres like Pindar's why tradition made him not only a sage but a miser. Of the two the role of sage is easier to account for. Fifth-century lyric derives from specific myths and incidents abstract statements about human experience: the power of the gods, the brief but memorable acts of men; the envy of the unsuccessful for the man who achieves. Plato cites verses from a poem by Simonides for Scopas of Thessaly (*PMG* 542) which comments on an apophthegm of Pittacus about the vicissitudes of life and the limits of human excellence.[1] Analogues to his observations can be found in the victory odes of Pindar and Bacchylides: the futility of fighting against necessity; the inability of any man to have complete good fortune.[2] A scrap of papyrus from one of

[1] Wehrli 1973, 199–200.
[2] Dickie 1978, 21–33.

Simonides' victory odes preserves part of a statement about fate (*PMG* 519 fr. 79, cf. 514); another ode compares good fortune to the period of winter weather known as halcyon days (508). Pindar speaks of human hopes whirled up and down by the wind (*Ol.* 12.5–6a).[3] Sentiments about the frailty of human life are cited from Simonides' *Lamentations* (*PMG* 520–2); quotations from Pindar's suggest that he offered consolation by describing happiness in the next world (130–4; cf. 129).

Gnomic statements in Pindar's victory odes are so abstract that they can seem almost trite when separated from the particular situation that they describe (e.g., *Ol.* 1.113). But Simonides' comments, like Solon's, make sense out of context because of their directness and the precision of his metaphors (e.g., *PMG* 521.3–4); his style makes him sound more like an adviser than a poet whose verse is memorable for the originality of its narrative and its dramatic phrasing. None of the sayings attributed to Simonides by Xenophon in the fourth century or by later biographers bears close resemblance to any of Simonides' poetry known to us, but the clarity of his observations retains some sense of the character of his style. Thales was said to have advised 'be envied rather than pitied' (1 p. 64 §9 DK).[4] Pindar in his *First Pythian Ode* tersely tells Hieron: 'Envy is better than pity; don't pass over what is beautiful' (85–6). But Simonides in Xenophon's dialogue *Hieron* concludes by explaining to the tyrant why this 'philosophy' works: if you enrich your friends, you make yourself powerful and loved; 'so being fortunate you won't be envied' (XI.15).

Even less survives to suggest why Simonides became known as a miser, and was portrayed as a parasite at the banquets of the rich. According to tradition he was the first poet to compose for pay. The source of this information is a scholium on Pindar's *Isthm.* 2: when Pindar says the Muse now is paid for her services, the commentators and the Alexandrian poet-scholar Callimachus understood him to be referring specifically to Simonides (schol. *Isthm.* 2.9a, III p. 214 Dr; Callim. fr. 222).[5] But in

---

[3] Nisetich 1977, 255–64.
[4] Milobenski 1964, 1–2.
[5] Bell 1978, 29; Woodbury 1968, 529.

the scholia to Pindar, a compliment to a patron for his generosity is often interpreted as a reference to payment. For
example, the commentators account for a prominent statement
about men's respect for gold by explaining: 'We know that
Pindar was completely avaricious ("a gold-lover"). He testifies
to his own miserliness ("love for silver") here when he praises
wealth and hints that it is appropriate for those who are praised
to repay Pindar with gold' (schol. *Isthm.* 5.2a, III p. 242 Dr).[6]
When Pindar contrasts his winged verse with the stationary art
of a sculptor, an ancient commentator explained that Pindar
had asked three thousand drachmas to write an ode, and the
family had replied that for the same price they could have a
statue; later they gave in and paid him, but he began the poem
by referring to a statue in order to reprove them (schol. *Nem.*
5.1a, III p. 98 Dr). The scholia suggest that Pindar omits
reference to an earlier victory because 'perhaps' he had not
been given the commission to write its victory ode (schol.
*Pyth.* 10 inscr. II p. 242 Dr). 'The wise are not hurt by gain' is
taken to mean that victors should pay to be immortalised
(schol. *Nem.* 7.25a III 120).

But these stories about Pindar's concern with money were
never put into a collection of anecdotes.[7] Pindar's statements,
unlike Simonides', are intricately involved with other forms of
praise and so do not lend themselves to ready summarising or
quotation.[8] In *Isthmian Ode* 2, for example, he observes that the
Muse (i.e., poets) must now be paid as affirmation that despite
his being hired his admiration for the victor is sincere.[9] Bacchylides' references to wealth inspire no anecdotal explanations
because he tends to detach himself from them: Hieron will be
honoured for having 'shown the flowers of his wealth to mortals',
the poet for the beauty of his song (Ode 3.92–8). But anecdotes
are told about Simonides because like Pindar he made references to his patron's wealth in the first person (e.g. 542.11, 21,
26f., 36f.), and also because unlike Pindar the lucidity of his

[6] Lefkowitz 1975, 82; Bell 1978, 61. Cf. also schol. *Nem.* 7. 25a, III p. 120;
schol. *Pyth* 11. 58a, II p. 260.

[7] Cf. Austin 1967, 10.

[8] Cf. p. 57 below.

[9] Bell 1978, 61; Woodbury 1968, 538–42.

style made his comments detachable from their original settings.

The natural setting for poets to meet with patrons was the symposium. Pindar and Bacchylides pay tribute to their patrons' hospitality (e.g. *Ol.* 1.11, *Nem.* 1.19–22, Bacch. 3.15); they contrast themselves with abusive poets who fatten themselves on hatred (*Pyth.* 2.54, 55; Bacch. 3.68).[10] In comedy the poet becomes a parasite. In Aristophanes' *Birds* a lyric poet sings songs 'à la Simonides' (919) and recites some Pindar (941ff.) in the hope of getting food and a new cloak.[11] Chamaeleon in his biography of Simonides tells how the poet complained when he did not receive a share of the roast hare served to Hieron's other guests (fr. 33 Wehrli). We might compare how obscure references to greed and to slanderers in Pindar's *Pythian* 2 led ancient commentators to suggest that Pindar was criticising Hieron for giving the commission for the ode not to himself but to Bacchylides (e.g. schol. *Pyth.* 2.131a, II p. 53 Dr).[12] In these stories the hospitable home of the epinician poet's patron (e.g. *Ol.* 1.11, *Nem.* 1.21–2) becomes the setting of a dinner-party where the poet must beg for his food.

Since Xenophanes in the early fifth century is said to have called Simonides a 'miser' (21B DK), anecdotes about him were apparently put into circulation during his own lifetime, at first in the form of comic parody. Xenophanes' comment about Simonides is cited to explain a joke in Aristophanes about Simonides being old and shabby and ready to go to sea on a mat in order to make money (*Peace* 695ff.).[13] Xenophanes made fun of Homer and Hesiod as well as of Simonides in his *Silloi*: he wished to show that the poets most esteemed for their wisdom (21B10) were not so clever after all, because they never questioned the logical flaws in conventional religion (e.g. 21B11, 12, 14).[14] By the end of his lifetime the poet Anacreon was portrayed in vase painting wearing a woman's headdress while singing.[15] Although like his contemporary Simonides he

[10] Milobenski 1964, 4n.15; on the greed of the envious, Nagy 1979, ch. 12, §10.

[11] Bell 1978, 40.

[12] Lefkowitz 1975, 81–2.

[13] Cf. Bell 1978, 35.

[14] Cf. p. 3 above; Heraclitus 22B56–7 DK; Kirk and Raven 1957, 167–9.

[15] Boardman 1975, 219.

wrote poems for a variety of occasions (e.g. on war, *PMG* 504), Aristophanes in the *Thesmophoriazousae* talks about him wearing a woman's headdress and dancing in an effeminate manner (163) so that his manners would match his poetry (150).[16] Critias called Anacreon 'sweet weaver of womanish song, rouser of symposia, rival of flutes, lover of the lyre' (88B1 DK = *PMG* 500). His Suda biography says 'his life was devoted to love and song'; he was said to have died by choking on a grape-pip (Val. Max. 9.8).

In the fourth century Simonides' interest in money took on a positive ethical function.[17] He advises friends and patrons to conserve resources and guard against other men's greed. Xenophon has Hieron ask Simonides how to conduct himself as tyrant and question him about general philosophical issues.[18] Aristotle quotes from what Simonides said to Hieron's wife about 'wisdom and wealth' (*Rhet.* 1391a8);[19] a collection of these sayings about expenditures, 'respected for their truth' was circulating in Egypt in the third century (*PHibeh* 1.17).[20] Theocritus could count on his audience in Alexandria and King Hieron II of Syracuse to understand Simonides in his poem to represent himself, a poet justified in asking for support.[21] Unlike Callimachus, who based his allusion to Simonides' 'hired Muse' on Pindar's verse (fr. 222),[22] Theocritus drew on the biographical tradition that gave Simonides' views on wealth a moral purpose. Chamaeleon tells how Simonides sold most of the daily allotment of food given him by Hieron (fr. 33 Wehrli). The same story was told as a criticism of Themistocles (Plu., *Them.* 5.1), but Chamaeleon has Simonides claim that his conduct serves as an example of Hieron's generosity and his own moderation.[23]

---

[16] Cf. Anacreon *PMG* 388, 424.

[17] Wehrli 1973, 202–3.

[18] Cf. Cic., *Nat.D.* 1.22.

[19] Aristotle also refers to Simonides' 'Tall Tales', *PMG* 653.

[20] Cf. collections of advice in mythological settings, such as the *Sayings of Admetus*, *PMG* 749; *Chiron's Precepts*, Hes. fr. 283–5 MW; Wehrli 1973, 195n.12, 197–8.

[21] Austin 1967, 11–12.

[22] P. 50 above.

[23] Bell 1978, 41, 63–6.

In later tradition Simonides was also known for his invention of mnemonic devices. The Suda biography states simply that Simonides had a remarkable memory, but a papyrus of the third century A.D. indicates that this information, like the stories of his miserliness, originated in his poetry: 'Some attribute to him the discovery of mnemonics and he demonstrates this somewhere by means of his epigrams' (*POxy* 1800 i.36).[24] His surviving poetry displays an interest in the meaning of words; he anticipates Socrates by using antithesis as a means of definition (e.g., 'if the dreadful were dreadful to you,' *PMG* 543.18; cf. *EG* 271, 415).[25] His skilful use of antithesis, assonance and alliteration helps make his epigrams easy to remember (e.g. 167–8, 216–17, 416). Word play in poetry provided occasion for elaborate biographical aetiologies.[26] Chamaeleon provides detailed stories as 'solutions' to riddles attributed to Simonides (fr. 34 Wehrli/Ath. 456c).[27] When Pindar says in a dithyramb, 'In past times song was long drawn out and the letter *san* (*s*) was counterfeit', the fourth-century biographer Clearchus explained that Pindar had been criticised for using *s* too much (fr. 88 Wehrli/Ath. 455c/Pind., fr. 70b 1–2). The Suda biography says Simonides invented the signs for the long vowels *ēta* and *ōmega*, and the double letters *xi* and *psi*. Did a poem attributed to Simonides refer to these 'new' letters in the Attic alphabet?[28]

The writer of the papyrus biography (or his source) also had access to lines that could be directly understood as biographical testimony to Simonides' extraordinary mental powers. Two epigrams attributed to Simonides claim that he taught choruses and won prizes when he was very old (189–90, 181–4). Another epigram, varying the same theme, states that 'no one's memory compares with Simonides' at eighty' (14 W).[29] Satyrus tells a story that claims extraordinary competence in old age also for Sophocles. The dramatist responded to his son's criticism that

[24] Slater 1972, 236.
[25] Bell 1978, 82.
[26] E.g. also Ath. x. 453cff.
[27] On riddles in symposia, Bell 1978, 59n.118; also Cleobulia, West 1971b, II 50–1; Clearchus fr. 84–5 Wehrli.
[28] On the alphabet, Buck 1933, 71–3.
[29] Cf. Slater 1972, 236.

he was senile by producing the *Oedipus at Colonus* (*FHG* 3.162/ *Vit. Soph.* 13).[30] Behind both stories lies the comic figure of the energetic old poet refusing to make way for younger men.[31]

Third-century authors added to the portrait of Simonides the miser and mnemonic expert more conventional indications of his importance as a poet. Callimachus relates how Simonides was buried in Acragas (fr. 64), away from his home like Homer and Hesiod. He has the dead poet claim that his tomb was torn down by an evil man, a general who did not fear the Dioscuri; they had taken the poet outside just before the house fell down on his patrons the Scopadae. Further details are given in Cicero's version of the story (*De Orat* 2.86/*PMG* 510): Scopas had complained that Simonides had devoted so much of his song to the praise of Castor and Polydeuces that he should ask them for half the fee.[32] Afterwards Simonides was able to identify the bodies by recalling the seating arrangement.

The ambience of a dinner party is characteristic of fourth-century biographies of Simonides, but the rest of the story sounds Hellenistic. Pindar, according to the scholia, criticised Simonides for his digressions (schol. *Nem.* 4.60b); Alexandrian scholars tended not to understand the function of myth in archaic poetry.[33] Commentators explained Pindar's statement that he was not a sculptor by relating how the victor's family complained about Pindar's price for the ode.[34] The story of the miraculous rescue that confirms the poet's honesty resembles Eratosthenes' account of how Hesiod was found to have been falsely accused and his murderers identified and sacrificed to the god of hospitality.[35] The improbable notion of the falling roof could derive from a mistaken interpretation of a term like *oikos* (house in the sense of family) in the original poem,[36] in the way that Solon's *agorē* ('speech') was later understood as

[30] Pp. 84–5 below; cf. Hesiod's old age, p. 3 above.
[31] Pp. 52 above, 85 below.
[32] Other examples of piety in his poetry are *PMG* 526m, 581.5.
[33] Slater 1972, 234; Lefkowitz 1975, 80–1.
[34] P. 51 above.
[35] P. 6 above; also Jacoby on *FGrHist* 244F67. Cf. the story of how Simonides was saved by the ghost of a man he buried, which explains *EG* 412ff.; also Ibycus' cranes, p. 37 above.
[36] Slater 1972, 238.

'market-place'.[37] Inconsistency in the tradition suggests that some authorities did not directly consult Simonides' text.[38] Quintilian notes the different sites for the banquet and names of the patrons; he thought the story fictitious, since he could find no reference to it in Simonides' poems, and felt certain that the poet would have mentioned such a complimentary tale if he had known it (*Inst. Orat.* xi.ii.11–16).

Since stories about Simonides were told as early as the fifth century and relatively few citations of his lyric verse survive, it would seem that by the fourth century the poet's biography had become more interesting and accessible than much of his poetry. An indication of its importance is that Horace claims authority by acting as well as by writing like a moralistic poet; he does not say that the Muses spoke to him (cf. Callim. fr. 2, 1.21–2) but describes how on a number of occasions the gods kept him safe from danger (*Carm.* 3.4.9–28).[39] The way Simonides is characterised in the tradition serves as an index of popular taste: the content of poetry matters more than its style; specifics disappear into the generic;[40] the status of poet is reduced from honoured guest to learned dependent. Of his poetry, more epigrams are preserved because their general reflections better suit his character in his biography. Epigrams in his style were steadily attributed to him;[41] as in the case of later additions to the collection of Theognis' poems,[42] the new verses were not meant simply to deceive but also to represent, like the biographies, a contemporary understanding of the poet.

[37] P. 40 above.
[38] See esp. Pfeiffer on Call. fr. 222; Page on *PMG* 510.
[39] Cf. his use of the notion of Euripides' metamorphosis into a bird, Satyrus fr. 39.xvii; see p. 169 n.13.
[40] Wehrli 1973, 203–4.
[41] On authenticity, Gow-Page 1965, II 516.
[42] On additions to the Theognidean Corpus, West 1971b, I 172–3, II 93; cf. also Menander's *Maxims*, by various poets, Lesky 1966, 646.

# CHAPTER SIX

# Pindar

Pindar's poetry testifies that like Simonides he was entertained by Hieron of Syracuse (e.g. *Ol.* 1.10–11). But in the commentaries and the Lives Pindar does not play the detached role of the wise adviser, because he portrays himself in his first-person statements as grappling with the same dangers as his patrons.[1] He calls hopes winged, but that is also how he describes his own poem (*Pyth.* 8.90–1, 33–4). He states that mortals should search for what is possible and realise their limitations, but also that a poet too should 'not strive for immortal life, but drain his practical skill' (*Pyth.* 3.59–61). Simonides instead separates himself from ordinary men, e.g., 'I will never look for the impossible and throw my life away in empty hope' (*PMG* 541.21–3).

In speaking of himself as if he were an athlete, Pindar meant to express his understanding of victorious achievement.[2] But ancient commentators tended to read sentences one by one, out of context, and thought that what he said referred primarily to himself.[3] When he uses metaphors to describe his supremacy, the scholia suggest that he is hinting at the weaknesses of poetic competitors. A pair of crows chattering against an eagle are Bacchylides and Simonides (schol. *Ol.* 2.154b). Jackdaws that keep low while the swift eagle catches his prey are identified with Bacchylides (schol. *Nem.* 3.143); so are an ape's cleverly deceptive antics (schol. *Pyth.* 2.163b, 166d, 171bcd). Unnamed envious 'enemies' (schol. *Nem.* 4.60b) and the 'greedy muse who works for money' (schol. *Isthm.* 2.9a,b, 15a) are construed as references to Simonides.[4]

---

[1] Lefkowitz 1980, 29–49.
[2] Ibid., 37ff.
[3] Lefkowitz 1975b, 1977.
[4] Lefkowitz 1975, 79–82; Podlecki 1979, 13ff.

A statement about what he has not done in an ode is read as an apology: that the short measure of a song prevents him from saying everything indicates that he was only paid to sing one triad (schol. *Isthm.* 1.85b); that he is not a maker of statues means that his patrons thought he charged too much for an ode (schol. *Nem.* 5.1a; p. 51 above); failure to mention a victory means that he wasn't paid to sing about it (schol. *Pyth.* 10. inscr., II p. 42);[5] that he 'did not savage Neoptolemus in ruthless words' suggests that he was being criticised by the Aeginetans for what he said in another song (schol. *Nem.* 7.150a). That Rhadamanthys didn't enjoy deceptions means that Hieron shouldn't listen to slander about Pindar (schol. *Pyth.* 2.133a); 'it is likely,' the commentary suggests, that Pindar was accused of being friendly with Thrasydaeus, the son of Hieron's rival Theron (schol. *Pyth.* 2.132b). His not wishing to comment on 'acts done justly and unjustly' is also interpreted as a reference to the quarrel between the two Sicilian tyrants (schol. *Ol.* 2.29c). Characteristically, Simonides is credited with having made peace between the two rulers by his timely intervention (schol. *Ol.* 2.29d).[6]

Asking a rhetorical question is interpreted as a sign of insecurity.[7] Pindar in his encomium for Xenophon of Corinth wrote: 'I wonder what the Lords of the Isthmus will say of me, who am composing this beginning for a song thought honey-sweet, as a companion of shared women' (fr. 122.10ff.). Chamaeleon, taking the lines out of context, explained: 'It is evident when Pindar speaks to the prostitutes that there was concern about how the matter would appear to the Corinthians. Trusting in himself, as seems likely, he wrote immediately: "We have taught how to test gold with a clean touchstone"' (fr. 31 Wehrli). The phrases 'it is evident' and 'as seems likely' indicate that Chamaeleon is offering his readers what he believes to be a logical interpretation.[8] But behind what he says is an assumption of strained relations between the poet and his

---

[5] Bundy 1962, I 33; cf. schol. *Ol.* 10. 1b.
[6] Cf. Timaeus *FGrHist* 566F93. In Diod. Sic. 11.48.7 Hieron himself is peacemaker; Podlecki 1979, 8–9.
[7] Cf. schol. *Nem.* 3.45c: 'he sees he is digressing'; also schol. *Pyth.* 11.58b.
[8] Cf. Lefkowitz 1975, 76.

public: Pindar speaks of Lords of the Isthmus, that is, the judges at the Isthmian games; Chamaeleon assumes that he means the citizens of Corinth, the way Aristodemus has Pindar in *Nem.* 7 apologise not to his patron but to the Aeginetans in general.[9]

But it is an indication of Pindar's relative importance as a poet that the Byzantine Vitae preserve stories of his early recognition.[10] An anecdote attributed to the biographers Chamaeleon and Ister has him discover his talent on Mt. Helicon (*Vit.* 1.1.6ff.), where the muses spoke to Hesiod and gave him his laurel branch.[11] But Pindar's experience occurs while he is asleep: he awakes to find that bees have built a honeycomb in his mouth.[12] Pindar describes his song 'like a bee (*melissa*) rushing from story to story' (*Pyth.* 10.45); in Hellenistic epigrams his song (*melos*) was said to sound like a bee's (Ant.Sid., *EG* 3446–7).[13] Simonides was called Melicertes because of his sweetness (Suda). Some of Pindar's biographers said he only dreamt about the honeycomb, but Chamaeleon's and Ister's version give the traditional metaphor a contrived and ludicrous tangibility; cf. the sixth-century A.D. epic poet who described how on a bronze statue of Homer 'a Pierian bee wandered about his divine mouth, bringing forth a dripping honeycomb' (*AP.* 2.342–3).[14]

The first public recognition of Pindar's talent occurs significantly in Athens: his teacher Agathocles or Apollodorus was away, and entrusted the training of the cyclic choruses to Pindar even though he was a boy (*Vit.* 1.1.11). The next anecdote in Pindar's *Vita* also gives the Athenians credit for recognising his talent: when he wrote a dithyramb praising Athens (fr. 76) the Thebans fined him a thousand drachmas, which the Athenians paid (1.1.16). The story about his doing a man's work as a child has analogues in folktale: in the Herodotean life of Homer the school-teacher Phemius recognised the boy

[9] P. 58 above.
[10] See Appendix 2.
[11] P. 2 above.
[12] The same story is also told of Plato; Riginos 1976, §3; cf. Lefkowitz 1975b, n.28; Lefkowitz 1975, 73n.8; Bell 1978, 58n.116; p. 9 n.35 above; p. 80 below.
[13] For the pun, cf. *Nem.* 11.18; *APl* 305; Gow-Page 1965 on 284.
[14] P. 24 above.

Melesigenes' talent and left his school to him when he died
(*Vit.Hdt.* 5).[15] But the stories also testify to the importance of
Athenian culture; in the fourth century the Spartan poet
Tyrtaeus was said to have been an Athenian.[16]

The next anecdotes reported in the *Vita* offer testimony of
divine and posthumous recognition.[17] Pan was heard singing
one of Pindar's odes (fr. 95).[18] Demeter appeared to Pindar in
a dream and demanded a hymn for herself; he wrote the song
(fr. 37) and built an altar to her.[19] He was born (as his own
words suggest, fr. 193) during the Pythian festival; Euripides
was born on the day of the battle of Salamis.[20] When Thebes
was destroyed Pindar's house was preserved by the Spartan
general Pausanias; someone had written a trochaic line on the
house, 'Don't burn the house of Pindar the Muses' poet'; the
same story was later told about Pindar's house and Alexander
(1.2.10–14; cf. 1.5.11–14). Pindar's name is called every day
when the priest closes the temple of Apollo at Delphi. Pilgrims
to the shrine of Ammon asked what would be best for Pindar,
and the poet died on the same day (1.2.19). The Suda biography
says that Pindar himself asked to be given what was best and
died in the theatre while lying in the arms of his beloved
Theoxenus of Tenedos, for whom he wrote an encomium
(fr. 123).

In his version of the story of Demeter's epiphany, Aristodemus (*FGrHist* 383F*13) assigned an important role to the
ordinary people involved with the great poet: 'Pindar was
giving a lesson to Olympichus the flute player when there was
a noise and flame on the mountain where they were practising.
Pindar thought that he saw a stone statue of the Mother of the
gods in front of him, and set up a statue near his house of the
Mother of the gods and Pan; the citizens of Thebes sent an
inquiry to the Delphic oracle about what had happened, and
the oracle confirmed that a shrine be established to the Mother

---

[15] P. 20 above; Lefkowitz 1975, 73.
[16] P. 38 above.
[17] Lefkowitz 1975, 73–4.
[18] Lehnus 1979, 57–68.
[19] Lehnus 1979, 1–55.
[20] P. 92 below.

of the gods. The citizens were amazed that Pindar had antici-
pated the oracle and honoured Pindar equally in the ritual to
the goddess' (schol. *Pyth.* 3.137b). In his explanation of Pindar's
statement that he did not savage Neoptolemus with ruthless
words, Aristodemus has Pindar apologise not to the victor or
his father but to the citizens of Aegina (schol. *Nem.* 7.150a).
Callimachus, elaborating on a standard form of epitaph, has
the dead Simonides engage the audience directly in the story
of the desecration of his grave (fr. 64); Eratosthenes has
Hesiod's dog identify his murderers (fr. 19 Powell).[21]

Aristodemus' account may in part be based on Pindar's
original hymn.[22] Pindar describes an epiphany of the hero
Alcmeon in *Pythian* 8;[23] the *Homeric Hymn to Dionysus* describes
how a ship's crew reacts to the god's presence and how the
captain establishes his cult. But Aristodemus' story, unlike a
hymn (e.g. Pindar fr. 33e) concentrates on human responses
more than on the divinity, and the original hymn would not
have mentioned the 'equal' honour given by the Thebans to
Pindar himself. Since Pausanias gives a different account of
the hymn's origin, the hymn itself must have provided no
indication of exactly how the poet came to write it: Persephone
(not Demeter) appeared to Pindar in a dream; Pindar wrote
the song for her after his death; the poet recited it in a dream to
an old woman relative, who wrote it down from memory
(9.23.2). The location, Pindar's house, may have been suggested
by his stating in *Pyth.* 3: 'I will pray to the Mother whom girls
sing to at night with Pan beside my door' (77–9).[24]

The anecdote in the *Vita* about Pan singing a song (or Paean)
of Pindar also could have been deduced from allusions to the
circumstances of performance in the song itself (e.g. in Pindar
fr. 107ab),[25] or from a direct request to the god to join in their
song. Sappho addresses Aphrodite frequently in her poems (e.g.
fr. 1, 2); a third century biography gives special emphasis to

---

[21] Pp. 55, 6–7 above.
[22] Lehnus 1979, 55 28n.93; Lefkowitz 1975, 74.
[23] Lehnus 1979, 37; Page 1955, 40–1.
[24] Cf. p. 63 below.
[25] E.g. *panistai* in Menander, *Dysc.* 222 Gomme-Sandbach; cf. Lehnus
1979, 67.

her relationship with the goddess: 'she was in such high favour with the citizens that Callias of Mytilene said in . . . Aphrodite' (*SLG* 261, 11–16).[26] Once the deities themselves were thought to intervene only in human incarnation, the direct encounters described by archaic poets could no longer be understood. The scholia do not accept that Pindar in *Pyth.* 8 literally meant that he met Alcmeon; they proposed instead that the chorus was speaking about a local hero shrine, or that he was referring to the hero-cult in Thebes of Alcmeon's father Amphiaraus (schol. *Pyth.* 8.78ab).[27] Tzetzes insists in his biography that Hesiod's encounter with the Muses was meant allegorically, or took place in a dream (p. 46 W).[28] So in the anecdotes about Pindar's hymn to Pan the imagined circumstances of performance are more carefully preserved than the poet's words, and the poet's response becomes as important as the god's singing.[29]

Pindar's biographers preserve details about Pindar's family that do not seem to have been available to biographers of other poets. Their source material was poetry about him or by him, some of it poetry for local celebrations with a high preponderance of proper names. A biography of the second or third century A.D. records that 'according to Corinna and other poetesses he was the son of Scopelinus; according to most poets he was the son of Daiphantus' (*POxy* 2438.1–4).[30] The Suda biography of Pindar prefers Daiphantus, because 'Scopelinus' son is less famous and a relative of Pindar's'; the *Vita* says Scopelinus according to some authorities was Pindar's uncle and aulos-teacher (1.1.3–5).[31] If the names Scopelinus and Pindar were linked in a poem by a Boeotian poetess like Corinna or Myrtis, it was in a manner sufficiently ambiguous to suggest a variety of interpretations.[32]

---

[26] Gronewald 1974, 114–16; Dover 1978, 174.

[27] Lefkowitz, 1975b, 179ff.    [28] P. 9 above.

[29] E.g. there is no reference to a myth, Lehnus 1979, 127; all citations are listed in ibid., 57–8.

[30] Text in Gallo 1968, 49ff.

[31] The Thomas *Vita* (1.4.11) makes Scopelinus Pindar's stepfather and teacher; Scopelinus passed Pindar on to Lasus for instruction. The anecdote suggests that Pindar was thought to be influenced by Lasus; Fairweather 1974, 256–7 and pp. 128–9, 131 below.

[32] Lehnus 1977, 78–82.

Only a few lines survive to indicate the kind of testimony the biographer may have been drawing from 'Corinna and other poetesses'. Corinna is said to have written, 'I blame clear-voiced Myrtis because being a woman she entered into rivalry with Pindar' (*PMG* 664a). The citation gives no indication of the context of these lines, but only in partheneia does the 'I' involve herself so directly in the judgment of other people. Alcman's chorus of girls says 'Our famous chorus-leader won't let me praise or blame [Agido]' (*PMG* 1.43–44); 'The [Doves] . . . fight for us' (60–3); 'It is through Hagesichora that the girls have reached the peace they long for . . .' (90–1).[33]

Other family names come from Pindar's own partheneia.[34] The *Vita* says he wrote a partheneion for his *son* Daiphantus (1.3.4–5). Since sons were often named after their grandfathers, presumably Daiphantus would have been Pindar's father's name as well. Sappho speaks of a *pais* (child or slave) Cleis (fr. 132), who was understood by biographers to be her daughter (*POxy* 1800.i.14); the Suda biography gives Cleis also as the name of Sappho's mother.[35] According to the papyrus biography, Pindar 'mentions' his daughters Protomache and Eumetis in the same partheneon as Daiphantus (fr. 94c; *POxy* 2438.24–5, 28–30). Was their relationship explicitly stated, or was it rather *inferred* from the song by biographers?[36] The names of all the girls in the chorus are listed in Alcman's *partheneion* (*PMG* 1.70–7).[37] The reference to '*korai* (girls or daughters) who sing at night to the Mother with Pan near my door' (*Pyth.* 3.77) suggested that Pindar had daughters (schol. *Pyth.* 3.139a), the way Hesiod's statement 'Neither may I nor my son be called a just man' encouraged his biographers to suggest that Hesiod raped Stesichorus' mother.[38] Theban maidens also sing to Pagondas, one of the names suggested for Pindar's father (fr. 94b, 10).

[33] Cf. Pind., fr. 94b 66–76.
[34] Lefkowitz 1975, 75.
[35] Fr. 98a.1 refers to her mother without a name.
[36] They are mentioned in an epigram about Pindar's death; cf. p. 10 n.37 above.
[37] Calame 1977, II 32.
[38] P. 4 above. Rose 1931, 121–2 dates the epigram to the late third century; cf. Aristodemus' aetiology of Pindar's Demeter hymn (p. 60 above).

Names of other relatives appear simply to represent aspects of Pindar's professional achievement. According to the Ambrosian *Vita* Pindar's mother was called Cleodice or Cledice ('justly famous').[39] His wife has the equally suitable name Megacleia ('of great fame'), or in the Metrical *Vita*, Timoxeine ('honoured by strangers'). The Metrical *Vita* also gives Pindar a twin brother, Eritimus ('honoured in strife'),[40] who was a boxer and a wrestler, as if to account for Pindar's knowledge of athletics. Like Hesiod's mother Pycimede ('very clever') and his sons Mnasiepes and Archiepes ('rememberer and beginner of epic verse'),[41] none of these names occurs in Pindar's surviving poetry; their inconsistency suggests that they derive from no single source or tradition.[42]

Corinna's verses 'I blame Myrtis . . . because being a woman she entered into rivalry with Pindar' provide the basis for deductions about poetic training and competition in Boeotia.[43] Corinna is said to have been a pupil of Myrtis, and Pindar (as if the biographer had Corinna's lines in mind) a pupil of 'the woman Myrtis'. The statement in Sappho's Suda biography (fr. 253) that 'Anagora' was Sappho's pupil derives from references to Anactoria in Sappho's poems (e.g. 16.15, 95.4).[44] Alcman's chorus members speak of their leaders 'fighting' for them and bringing them 'peace'.[45] When Pindar advises himself to hold out 'against counter-strategies' like a wrestler, the commentators interpreted the metaphor as a reference to poetic rivalry with Simonides, and contrasted the two poets' styles: 'This seems to refer to Simonides; he usually used digres-

[39] In the Thoman Vita (1.4.11) she is Myrto, cf. Myrtis.

[40] Lefkowitz 1975, 74.

[41] P. 6 above.

[42] Cf. the names given to Hesiod's murderers by Alcidamas (Amphiphanes and Ganyctor, sons of Phegeus p. 4 above) and Eratosthenes (Ctimenus and Antiphus, sons of Ganyctor, p. 6 above).

[43] The ancients considered them contemporaries; cf. the story about Simonides competing with Lasus, Ar., *Vesp.* 1410–1. But cf. Page 1953, 68–84.

[44] The information in an ancient commentary that she educated the noblest girls in Ionia (*SLG* 261, p. 36 above) may also be based directly on her poetry. Anacreon, who mentions a girl from Lesbos in a poem (*PMG* 348) was said to be Sappho's lover (fr. 219=Chamaeleon fr. 26 Wehrli); p. 125.

[45] Cf. Pind., fr. 52b.31–4.

sions' (schol. *Nem.* 4.60b).[46] Biographers derived from Hesiod's account of his victory at Chalcis the notion of an actual contest between Hesiod and his 'rival' Homer.[47] The Suda biography notes that 'as the story goes' Corinna was victorious five times over Pindar.

An anecdote about Corinna's victory in local competition draws on Pindar's claim of sophistication in *Ol.* 6.90 (schol. *Ol.* 6.132; cf. fr. 83). In the story Pindar behaves like the defensive poet of the commentaries on the victory odes; he criticises the Thebans' lack of musical taste, and calls the victorious Corinna 'a Boeotian swine' (Ael., *VH* 13.25). Plutarch tells a story of how Corinna first criticised the young Pindar for using too little narrative in his songs, and then for including too many stories at one time. (*Mor.* 347f.). The story explains why Pindar tells three myths about Thebes in quick succession at the beginning of a song (fr. 29a). Ancient commentators apparently did not understand that this characteristic rhetorical device was intended to praise rather than to defend.[48]

When Pausanias made his tour of Boeotia in the second century A.D., he saw at Thebes the ruins of Pindar's house and the tablet on which Pindar's hymn to Ammon (fr. 36) had been inscribed (9.25.3, 16.1); at Tanagra he saw a memorial depicting Corinna's victory over Pindar (9.22.3). At Delphi in the temple of Apollo he was shown the iron chair where Pindar was said to have composed his songs for the god (10.24.3). Of these relics, only Pindar's house is mentioned in his surviving poetry (*Pyth.* 3.78). The others offer mute testimony to events in his *biography*: his competition with Corinna; Ammon's debt to him; Pindar's importance in Delphic ritual.

By the third century B.C. Pindar's poetry was represented primarily by his 'Life'. Callimachus knew and imitated phrases from Pindar's poetry (e.g. 480, 597, 384).[49] His claim to poetic authority in the Prologue to the *Aetia* is based in part on Pindar's *Paean* viib (fr. 52b). There Pindar claims to be different from

[46] Cf. p. 55 above.
[47] P. 5 above.
[48] Bundy 1962, 16, esp. n.21. Aristarchus thought the priamel in *Isthm.* 7 was directed against the Spartans, schol. *Isthm.* 7.23a, cf. schol. *Ol.* 1.1b, 1f.
[49] Pfeiffer 1949 on fr. 383. 1; Parsons 1977, 45–6.

poets who 'go down Homer's worn wagon-road' and that men who do not compose poetry have 'blind hearts' (11ff., 19–20). Callimachus in his adaptation speaks of finding a path that is not only untrodden but narrow; then he describes *himself* in terms of his art, as the 'slight one, the winged' (23ff.). He prefaces his characterisation of himself by describing what his envious enemies the Telchines, 'ignorant men, no friends of the Muses' say against his kind of poetry and what he replies in defence (1–20).[50] Pindar describes envious slanderers in *Pyth.* 2 in order to illustrate the dangers of ingratitude, but the scholia interpret his lines as a defence of his poetry against criticism by his political and poetic rivals.[51]

[50] Pp. 118, 123–4 below.
[51] Pp. 57–8 above.

# CHAPTER SEVEN

# Aeschylus

The lives of archaic poets derive from the 'autobiography' of their first-person statements, supplemented by 'facts' gathered from their poetry. The primary source material for the lives of the tragic poets are the dramas themselves; but since tragic poets do not speak directly in their own persons, stories about the tragic poets derive from impressions about their style and 'representative' verses in their poetry.

Anecdotes about the tragic poets were told by the comic poets; Aristophanes in the *Frogs* refers to Phrynichus (910) as well as to Aeschylus and Sophocles. Euripides appeared as a character in the *Thesmophoriazousae* and *Acharnians* while he was still alive and in the *Frogs* after his death. Biographers today draw on jokes and parody selectively; but ancient biographers, and more particularly their excerptors, reported the comic anecdotes as if they were serious judgments. They also had access to anecdotes about poets included in the *Visits* of Ion of Chios, a contemporary of Sophocles. Ion told an anecdote about Sophocles' conversation at a dinner party on his island (*FGrHist* 392F6 = Soph. T75 Radt); Plutarch recounts a conversation between Aeschylus and Ion at the Isthmian games (*FGrHist* 392F22). But these need not have been more accurate transcripts than the anecdotes preserved by Aristotle and by Xenophon about dinner-table repartee of Simonides and Hieron (or Hieron's wife).[1] Aeschylus is portrayed discussing discipline and courage, Sophocles seducing a young boy at a dinner party; the story shows him to be a more successful strategist in private life than on the battlefield, witty and urbane in social situations. Since the original context is lost, it is impossible to say whether Ion meant the anecdotes to have

---

[1] Cf. p. 53 above. On Ion, Fairweather 1974, 213.

any bearing on the composition of particular dramas. As they stand they provide a contemporary assessment of the poets' styles: Ion's portrayal fits in generally with Euripides' characterisation in the *Frogs* of Aeschylus as inspiring the Athenians to fight for their country (1016ff.) and of Sophocles as 'easygoing' (*eukolos*, 82, cf. Phryn., *Muses* fr. 31; Ar., *Pax* 696).

Aeschylus in the *Frogs* has a character like his poetry, and speaks in his own style, with complex compound adjectives (841ff.). His hostility toward popularisation and immorality makes him sound like the 'well-born people' he says drank hemlock because they were disgraced by Euripides' Bellerophons (1050–1, cf. 1031); the *Vita* states that 'his family was aristocratic' (1.2). In the *Frogs* Aeschylus is distinguished from Euripides by his piety; he begins the contest by praying to Demeter 'who has nourished my mind; may I be worthy of your mysteries' (886–7). The *Vita* says that Aeschylus came from the deme of Eleusis. This sounds plausible, because there was an Eleusinian Aeschylus in the fourth century.[2] But it is also significant that Aeschylus wrote about the Mysteries in his poetry, in dramas like the *Eleusinioi*. An anecdote told by the unreliable Heraclides Ponticus[3] says he was put on trial for profaning them, and then let off because he and his brother had fought and been wounded at Marathon (fr. 170 Wehrli = T 44 Wil). Heraclides' source may have been a scene in comedy; Chamaeleon (or his source) deduced from Aeschylus' portrayal of drunkards in his satyr play *Cabiri* that 'what the tragedian did himself he has fastened on to his heroes—he wrote his tragedies while he was drunk'; he quotes Sophocles as saying, 'You write what you ought to write but without knowing it' (fr. 40ab Wehrli). Euripides in the *Frogs* accuses Aeschylus of babbling about whatever came into his head and confusing the audience by breaking in in the midst of the action (945).[4]

In the *Frogs* Aeschylus acts as warlike and angry as Achilles (992); he embodies the sophist Gorgias' characterisation of his

[2] Davies 1971, 6–8.
[3] See pp. 172–3.
[4] Cf. Dioscorides *EG* 2852ff., '[Aeschylus] carved letters not chiselled but as washed out by rain torrents'; Gabathuler 1937, 84; Gow-Page 1965, on 1594.

*Seven against Thebes* as 'full of Ares' (82B24 DK; *Ran.* 1021); he cites his war plays the *Seven* and the *Persians* as evidence of his patriotism (1091ff.). Dionysus suggests that he modelled his lyric verses on 'rope-twisting songs from Marathon' (1296–7). His *Vita* reports: 'They say that he was heroic and that he fought in the battle of Marathon along with his brother Cynegirus, and in the naval battle at Salamis along with his younger brother Ameinias, and also in the infantry battle at Plataea' (1.9ff.).[5] Herodotus records that Cynegirus son of Euphorion lost an arm and died at Marathon; Euphorion is given in the Suda as the name of both Aeschylus' father and son (T41 Wil).[6] But Ameinias, a hero of the battle at Salamis, according to Herodotus comes from Pallene, not Eleusis (vii. 84). He appears to have been linked with Aeschylus first by Ephorus (Diod. Sic. xi.27 = T27 Wil), the author of the genealogy which makes Homer and Hesiod cousins (*FGrHist* 70F1), and of the allegorical names of Hesiod's parents Dios and Pycimede.[7]

Since Aeschylus' traditional dates make him a suitable age, there is no reason to doubt that he fought in any of the battles;[8] but the *evidence* that he participated may derive from his poetry rather than any independent source. Ion in his *Visits* wrote that Aeschylus fought at Salamis (*FGrHist* 392F7). But Ion is cited in the scholia to *Pers.* 432–3: 'Understand this clearly, never did so great a multitude perish in a single day', lines that could be taken as evidence that Aeschylus was an eye-witness at the battle. The notion that he fought 'heroically' could be inferred from his characterisation in Aristophanes and then strengthened by association with the hero Cynegirus and finally with Ameinias. In popular imagination his military service came to represent what his poetry stood for. The epitaph preserved in the *Vita* makes no reference to what he wrote, but claims that 'the famous grave of Marathon could tell of his courage and the

---

[5] See Appendix 3.
[6] Cf. how Sappho's mother acquires the name of Sappho's daughter (?) Cleis, p. 63 above; inconsistency suggests the name of Aeschylus' second son (Euaion, Eubion, Bion) was invented, p. 64 n.42 above.
[7] P. 6 above.
[8] Lefkowitz 1978, 464.

*Indo-European.*

long-haired Mede knew it well' (25). An unnamed figure in the Stoa Poikile painting was represented to Pausanias as Aeschylus at Marathon.[9]

The literary history in the *Vita* also comes directly from the *Frogs*. Aeschylus says: 'I brought my songs for a noble purpose from a noble source, so that I wouldn't be seen plucking them from the same holy meadow as Phrynichus' (1298–300); the *Vita* reports that 'he raised standards far above his predecessors' (1.4).[10] The *Vita* emphasises his innovations in staging, the splendour of his choral productions and costumes, and the seriousness (*semnotēs*) of his choral songs. The chorus in the *Frogs* addresses him as 'you who first built towers of serious (*semna*) speeches and adorned the tragic lyre' (1004–5); Euripides accuses him of using 'boastful language and driving [the audience] out of their minds', and of 'terrifying them' with characters in martial costume (961ff.). Euripides criticises Aeschylus for his ponderous style and the lack of action in his plays (911ff.); Aeschylus himself speaks with complex compound adjectives (841ff.). According to the *Vita* 'in the composition of his poetry he strove for a grand style, by using compound words and epithets, and also metaphors and every other device that could lend weight to his diction; the plots of his plays do not abound in reversals and complexities like those of later poets, for he aimed solely at investing his characters with dignity; he thought heroic grandeur struck the appropriate archaic note' (1.13ff.).

Euripides says in the *Frogs* that he improved tragedy by putting her on a diet (938ff.), simplifying diction and giving excitement to narratives, and by bringing in ordinary people as characters 'in a democratic manner', actions for which Aeschylus suggests that he should have been executed (950). Euripides in Aristophanes claims that he taught the audience how to use sophistic arguments (959–60) and that he 'explained to them how to think, by putting Reasoning in my art and Inquiry' (972ff.). Aeschylus, according to the *Vita*, believed that 'cunning ingenuity and sententiousness were foreign to tragedy' (1.20–1).

[9] Ibid., 465n.32.
[10] Cf. Dioscorides, *EG* 2853ff. (p. 68 n.4 above).

The *Vita* explains that 'it was for this reason that Aristophanes made fun of him in his comedies' and summarises the scenes with the silent Niobe and Achilles that Euripides makes fun of in the *Frogs*.[11] As in the case of Solon's poem on Salamis 'before the agora'[12] the explanation of the poetry has become 'history', of which the poetry itself is then cited as confirmation.

Two stories in the *Vita* about Aeschylus' contests with other poets account for why Aeschylus had a tomb in Gela rather than in Athens (2.7ff.). The first explanation is that 'he was criticised by the Athenians and defeated by Sophocles when the latter was a young man'; the second claims that he was 'defeated by Simonides in an elegy for those who died at Marathon' and so left Athens for Sicily. 'Literary history' is cited in confirmation of the judgment in favour of Simonides: 'Elegy in particular needs to have the conciseness necessary to arouse emotion, and Aeschylus' poem, as the story goes, was not suitable.' The impression that Aeschylus' poetry contained 'few pathetic scenes or other effects calculated to produce tears' (2.3ff.) of course derives from the characterisation of his poetry in the *Frogs* as weighty (924–5), long-winded (914–15), and boring (1018), and of his verse as monotonous (1261–2). In the *Lives*, contests frequently account for a poet's disappearance: the seer Calchas dies after being defeated by the seer Mopsus (Hes., fr. 278); Homer dies after failing to answer the riddle of the fisher boys;[13] Pindar was defeated in his native Boeotia by Corinna.[14]

Finally the *Vita* proposes a third reason for his departure from Athens: 'Some say that during the performance of the *Eumenides*, when he brought on the chorus one by one, he so frightened the audience that children fainted and unborn infants were aborted' (2.11f.). Detail makes the story sound plausible; but the text of the *Eumenides* indicates rather that the chorus were already on stage asleep at the beginning of the parodos, and *wake* each other from sleep one by one: 'Wake up; and you wake her up; I'll wake you up' (140).[15] After their

[11] Lefkowitz 1978, 464–5. Taplin 1972, 58–64.
[12] P. 40 above.     [13] P. 18 above.
[14] P. 65 above.
[15] Cf. Eur., *Hec.* 52ff.; Taplin 1977, 134ff., but cf. 141, 372.

song Apollo states that they belong not in his temple but in places where 'the manhood of the young is ruined by the destruction of seed' (187–8); they themselves sing a song that drives men mad and is 'withering to mortals' (328ff.). They claim: 'I have chosen the ruin of houses' (354). They threaten Athens with 'canker, blasting leaves and children' and to 'cast upon the land infections that destroy its people' (785–7). In the *Frogs* the character of Aeschylus was based on his style ('terrible things with bogey faces', 925); in the anecdote the words of the Furies are taken to represent the intentions of the poet.

It is significant that the *Vita* offers these three negative reasons for Aeschylus' visit to Sicily, rather than simply stating that he went there because he was invited to Hieron's court, like the lyric poets Simonides and Pindar. The notion that the Athenians were dissatisfied with him makes his invitation to Gela seem like an exile, instead of an indication of his success and international recognition. The Suda biography explicitly states that 'he went into exile in Sicily because the stage fell down when he was putting on a performance' (T41 Wil). The *Vita* relates that he put on the *Women of Aetna* to celebrate the founding of Aetna (the occasion is commemorated also in Pindar's *Pyth.* 1) and that 'he was greatly honoured both by Hieron and the people of Gela and lived there for two years before he died' (2.13–17). But then the *Vita* gives an account of his death that both marks Aeschylus as extraordinary and at the same time demeans him. He had received an oracle 'something thrown from the sky will kill you' and he was killed when an eagle dropped a tortoise on his head (2.17–21). The account in the *Vita* omits a detail that makes the poet's death sound even more comic: that the poet was bald and the eagle mistook his head for a rock on which to break the tortoise's shell (T32 Wil).

Death as a result of a misunderstood oracle gives Aeschylus the stature of a famous poet: Hesiod avoided the famous grove of Nemean Zeus in order to die in Nemean Locri; Homer did not heed the oracle's warning about Ios and the riddle posed by young men. As in the case of the other poets, the setting of Aeschylus' death has an inverse relation to his poetry: Hesiod wrote the *Theogony* in praise of Zeus; Homer was alleged to be the wisest of all Greeks; Aeschylus the poet is killed by a tortoise, the animal whose shell is used to make a lyre. In an analogous way, Tiresias' vague prediction in the *Odyssey* that 'death will come to you from the sea' became in cyclic epic an account of how Odysseus' son Telegonus killed him with the spine of a roach-fish, which he was using instead of a spear (Procl. *Chrest.* 324).[16] At the end of Aeschylus' *Vita* the oracle about his death is cited in verse form as 'an inscription on his tomb: "I died, struck on the forehead from an eagle's claws"'. Without reference to the tortoise the 'inscription' sounds less comic and more like Archilochus' final encounter with the mysterious Calondas Corax ('crow').[17]

By suggesting that Aeschylus went to Gela because the Athenians were dissatisfied with him, the *Vita* implies that Aeschylus received greater honour after his death than during his lifetime (2.21f.). The people of Gela 'buried him richly' and 'honoured him extravagantly' with the epigram about his having fought at Marathon (*EG* 454ff.). 'All who made their living in the tragic theatre went to his tomb to offer sacrifices and recited their plays there. The Athenians liked Aeschylus so much that they voted after his death to award a golden crown to whoever was willing to put on one of his dramas.' Homer was buried by the people of Ios, and honoured with an epigram (*Vit.Hdt.* 36);[18] Hesiod's innocence was recognised after his death and his bones moved to Orchomenos.[19] After the difficulties in their lifetimes, the posthumous honours give them heroic stature; but in Aeschylus' case it is possible to see that the pattern is not inherent, but rather imposed on the few 'facts' that could be deduced from his poetry or poetry about him.

The list of discoveries attributed to Aeschylus in the *Vita* should be regarded with equal caution.[20] The phrase 'highly

---

[16] Fairweather 1974, 271. Hartmann 1917, 108 suggests that the story of Aeschylus' death may derive from a comic parody of Aeschylus' *Psychagogoi*.

[17] P. 29 above.

[18] P. 21 above.

[19] P. 10 above.

[20] Taplin 1977, 44–6, 438; Lloyd-Jones 1966, 19.

heroic effects' (*gennikōtatois pathesi* 3.6) summarises Aeschylus' description in the *Frogs* of how his dramas the *Seven* and the *Persae* made the citizens 'heroic' (*gennaious*, 1017). Chamaeleon's claim (fr. 41 Wehrli) that Aeschylus first created choreography (*prōton schēmatisai*) is based directly on the lines given the poet in a lost play (fr. 677) of Aristophanes: 'I myself made the arrangements [*schēmata epoioun*] for choruses' (T38 Wil). Special stage effects and scenery listed in the *Vita*, 'altars, tombs, trumpets, images and Furies' are mentioned in the text of his dramas (altars and tombs, *Cho.* 160, trumpets,[21] *Eum.* 568 and *Ran.* 1041; Furies, *Eum.*). Aristotle in the *Poetics* (1449a) says he was the first to use two actors; the *Vita* (3.11) gives their names, Cleandrus and Mynniscus, but then adds that he 'invented the third actor, though Dicaearchus of Messene says it was Sophocles'. Dicaearchus got this information from his teacher Aristotle, who claimed that Sophocles added the third actor and scenery; but all of this 'data' can be deduced from the texts of their plays.[22] In the *Persae* and *Septem* Aeschylus uses two actors, but in the *Oresteia* he uses three. Aristotle's scheme makes a neat progression out of a continuing process of experimentation.[23] Aeschylus may have been the first to equip the actors with gloves and robes and higher buskins; but it is likely that these discoveries were imputed to him by later critics primarily because he was considered the first major dramatist.

---

[21] Taplin 1977, 393n.2.
[22] Knox 1979, 40–1.
[23] Cf. also TT36–40 Wil.

# CHAPTER EIGHT

# Sophocles

The compiler of the Life of Sophocles[1] evidently had before him several biographies of the poet from which to draw his information. He selects data with some discrimination, discarding information that runs contrary to common sense. He declares that Aristoxenus was wrong to call Sophocles' father Sophillus a carpenter (fr. 115 W), and Ister to say that he was a bronze-smith or sword-maker (*FGrHist* 334F33) because a man descended from a tradesman would not have held generalship 'along with Pericles and Thucydides, who were the most important men in the city'. He also says that Ister is not to be believed when he said that Sophocles was a Phliasian by birth,[2] because the information is to be found only in Ister. So he concludes that Sophocles was an Athenian by birth, from a good family, though he does not cite Ion of Chios, Sophocles' contemporary, who says Sophocles behaved like 'any other Athenian aristocrat' (T75.32/35 W) nor does he observe that Sophocles must have come from a leading family since he participated (as he says later) in Athenian cult.

But even though the compiler distinguishes between sensible and fanciful (or likely and less likely) information, he does not inquire into the nature of the source material on which Aristoxenus and Ister drew. He observes that 'indeed if his father had been a tradesman, he would not have got off without abuse from the comic poets';[3] but he does not note

[1] See Appendix 4.

[2] The satyr plays on which tragedy was thought to have been based were invented by Pratinas of Phlius, cf. Dioscorides *EG* 286o (T179); Gow-Page 1965, on 1599; did Ister misunderstand his source?

[3] The joke would only make sense if Euripides' parents were well-born; apparently no one made fun of Socrates because his mother Phaenarete was a midwife, *Theaet.* 149a; Herodicus apud Ath. v.219b; pp. 127–8 below.

that the comic poets were the most ready source of Aristoxenus' and Ister's information. The fourth-century historian Philochorus denied the comic poets' allegations that Euripides' mother was a vegetable seller; 'actually both his parents were well-born' (*FGrHist* 328F218).[4] But he might simply have deduced this information from accounts of Euripides' participation in Attic cult.[5]

Sophocles' biographer does not question Ister or his other sources when they provide plausible information: 'He trained with the other boys both in wrestling and in music, and won crowns for both, as Ister says' (*FGrHist* 334F35); 'Satyrus says that Sophocles invented the crooked staff himself' (*FHG* 3.161ff.); 'Ister also says [*FGrHist* 334F36] that he discovered the white half-boots that actors and chorus members wear, etc.' 'He won twenty victories, according to Carystius' (*FHG* 4.359). 'Sophocles was more pious than anyone else, according to what Hieronymus says' (fr. 31 Wehrli). But in Aeschylus' case the biographers' sources for plausible information were the same as for implausible: comedy and anecdotes based on the poet's own dramas.

Sophocles' biographer concludes his discussion of the poet's birth by reaffirming that he was an Athenian from the deme of Colonus: 'He was distinguished both because of his life and his poetry. He was well-educated and raised in comfortable circumstances, and he was involved in government and in embassies abroad.' Some of this information could easily be deduced from the very existence of his poetry; but there is independent confirmation that he came from Colonus and held public office. An inscription records that '[S]ophocles [from] Colo[nus]' was state treasurer in 443/2 B.C. (T18/*ATL* 2.18); according to the fourth-century historian Androtion he was one of the ten generals in the Samian war of 441/0 (*FGrHist* 324F38/T19). But this true information ironically became the source of influential false deductions: that the *Oedipus at Colonus* was in certain ways autobiographical, and that Sophocles' generalship had direct bearing on the date of his *Antigone* (T25 Radt = *Ant. Arg.* 1.15 Pearson).

---

[4] Jacoby on *FGrHist* 328F218.    [5] See below, p. 92.

After the long opening statement about Sophocles' birth, his biographer gives his birth date (495/4) and his age in relation to Aeschylus (seven years younger) and Euripides (twenty-four years older). He then records evidence of the poet's talents: according to Ister 'he trained with the other boys both in wrestling and in music and won crowns for both' (*FGrHist* 334F35); 'he studied music with Lamprus, and after the naval battle at Salamis [in 480, when Sophocles was fifteen], when the Athenians were standing round the victory monument, Sophocles with his lyre, naked and anointed with oil, led the chorus which sang the paean at the victory sacrifice'. An anecdote preserved by Athenaeus and the scholia on Homer says that he played ball excellently when he acted the part of Nausicaa (T25–30). These anecdotes, like Ister's information that Sophocles' father was a bronze-smith or sword maker, are meant as representations of the poet's heroic stature, not as statements of literal fact; the same impulse emphasises the importance of Aeschylus' military service in his biography. They also show that the poet's talent was evident when he was very young. As in Pindar's case, early recognition helps account for extraordinary productivity over a long period of time—in both cases, ancient dating suggests almost half a century. 'He learned about tragedy from Aeschylus' is another representative statement, meant to indicate his place in the succession; it accounts for a different 'fact' from the contradictory information in the Aeschylus *Vita*, which claims that Aeschylus was defeated by Sophocles as a young man, and so left Athens for Sicily (II.61 Soph. T36–7).

Aristotle said that Sophocles invented the third actor (*Poet.* 1449a15/T95). Sophocles' biographer reports this 'fact' without adumbration. But since Aeschylus also used three actors (T96 Radt = Aesch. *Vit.* 3.12), the notion[6] that Sophocles invented the practice is simply representative, an indication that with Sophocles tragedy attained what Aristotle regarded as 'its natural form' (1449a15); the statement that he increased the size of the chorus from twelve to fifteen belongs in the same category. Sophocles' biographer 'confirms' that Sophocles

[6] P. 74 above.

discovered the third actor by an explanatory anecdote:
Sophocles 'broke the tradition of the poet's acting because his
own voice was weak—in the old days the poet himself served as
one of the actors' (4). The idea that the poet himself led the
chorus is inherent in Aristotle's derivation of tragedy from
'those who led dithyrambs' (*Poet.* 1449a11). Poets speak of
'leading' choral song; for example, Archilochus' verses 'I
know how to lead a beautiful song to lord Dionysus, a dithyramb' (fr. 120 W). It seems unlikely that Sophocles' biographer,
writing centuries after tragedy had ceased to be performed,
had access to any other source of information about the poet's
acting. The notion that Sophocles' voice was weak was
apparently intended to explain only his use of three actors,
since it is contradicted by three other anecdotes: (1) a picture
of Sophocles playing a lyre in the Stoa Poikile painting (*Vita* 5),
(2) the story that he choked to death while reading the *Antigone*
(*Vita* 14), (3) the story that he played the part of Nausicaa in
the *Washerwomen* (T28–30).[7] Sophocles' biographer is aware of
the inconsistency because he explains 'only in the Thamyris
did he ever sing'. Did the Thamyris seem particularly suitable
because it told the story of a bard who competed with the
Muses (*Il.* 2.549ff.)?[8] When Pindar tells Aeneas in *Ol.* 6.87ff.
to rouse his comrades to sing, the scholia explain: 'Aeneas was
the chorus-leader. He used him because of his weak voice and
because of not being able to recite to choruses himself, as most
poets did for themselves when they competed' (Schol. *Ol.*
6.149a 188).[9]

Aeschylus is said to have 'equipped the actors with gloves
and dignified them with long robes and elevated their stance
with higher buskins' (3.9ff.); Sophocles, according to Satyrus
(*FHG* 3.161ff.) 'invented the crooked staff himself; according
to Ister (*FGrHist* 334F36), he 'discovered the white half-boots
that actors and chorus members wear, wrote his dramas to suit
their characters, and organised a thiasos to the Muses'. At the
end of the *Vita*, Sophocles' biographer records that Aristoxenus
in his *History of Music* said Sophocles was the first Athenian to

[7] P. 77 above.
[8] Pp. 12, 33 above; cf. Soph. T99b.
[9] Bell 1978, 62.

use Phrygian music and to mix in the dithyrambic style
(fr. 79 Wehrli). The source of virtually all of Aeschylus'
biographer's information about Aeschylus' scenic innovations
was Aristophanes' *Frogs*.[10] The fragments of Satyrus' *Life of
Euripides* indicate that his principal source material also con-
sisted of comedy and Euripides' own plays.[11]

The notion that Sophocles wrote his dramas to suit his
actors' characters cannot reflect fifth-century practice, since
the archons assigned protagonists to the dramatists by lot (Suda
s.v. *nemesis hypokritōn*).[12] Though the idea may reflect
changes in the fourth century, the most likely source of the
information is comedy. Aristophanes has Agathon dress in
women's clothes and argue that poets ought to adapt their
habits to their poetry (*Thesm.* 149–50): poets who write Ionic
rhythms like Ibycus, Anacreon, and Alcaeus, ought to wear
effeminate Ionic dress (*Thesm.* 159ff.).[13] In context the proposal
is meant to sound ridiculous; but there is (as in all good jokes)
a basic reality behind it: Anacreon was already represented in
vase painting in a woman's Lydian cap.[14] In the third century
Satyrus cited Aristophanes to explain Euripides' anti-social
behaviour: 'He is like what he makes his characters say' (fr. 59
Austin).[15]

That Sophocles organised a *thiasos* of cultivated people could
be based on historical fact; a fifth-century inscription records
the seating-plan of a *thiasos* to which the poet Aristophanes
belonged, with two men he mentions in his comedies.[16] But
since ancient biographers appear rarely to have consulted
anything other than literary documents, it seems more likely
that the notion of Sophocles' *thiasos* derives from a representation in comedy or in a dialogue which like Plato's *Symposium*
describes the gathering (and seating arrangement) of learned
friends at the home of the tragic poet Agathon.[17]

The next statement in Sophocles' *Vita* comes directly from
comedy: 'In a word his character was so charming that he was
loved everywhere and by everyone' (7). Aristophanes in the

[10] Pp. 70, 73–4 above.
[11] P. 99 below.
[12] Owen 1936, 148–9.
[13] Pp. 52–3 above.
[14] Snyder 1974, 243–6.
[15] P. 166 n.7 below.
[16] See p. 88 n.3.
[17] Dover 1980, 10.

*Frogs* characterised Sophocles as 'easy-going here [i.e. in this world] and easy-going there [in Hades]' (8);[18] one of Hades' servants described Sophocles as readily yielding first place to Aeschylus: 'he kissed Aeschylus, when he came down here, and grasped his right hand, and he stood back from the Chair' (788–90) (T101, 102).[19] According to Phrynichus (T105) 'he lived for many years and died a happy man and clever; after writing many good tragedies he died well, without having suffered any impairment'. Ion of Chios describes how Sophocles contrives without force to get a young boy to kiss him, while carrying on a witty conversation. The characterisation may have some foundation in fact: Sophocles was repeatedly elected to public office; he is said never to have won third prize. But to some extent at least the notion of charm and ease may reflect ancient assessments of his style (T 108ff.). His biographer later paraphrases a fragment of Aristophanes about Sophocles' mouth being anointed with honey (22/cf. T108 = fr. 581 Kock), and claims he was called 'the bee' because 'he culled the best from all his predecessors'.[20] Aristophanes said of Phrynichus (the tragic poet) 'like a bee he sucked the fruit of melodies immortal, ever carrying away sweet song' (*Av.* 748–50). But this traditional characterisation of lyric style was applied by literary critics particularly to Sophocles, because it places him midway in a linear progression between Aeschylus' rough archaism and Euripides' smooth sophistry.

To support the statement that Sophocles was loved by everyone, the biographer supplies two anecdotes testifying to his popularity: (1) the Athenians elected him general when he was sixty-five years old, seven years before the start of the Peloponnesian war (431/0);[21] (2) 'he was so loyal to Athens that when many kings sent for him he did not want to leave his country'. Plutarch knew the story about his second generalship (T26), which sounds as if it were designed to put two famous men, Sophocles and Nicias, together; Plutarch's punch-line

---

[18] P. 68 above.
[19] Stanford 1963, 139.
[20] P. 59 above.
[21] Woodbury 1970, 214–15; Friis Johansen 1962, 110.

emphasises Sophocles' linguistic skill, like Ion's story about the symposium in Chios.[22] Ion (*FGrHist* 392F6) and Androtion (*FGrHist* 324F38) mention only his service in the Samian war of 441/0. His loyalty to Athens sets him apart from Aeschylus, who went to Sicily, and Euripides, who according to Aristotle went to the court of Archelaus king of Macedon. The patterns of these poets' lives, and Homer's, may have suggested to biographers that foreign kings might have been interested also in Sophocles. In any case the notion of their interest could easily have been pointed out by a comic poet: Aristophanes boasts that the king of Persia wanted to know whom Aristophanes was criticising in his poetry because his advice is so good (*Ach.* 646ff.). The joke was taken seriously by his biographer.[23] The fourth-century poets Menander and Philemon were said to have been invited to Alexandria by Ptolemy Soter; the story (recorded in one of Alciphron's imaginary letters, iv. 8.4–5 = Menander fr. 12 K-Th) may have been based on the actual experience of the Athenian writer and statesman Demetrius of Phaleron, who went in exile to Alexandria and became librarian under Ptolemy Philadelphus.

The relation between Sophocles' generalship and his poetry was of great interest to his biographers. Aristophanes of Byzantium notes in his hypothesis to Sophocles' *Antigone* that 'Sophocles was judged worthy of the generalship in the campaign against Samos, because of the high reputation he had won from having put on the Antigone' (T25). Ion, in his anecdote about Sophocles' visit to Chios, also implies that there is some relationship between his reputation as a poet and his serving as general (T75 = *FGrHist* 392F6). Sophocles uses an elaborate ruse to get a young slave boy to kiss him, and then observes ' "I am interested in strategy [*stratēgein*, being a general], gentlemen, although Pericles said I can write poetry, but don't understand strategy; but now didn't that strategy of mine work out perfectly?" ' Ion's anecdote gives Sophocles more credit for his wit than for his success in public office: 'He said and did many things cleverly when he was drinking, but in

---

[22] P. 67 above.
[23] Lefkowitz 1978, 459; p. 111 below.

political matters he was no more clever or persuasive than any other Athenian aristocrat.'[24]

Ion's anecdote, at least in the form we have it, does not say anything specific about the *Antigone*. The only ancient evidence that links the *Antigone* specifically with Sophocles' generalship during the Samian campaign is Aristophanes of Byzantium's hypothesis (T25).[25] Aristophanes could have discovered the date of the play from chronological information in Callimachus' *Catalogues* (*Pinakes*); but a quite different date was suggested by Callimachus' contemporary Satyrus, a generation before Aristophanes. An anecdote is preserved in Sophocles' *Vita* that according to Satyrus Sophocles died while reciting a passage from the *Antigone*, or as 'others' said, he died of joy when he had recited the play and heard that he was proclaimed victor (14), that is, in 406/5 B.C. The co-existence of these stories suggests that in the third century there was no fixed information available about the date of the *Antigone*.[26] Aristophanes, in suggesting a link between Sophocles' term as general and the composition of the play, might only have been making a logical conjecture, the way he claimed that the *Odyssey* ended at 23.296, after Odysseus and Penelope were reunited.[27]

The subject matter of the *Antigone* apparently suggested to biographers that it was performed at the time of a political crisis. The Samian revolt challenged the authority of the Athenian empire;[28] Sophocles died not long before Athens was defeated in the Peloponnesian war. It is conceivable that Sophocles could have written some portion of the *Antigone* as commentary on a particular event; but in practice fifth-century dramas appear to offer general warnings rather than to respond to specific political situations. Aeschylus' *Persians*, produced eight years after the defeat of the Persian navy at Salamis, portrayed the dangers of *hybris*; Herodotus finished his books about the defeat of the Persians as Athens was developing her

---

[24] Cf. Aeschylus composing while drunk, p. 68 above.
[25] On the evidence, Woodbury 1970, 210–24.
[26] P. 86 below; cf. Woodbury 1970, 223.
[27] Pfeiffer 1968, I 175; Rossi 1968, 151–63.
[28] Hammond 1959, 314–16.

own empire.[29] Euripides' *Trojan Women* was produced in 415, the year that Athens put down the Melian rebellion and prepared her expedition against Sicily; but the general issue of how to deal with dissident allies had already been raised by the Mytilenean revolt of 427, at the very beginning of the war. Sophocles' service as Hellenotamias in 443/2 and as general in the war against the Anaeans in 438 (?) need not have had any more direct bearing on his poetry than Aeschylus' service as soldier in the Persian wars.[30]

Since Sophocles' biographer wishes to present a favourable picture of the poet he does not include any reference to allegations of misconduct in public office, e.g. Aristophanes' claim in 421 in his comedy *Peace* that Sophocles turned into Simonides, because he was 'old and debauched and ready to go to sea on a raft in order to make money' (697).[31] One of the scholia on the line explains that both poets were guilty of 'loving money' and that Sophocles 'made money out of his generalship in Samos' (T104c). Another scholion denies the story (T104d); charges of corruption were made routinely in comedy against important public figures,[32] and Aristophanes did not hesitate to make fun even of members of his thiasos for 'impiety' and sexual misconduct.[33]

After the anecdotes about Sophocles' political status, his biographer provides two illustrations of his piety: he held the priesthood of the hero Halon (maintained after his death by his son Iophon); according to Hieronymus (fr. 31 Wehrli) he established a shrine to Heracles Informer as a result of a dream in which Heracles told him where to find a golden crown that had been stolen from the Acropolis.[34] Sophocles used the reward for finding the crown to build the shrine. Both stories

[29] Fornara 1971, 89–91.
[30] Cf. Woodbury 1970, 213n.24; pp. 69–70 above.
[31] P. 52 above; cf. p. 108 n.9 below.
[32] A Creon served with Sophocles as one of the ten generals in 441/0, Androtion *FGrHist* 324F38; but cf. Woodbury 1970, 209–24.
[33] P. 89 n.3 below.
[34] Cf. Hieronymus' aetiology of an epigram addressed to Euripides about Sophocles' cloak (fr. 35 Wehrli = T75 Radt = Ath. 604d–f); the epigram is attributed to Sophocles (fr. 4 West = *EG* 462ff.), but its style (e.g. *speirōn* not as a metaphor) and content seem Hellenistic; West 1974, 20–1.

seem plausible enough; but since the other anecdotes in the life appear to be derived from poetry and hypothesis rather than independent sources, there is reason to be suspicious of the origin even of these stories. Halon is unattested elsewhere;[35] the biographer identifies him as 'a hero under Chiron's tutelage along with Asclepius' (11). Other anecdotes, not in the *Vita*, testify that Sophocles 'gave hospitality to Asclepius', that is, received the god in his house (T67), and that because of this act Sophocles himself was later worshipped as the hero Dexion ('Receiver', T69). Like Aristodemus' story of Pindar and the cult of Demeter,[36] the anecdotes about Sophocles appear to represent recognition given to the poet in the Hellenistic period and after. Dexion is mentioned in inscriptions of the second and third centuries A.D. (T70–1),[37] but in actual cult practice adult heroes are worshipped under their own names and do not acquire new identities.[38] Sophocles is said to have written a paean for Asclepius (T73a = *PMG* 737); were stories about his priesthood created to explain references to himself in the ode, like the stories about Pindar's *Hymn to Demeter*? Was the story about the shrine of Heracles Informer also intended to explain the existence of a particular poem, like the stories about Pindar's *Hymns* to Pan and Ammon?[39]

Behind the idea of Sophocles being worshipped as the hero Dexion lies the plot of the *Oedipus at Colonus*. The old Oedipus wants to be buried at Colonus, near Athens, 'to bring gain to the house of those who receive me and destruction to those who sent me away' (92–3). In the play, he curses his son Polynices who tries to make him go back to Thebes. This scene is the source of the next anecdote (13) in the *Vita*, which tells how Sophocles 'at some point' brought a law-suit against his son Iophon because of Iophon's jealousy of Sophocles' favouritism

[35] Friis Johanssen 1962, 110.

[36] Pp. 61–2 above.

[37] The name expresses the kindly aspect of the dead hero; cf. Hypodectes (*IG*[2] II 1061), Dexamenos; *dechomai* can denote divine protection (e.g. Pind., *Pyth.* 8.5, 19; 9.73).

[38] Change of name signifies a change from child to adult, Brelich 1958, 128; when Melicertes becomes a god he acquires the name Palaemon; schol. Pind., *Isthm.* hypoth., III p. 192.

[39] P. 60 above.

for his other son Ariston's child who was also called Sophocles. 'Once in a drama he portrayed his son Iophon as being envious [of the young Sophocles] and as making accusations to his clansmen that his father had lost his mind in his old age. They censured Iophon. Satyrus says the poet said: "If I am Sophocles I'm not out of my mind; if I am out of my mind, I'm not Sophocles", and then he produced the *Oedipus [at Colonus]*.' The punch line 'if I am Sophocles' expresses the same general sentiment as the epigram 'No one's memory compares with Simonides' at eighty' (fr. 14 W). Biographers needed to account for extraordinary competence in old age.[40]

The source of Satyrus' anecdote about Sophocles and Iophon appears to be a comedy about Sophocles' family:[41] 'In a drama he portrayed his son Iophon as being envious'; 'He made accusations before his clansmen'; 'Sophocles brought a lawsuit' suggests the setting of at least two of its scenes. The anecdote preserves the names of the characters: Sophocles, Iophon, his son by Nicostrate, Ariston, his son by Theoris of Sicyon, her child Sophocles. The subject of the dispute— distribution of attention or affection—is a comic reduction of real-life litigation among step-children over distribution of property. In his *Life of Euripides* Satyrus combines the plot of Aristophanes' *Thesmophoriazousae* with a quotation from Euripides' *Melanippe* to create an incident in the poet's life: that the women of Athens threatened him but let him off when he promised never again to say anything bad about them; he even cites the 'decree' against Euripides from *Thesm.* 335ff.[42] Aristophanes has Dionysus joke about Iophon's dependence on Sophocles (*Ran.* 73ff.); but Sophocles' biographer lists Iophon as one of Sophocles' rivals in poetic competitions (19).

After the anecdote about Sophocles as an old man, his biographer provides three different accounts of his death, without judging which is the most likely: (1) Sophocles choked on an unripe grape at the festival of the Choes; (2) he lost his

---

[40] Pp. 54–5 above.

[41] See Radt ad loc.; Jebb 1900, xxxix–xliii; Ar., *Rhet.* 1416a3 cites Sophocles as saying to an 'accuser' that he trembled not in order to appear old, but from necessity.

[42] Pp. 89–90 below.

voice (and breath) while reading the *Antigone*; (3) after the drama had been recited he died of joy when he was declared victor. Like Aeschylus' death, each of these deaths is particularly appropriate for a poet, but at the same time degrading. The grape he choked on at the festival of the Choes was sent to him by Callippides the actor; the source of this story is Ister (*FGrHist* 334F37), whose account of Sophocles' birth the biographer disregarded; it was also recorded in Neanthes' account of amazing deaths (*FGrHist* 84F18). The original anecdote may have emphasised Sophocles' fondness for drink; 'He used to say and do many things cleverly . . . when he was drinking'.[43] The story that he choked while reading the *Antigone* is attributed to Satyrus (*FHG* 3.162);[44] as in the case of the story of Euripides and the women, and the tale of Sophocles' quarrel with Iophon, Satyrus connects events in the poets' lives with their art. The third story, attributed to no particular author, appears simply to offer a more sentimental form of death as the result of the *Antigone*. It is interesting that two anecdotes select Antigone rather than *Oedipus Tyrannus*, which Aristotle repeatedly uses to illustrate excellence in composition (e.g. *Poet.* 1453a); Dioscorides in his epigram about Sophocles picks *Antigone* or *Electra* as the 'top' (*EG* 2866–7).[45]

Like Aeschylus, Sophocles is recognised as a hero only after his death. Details are given about the location (eleven stades from the city wall) and decoration (a siren or Chelidon) of his tomb. The precise details suggest that in late antiquity a tomb was identified as Sophocles' and pointed out to tourists. An anecdote explains how he came to be buried in wartime. Dionysus twice appeared to the Spartan general Lysander in a dream; as in the story about Sophocles and the shrine of Heracles Informer,[46] divine intervention acknowledges his importance. The biographer appends an epigram provided by the literary forger Lobon, which emphasises Sophocles' piety: 'In this tomb I hide Sophocles who won first prize with his art, a most holy figure.' The account of his recognition concludes with a final anecdote from Ister (*FGrHist* 334F38): 'The

---

[43] Pp. 81–2 above.       [44] P. 82 above.
[45] P. 75 n.2 above.       [46] P. 83 above.

Athenians voted to sacrifice to him each year because of his excellence.' The original account by Ister may have referred to the cult of Sophocles as Dexion, but the biographer records only the information needed to show that by the Hellenistic age Sophocles had attained heroic status, like Homer in Argos, Archilochus in Paros or Stesichorus in Catana.[47]

As in Aeschylus' biography, the account of the poet's tomb is followed by statistics of his accomplishments: the number of dramas he wrote (123) and the names of some of his more famous competitors. The source of this information is likely to have been Aristotle's *didaskaliai*, which preserved the names (though not always the titles) of the competitors in most years.[48] The *Vita* then concludes with a general assessment of his style. The examples are different from the discussion of his poetry at the beginning of the *Vita*, but no less simple in character. There is a general estimate of his debt to Homer (vocabulary, plots, especially from the *Odyssey*): 'He delineated character, elaborated and used contrivances skilfully reproducing Homer's charm. For this reason a certain Ionian says that only Sophocles is a pupil of Homer.' The biographer rightly understands the 'certain Ionian's' remark as metaphorical statement about Sophocles' *poetry*. This, and his listing all three versions of the poet's death, suggest that he also considered much of his source material to be representative rather than historical.

---

[47] Pp. 19, 27, 34 above.
[48] Griffith 1977, 228-9.

# CHAPTER NINE

# Euripides

Euripides' *Vita* is of particular interest because we can trace in some detail the course of its development: anecdotes about Euripides were known to Philochorus in the fourth century: papyrus scraps preserve a sense of the contents and organisation of Satyrus' third-century biographical dialogue about the poet. Scholarly comment has concentrated on these earlier sources.[1] But since they survive only in fragments, more can be learned about the general nature and function of the fictions that comprise Euripides' biography from the later but complete *Vita* which is ostensibly the principal source of information about his life.[2] Close analysis again shows that virtually all the information in the *Vita* derives from comedy or Euripides' own dramas; that anecdotes endow the poet with both heroic capabilities and degrading weaknesses; and that over time these weaknesses gradually receive more emphasis in order to make the poet's achievement seem more comprehensible and accessible. Duplication and inconsistency suggest that the *Vita* has undergone a long and deteriorating process of condensation.

Euripides' biography is based on poetry about and by Euripides. Explicitly, the source of information about his mother's profession is 'the writers of Old Comedy who made fun of him in their plays by calling him the son of a woman who sold vegetables' (115). Three examples of the joke survive: 'Give me the herbs your mother gave you' (*Ach.* 479; also *Ran.* 840, *Thesm.* 387).[3] Aristophanes is also the source of several

---

[1] See esp. Arrighetti 1964, Kumaniecki 1929, Leo 1912, Delcourt 1933.

[2] See Appendix 5. Despite the issues raised by Stevens 1956, material from the *Vita* is regarded as historical by (e.g.) Webster 1967, Lesky 1966, 462–3.

[3] Also cf. *Ach.* 457, *Ran.* 947, *Eq.* 19; Méridier 1925, iii. Criticism of social background is a standard mode of invective; Nisbet 1961, 194. Ruck 1976, 14–32, supposes the herbs were aphrodisiacs; but it is a mistake to take at

other uncomplimentary anecdotes: (a) other people helped him write his plays (11–17, 99; when Euripides in the *Frogs* describes how he put Tragedy on a diet, Dionysus says 'mixing in Cephisophon for flavour', 944);[4] (b) Euripides had a long beard (27, a detail from a costuming scene in *Thesm.* 190 where Euripides says 'I'm grey-haired and have. a beard'); (c) Euripides had moles (28; Dionysus in the *Frogs* talks about the sties on Euripides' eyes, 1246); (d) Euripides was unpleasant to talk to (67; the play from which this line is quoted is lost— perhaps the speaker was describing a picture);[5] (e) Euripides hated women and the women wanted to kill him (70–1, 91, 100–4), but they spared him when he promised not to say anything else bad about them—this is simply a summary of the plot of Aristophanes' *Thesmophoriazousae*.[6]

By a similar process of inference and simplification, Euripides' dramas provide biographical data for the *Vita*. Deceptively, the anecdote is told first, and then the lines from which it is derived are cited as 'evidence'.[7] Dionysus in the *Frogs* teases Euripides for writing plays about adulterous women like Phaedra and Stheneboea (1043–4, 1080–1). In the *Vita* we are told that Euripides' wife was unfaithful, on more than one occasion (93–5, 22, 69–74), and that because of her infidelity he wrote the *Hippolytus* (70). When this wife remarried, Euripides gives her second husband advice in an iambic trimeter line that paraphrases what Electra says about her adulterous mother Clytemnestra in *El.* 923–4: 'Poor man [meaning the dead Aegisthus], if he thinks she won't be chaste in other's homes but

---

face value what Aristophanes says in a comedy about his friends. A member of his *thiasos* (*IG* II² 3.2343), Simon, is portrayed in *Nub.* 351 as a harpy and in 399 as a perjurer; Amphitheos, another member, boasts in *Ach.* 46 that he is immortal, descended from Demeter. See Dow 1969; Gelzer 1970, 1398.

[4] In *Thesm.* 1060ff. Aristophanes accuses him of plagiarising from himself; there is also Cratinus' notion of *euripidaristophanizein* (fr. 307); cf. schol. Pl., *Apol.* 19c.

[5] Cf. the note on Alex. Aetol. 7.1 (p. 126 Powell); P. 167 n.10 below. Charges of sternness and ugliness are standard in invective; Nisbet 1961, 195–6.

[6] Cf. Lesky 1966b, 361; Leo 1912, 377; Arrighetti 1964, 126.

[7] On the technique in general, Leo 1912, 377.

will be chaste in his.'[8] Lines about women's usefulness from *Melanippe* are cited in Satyrus and in the *Vita* as 'evidence' of his recantation.[9] In Satyrus' dialogue, lines from Euripides' *Ino* about metamorphosis into a bird are cited as evidence that he made 'so to speak, an obstructive plea' about his exile to the Athenians.[10] A trimeter verse about a mouth sweeter than honey and the Sirens (89–90) becomes the punchline for an anecdote about Euripides' bad breath.[11] In the *Bacchae*, the impious woman-hating Pentheus is torn apart by women led by his mother; in Satyrus and the *Vita* the woman-hater Euripides, friend of Socrates, is killed by a pack of hunting dogs descended from a bitch whose death Euripides had sanctioned.[12] In every case the poet and his work are regarded as synonymous.[13]

But the process of generating biographical data from poetry is best illustrated by the anecdote in Philochorus and the *Vita* about Euripides' cave (62–5). As in the case of the quotations from drama, what is given as the result of the story is in fact its origin: in order to explain why so many of Euripides' most beautiful lyrics describe the sea, it seemed logical to assume that he may have lived near the sea.[14] Other tragic poets speak

---

[8] *par' hōi men autēn sōphronein, par' hōi de mē* (*Vita*); cf. *dustēnos estin, ei dokei to sōphronein/ekei men autēn ouk echein, par' hōi d'echein* in *El*. Euripides himself appears as an adulterer in two anecdotes omitted in the *Vita*, Soph. T75 (p. 81 above) and Hermesianax 7.61ff. (p. 165 n.6 below).

[9] Cf. Stesichorus' palinode; Arrighetti 1964, 126–7; p. 33 above. The story of Chaucer's repentance at the time of his death may be based on his retraction at the end of *The Canterbury Tales*; Crow-Olson 1966, 547. Cf. the idea that the writer of the novel *Aethiopica* later became Heliodorus bishop of Trikka; Perry 1967, 107–8.

[10] The anecdote may have influenced Horace; Nisbet-Hubbard 1978, 334.

[11] A stock insult; cf. Brecht 1931, 95. But no such anecdote evolves from Aristophanes' similar line about the well-loved Sophocles, fr. 580A/*Vit.* 22.

[12] Nestle 1898, 141–4; but cf. Wilamowitz 1969, 1 17. The term *diasyrontes* ('tearing him apart', 122) also retains the metaphor (cf. Soph. fr. 767 of a hawk tearing at meat). The story in the *Suda* that Lucian was killed by dogs because he was 'rabid against the truth' appears to be based on *Peregr.* 2: 'I was almost torn apart by Cynics as Acteon was by dogs or his cousin Pentheus by women.' The phrase 'which he raised himself' (*has ethrepsato*) describes Archelaus' servant Lysimachus in the Suda biography (*hous autos etrephe*, p. 166 n.6 below). On dog sacrifice, see Greenewalt 1978, 31.

[13] Cf. also Euripides' 'trial' for impiety, p. 110 below; on misquotations, Dover 1976, 42ff.

[14] E.g. *IT* 392–420, *Hel.* 1451–64; Barlow 1971, 26–7; Padel 1974, 240.

of the sea; its random violence is an effective metaphor for the course of human fate.[15] But the same stories are not told about Aeschylus and Sophocles because they are not reported to have hated other people like Euripides (65–6, 118–20). Satyrus provides as documentation of his misanthropy a conveniently apt line from Aristophanes about Euripides being like the characters in his plays.[16] Hence the assumption that he would have lived in isolation, like the Cyclops in *Odyssey* 9 or Timon the misanthrope (Plu., *Ant.* 70).[17]

Since the most intriguing details in the biography are based on his own poetry or contemporary literature, one suspects the remaining anecdotes may derive from myth rather than history.[18] What happens to Euripides happens with remarkable frequency and symmetry to other poets. For example, Euripides' future promise was recognised early by an oracle, which his father at first misinterpreted and so had his son train first to be an athlete (4–7). Sophocles, according to his biographers, also studied wrestling along with poetry (*Vit.Soph.* 3). Archilochus' father was told that his son would be immortal.[19]

Euripides, we are told, had a second profession, painting (17–18). Aeschylus, according to his biographer, was an exemplary soldier (*Vit.Aesch.* 1.10).[20] Euripides' wife prefers the poet's slave to her husband (92–6). The wife of Aesop's master Xanthias also prefers his more capable slave (*Vit.Aesop.* 75,

[15] E.g. Aesch., *Eum.* 550–7, *Sept.* 158–76; Soph., *Ant.* 586–92; Easterling 1978, 145.

[16] Leo 1912, 382; Fairweather 1974, 234–5. Cf. the modern deduction that Shakespeare had boils because he wrote about them; Schoenbaum 1970, 756.

[17] Cf. also Phrynichus' *Monotropos*, fr. 18: 'I am called the solitary; I lead the life of Timon, without wife or mate, quick to anger, unapproachable, humourless, won't talk with anyone, prefer my own opinions.' On the attractiveness of the cave story and scholars' credulousness, see Jacoby *FGrHist* 111B586–7; Lefkowitz 1978, 466; Lesky 1966, 361. Cf. Wilamowitz 1969, 1 6 n.1. On the cave as a tourist attraction, p. 102 below.

[18] Lefkowitz 1978, 469; Momigliano 1971b, 14–15.

[19] P. 28 above.

[20] Plato was said to have been a wrestler, painter and poet; Riginos 1976, §§12–14. Socrates was said to have been a sculptor, D.L. 2.19 Paus. 1.22.8; cf. Calder, 1974, 274. Tisamenes misinterprets an oracle about winning contests in Hdt. 9.33.

p.95 Perry). Euripides was hated by his fellow Athenians but prospered in exile (87, 117–20). So did Aeschylus, at least according to his biographers (*Vit.Aesch.* 2.5), and Apollonius of Rhodes (*Vit.Ap.Rhod.* A p.1.10–12, B p.2.7–11 Wendel).[21] Euripides was worshipped as a hero after his death, like Aeschylus (*Vit.Aesch.* 2.26) and Sophocles (*Vit.Soph.* 17).[22] In the light of these recurrent events, it is no coincidence that Euripides was born on a significant occasion, the day of the battle of Salamis, like Hellanicus, whose name means 'victory for the Greeks' (19–21).[23]

Only two incidents in the *Vita* sound unique and therefore possibly of historical significance. But here again we may suspect that they found their origin in some literary source. Both are favourable to the poet. (1) Euripides acted as a torch-bearer in the rites of Apollo at Cape Zoster; stories about Pindar's poetry are offered as aetiologies of his hymns.[24] Was a passage from some play now lost cited to counter charges of Euripides' atheism, in the way that Satyrus describes how Euripides 'admirably incites the youth to valour and courage'?[25] The story could also be used to counter the jokes about his ancestry: Sophocles' biographer observes that Sophocles would not 'have been thought worthy of generalship along with Pericles and Thucydides' if his father had been an artisan as Aristoxenus and Ister alleged (*Vit.* 1).[26] (2) That Euripides was awarded the privileges of *proxenos* in Magnesia after his emigration there (22–3) could easily have originated from literal interpretation of a metaphorical expression of friendship: the scholia to Pindar offer concrete explanations for references in

[21] Pp. 72–3 above, 129 below.

[22] Apollonius was buried in Alexandria next to Callimachus (*Vit. Apoll.* B. 2.11–14); p. 129 below.

[23] Not that remarkable coincidence in itself constitutes disproof; the second and third presidents of the United States, John Adams and Thomas Jefferson, both died on 4 July 1826, the fiftieth anniversary of the Declaration of Independence.

[24] P. 60 above. Cf. how according to Theophrastus Euripides poured wine for Delian Apollo at Athens for the dancers who came from among the first families in Athens (Ath. 10.424E).

[25] Fr. 39 iv.33ff., omitted in the *Vita*.

[26] P. 75 above.

the *Odes* to *proxenia* with foreigners.[27] Similar privileges were awarded by Rhodes to Apollonius, but the story of his exile can be shown to be an aetiology for his epithet 'Rhodian'.[28] Custom would have located a commemorative inscription of Euripides' *proxenia* in Magnesia.[29] But since ancient biographers did not travel to pursue their research and did not have access to accurate descriptive geographies, they were no more likely to have seen it *in situ* than Themistocles' tomb.[30]

The ancient Greeks dealt with poetic achievement in the way that they coped with other unusual occurrences, by describing them in narrative form, telling myths of power, social isolation, exile, violent death. The pattern of events in Euripides' *Vita* follows at least the general outline of stories about the Greek heroes, both of legendary figures like Theseus or Heracles and of historical heroes like Themistocles or Alcibiades.[31]

*Early recognition of talent.* Euripides' father receives an oracle that his son will be a victor in contests where crowns are awarded (4–7). He was also born on a significant day, the occasion of the Greek victory at Salamis (2–4). Dionysus appeared to Aeschylus (who was guarding grapes) in a dream and told him to write tragedy (Paus. 1.21.2). Pindar, according to his biographers, also learned of his calling as a boy by means of special omens. (a) He fell asleep on Mt. Helicon and a bee built a honeycomb in his mouth (*Vit.* fr. 1.6–9 Dr). (b) He had a dream 'in which his mouth was full of honey and wax, and then he decided to write poetry' (1.1.9–11).[32] Archilochus

---

[27] *Nem.* 7.95*b*, III 129–30; *Ol.* 9.123c, I 296; Lloyd-Jones 1973b, 135.

[28] P. 130 below.

[29] Cf. the stele in Athens designating certain Selembryani as *proxenoi* of the Athenians, *IG*² I 116(409/8 B.C.). Thus Macedonia court historians could have had access to the decree of Philip's *proxenia* for Aristotle; cf. Düring 1957, 235.

[30] Lefkowitz 1975b, 180–1. Tombs of Themistocles were identified at Magnesia (p. 96 n.41 below) and at Athens, Plu., *Them.* 32.

[31] Nagy 1979, chs. 16, 17 suggests that a ritual pattern underlies the deaths of heroes and certain poets. To Euripides being torn apart by dogs, cf. the Lycaon werewolf ritual, Burkert 1972, 127–30. On the importance of hero worship in the fifth century, also Lloyd-Jones 1973b, 136–7.

[32] P. 59 above.

suddenly discovers a lyre at his feet and is stunned.[33] The warrior heroes of myths discover their calling early by performing special tasks. Theseus moves a stone which hides the sword and sandals hidden for him by his father (Plu., *Thes.* 3); the infant Heracles strangles the two snakes sent by Hera to kill him (Apollod. 5.4.8). But while these men establish themselves as heroes by deeds of strength, the poets discover their calling passively or accidentally.

*Versatility.* Even though Euripides' father misinterpreted the oracle, Euripides manages to be successful in the wrong field by winning a victory in games at Athens (7). He was also a recognised painter and served as a torchbearer in the rites of Apollo at Cape Zoster (18–19). Sophocles studied wrestling as a boy and led the chorus in the celebration of the victory at Salamis (*Vit.* 3). Later Sophocles was elected general (1, 9), though his skill in strategy is questioned in Ion's anecdote.[34] Sophocles was noted for his piety (11, 12). Aeschylus fought 'heroically' in all three of the important battles against the Persians (*Vit.Aesch.* 4). To these physically talented Athenian poets we might compare the poetically talented Athenian lawgiver Solon, the Athenian general Themistocles, with his many pithy sayings, and Theseus, who is celebrated as a founder of lawful government as well as a fighter and a general (Plu., *Thes.* 25). All follow the epic ideal 'to be both an orator of stories and a doer of deeds' (Phoenix's aim for Achilles, *Il.* 9.443).

*Accomplishments.* The great tragic poets can be distinguished from their colleagues simply by the quantity of their output. Euripides wrote 92 dramas, Sophocles 123, Aeschylus 70; Aeschylus' predecessor Phrynichus 9, Sophocles' contemporary Ion of Chios 40 (at most; it might have been only 30, or 12), Euripides' successful rival Nicomachus 11.[35] Heroes in

[33] P. 28 above.
[34] P. 81 above. Arist., *Rhet.* 1384b says that Euripides was a member of an embassy to Syracuse; Stevens 1956, 91. But his presence there may simply have been inferred by an ancient commentator from Aristotle's text, which mentions only 'Euripides' reply to the Syracusans'; cf. Jameson 1971, 533–4.
[35] This information from the Suda (s.vv.) may derive from Aristotle's *didaskaliai* (D.L. 5.26); Jaeger 1934, 326–7; Fairweather 1974, 253–4; Griffith 1977, 229–31.

art are distinguished from ordinary mortals by their size. They are heroes not because they have done one exemplary thing, but because they have committed many, and usually violent, acts. Heracles confronts a series of monsters; Theseus kills off a series of robbers. Each hero pursues repeatedly a special type of adversary; in Oedipus' case, it is his own family, father, mother-wife and sons.[36]

Historical heroes also are worshipped for having committed extraordinary damage, even though magnitude makes power indiscriminate and immoral.[37] In the early fifth century Cleomedes, who went mad and killed sixty boys in their schoolroom, was worshipped in Astypalea on the advice of the Delphic oracle as the 'last hero', an immortal.[38] Euripides' work, according to the biography, draws violent responses from his audiences, especially the women (77–80). Aeschylus' *Eumenides* so frightened the audience that 'children died and foetuses were aborted' (*Vit.Aesch.* 2.11).[39]

*Isolation, exile.* The Greek attitude toward extraordinary achievement is ambivalent. Though it seems strange to us, Greeks celebrated victory by both praising and blaming.[40] They would compare the victor to the gods but then assure him of the dangers he had risked by winning: the gods' jealousy, man's hatred, the certainty of eventual failure. Greek tragedy too celebrates this ethic of simultaneous love and hate. In drama a man of great stature, of singular ability like Oedipus or Heracles, confronts great challenge and fails. As a result he is banished from society, often by literal exile. In the biography, Euripides considers himself superior to other people: 'he spent his days in Salamis in a cave by the sea in order to avoid the public' (62–4). Euripides 'presumably was somewhat arrogant and kept away from ordinary people and had no interest in appealing to his audiences' (118–20). But, as in the case of Olympic victors and of war heroes, a superior stance invites

---

[36] Lévi-Strauss 1968, 88–91; Leach 1970, 80–2.
[37] Brelich 1958, 313–14; cf. Ar. fr. 58.4–5 Austin, 'heroes . . . stewards of good and of evil'; Nilsson 1967, 189–90; Burkert 1978, 318.
[38] Paus. 6.9.6–8; cf. Plu., *Rom.* 28; Brelich 1958, 320; Knox 1964, 56–7.
[39] P. 71 above.
[40] Lefkowitz 1976, 33.

envy and hatred (the Greek word *phthonos* essentially means both). 'The comic poets attacked him and tore him to pieces in their envy' (*phthonōi* 121–2). Euripides was accused 'enviously' (*hypo phthonou*) of having Cephisophon serve as coauthor of his tragedies (78–80). 'He was hated (*ephthoneito*) by the Athenians' (87).[41] 'A boorish youth said enviously (*hypo phthonou*) that Euripides had bad breath' (88).

When Euripides because of this attitude won few victories, he left Athens for Macedonia (118–24). Similarly, when Athenian audiences began to prefer Sophocles or Simonides, Aeschylus left Athens for Sicily (*Vit.Aesch.* 2.5). We are told that the Athenians loved Sophocles, but in one anecdote in his *Life*, even he briefly assumes the angry character of one of his most celebrated heroes, Oedipus at Colonus, who curses his son Polyneices. Sophocles quarrels with his son Iophon, who is envious (*phthonounta*) of his half-brother.[42]

*Violent death.* The heroes of tragedy die violent deaths in exile. The Theban Oedipus is swallowed by the earth at Colonus outside Athens. Heracles (another native Theban) has himself burned alive on Mt. Oeta in Thessaly. Euripides is torn apart by dogs in Macedonia (57–9). Aeschylus is killed in Sicily by being struck on the head by a tortoise dropped by an eagle (*Vit.Aesch.* 2.17). Sophocles died in Athens, but abruptly. He either choked on a grape or ran out of breath reciting *Antigone* or was overcome by joy at winning first prize with that same play (*Vit.Soph.* 14). Every way in which Sophocles dies is sudden and externally induced: he cannot die quietly in bed.[43]

The explanation lies once again in the Greeks' ambivalent

---

[41] The Athenians' envy of greatness was proverbial; cf. Diodorus on Aeschylus (*AP* 7.40 = *Garl.Phil.* 13 GP) and on Themistocles (*AP* 7.74 = *Garl.Phil.* 14 GP), also Antipater of Thessalonica on Themistocles (*AP* 7.236 = *Garl.Phil.* 115 GP). The practice of ostracism provided limited social sanction for these feelings; Schoeck 1970, 205–9.

[42] Pp. 84–5 above.

[43] Cf. Sotadea 15.5ff. Powell: 'all who wanted to make a great discovery or an artful poem or a clever bit of learning, all these have come to a bad end in their deaths and have suffered at the hands of the world's creator'; a list of the tragic poets' and philosophers' deaths follows. Here again what one writes may determine how one dies; Aristophanes simply dies without any special notoriety. Cf. Fairweather 1974, 270–1.

attitude toward extraordinary achievement. A great man, envied, hated and feared at the height of his power, becomes loved and respected once he has fallen.[44] The heroes Oedipus and Amphiaraus were worshipped where the earth had swallowed them. The Athenians offered yearly sacrifices to Sophocles (*Vit.Soph.* 17).[45] Aeschylus had a hero's shrine in Sicily and was honoured by the Athenians after his death (*Vit.Aesch.* 2.21).[46]

Euripides, once dead, is treated like a hero. Sophocles, his actors and the audience openly mourn for him (45–9). Dionysius the tyrant sent for his stylus and lyre and had them dedicated in the temple of the Muses (80–5). Like Amphiaraus and Themistocles, he has shrines in more than one place, the monument in Athens and a tomb in Macedonia.[47] Both were struck by lightning (45; *AP* 7.48). At the Macedonian tomb there were said to be two springs, one sustaining, the other destructive, as at Trophonius' shrine in Lebadeia.[48] Hellenistic epigrams locate this tomb both at Pella (*AP* 7.44, 49; Suda s.v.) and near Arethusa on the frontier, far from the Macedonian court (Adaeus, *AP* 7.51 = *Garl.Phil.* 3 GP).

Euripides' biography follows the general pattern of a tragic hero's life, but only in *outline*. The actual events that comprise the poet's life are too trivial to allow him heroic stature. Because many of the anecdotes derive from comedy, the poet often appears ludicrous and undignified. He is ugly, with moles on his face, unpleasant (28); he is set upon by women (100–2); he is sexually inadequate (92–6). Nor do the circum-

---

[44] Cf. Hor., *Ep.* 2.5–14; Fraenkel 1957, 386n.2; Pind., *Pyth.* 1.84, 2.55–6.

[45] Pp. 86–7 above.

[46] Cf. the cults of Homer at Smyrna (where like Pindar at Delphi he shares in Apollo's sacrifice), Sappho at Lesbos, and Aristotle at Stagira; Farnell 1921, 367, 421–6. Parmenides built a *hērōon* for his teacher Ameinias the Pythagorean, D.L. 9.21; Burkert 1969, 27–8.

[47] Farnell 1921, 58–61.

[48] Nestle 1898, 145–9; Vitruv., *De arch.* 8.16; Plin., *NH* 31.28. Cf. the springs of pleasure and grief at the site of the contest between Midas and Silenus, Theopompus *FGH* 1 289; Ael. *VH* 3.18. The presence of two springs also at Trophonius' shrine (Paus. 9.39.4) suggests that at Euripides' tomb they mark the ambivalence of a hero's power (p. 95 n.37 above), not as Nestle suggested (p. 149), the 'double nature' of Euripides' poetry.

stances of his death enhance his stature; its accidental character makes him seem more pathetic than heroic (56, 118–19). Aeschylus is degraded by being hit on the head by a tortoise, Sophocles by choking on a grape or on a line of *Antigone*, or even by dying of joy.

In emphasising Euripides' ineptitude and human failings, the biographers appear to be working in a tradition of narrative realism that began in the fifth century in the plays of Euripides himself.[49] As Sophie Trenkner observed, the character types and plots of Greek short stories virtually all have analogues in the exciting plots and naturalistic characters of the plays of Euripides.[50] It is Euripides who depicts Orestes as a born killer with incestuous tendencies and not as the noble, pious son who returns in the *Libation Bearers* to avenge his father's death.

Poets, starting with Hesiod in the eighth century, had always described themselves as isolated from and superior to other men.[51] But it is only in the fourth century, in the first literary biographies, that the poet's original heroic stance appears in completely naturalised form. Euripides is quite literally isolated, by living like a hermit in his cave. Sophocles is not simply 'servant of the Muses' (like Hesiod or Bacchylides) but an actual priest who tends the shrine of a local hero, Halon (*Vit.Soph.* 11).[52] The old heroes of myth, like Theseus and Heracles, often had gods for fathers. Homer, in some traditions reputed to be the son of a god, becomes in a fourth-century biography simply an illegitimate child.[53]

In addition to this trend toward naturalism, anecdotes drawn from comedy, once condensed, acquire a hostile tone. Exaggeration is funny only when set against true information; without perspective humour turns into criticism. Philemon's lines about wishing to hang himself to see Euripides become in the *Vita* evidence of excessive hero-worship (109–13). It does

---

[49] Jacoby 1933, 10.

[50] Trenkner 1958, 35ff.; Lloyd-Jones 1973b, 137; Lefkowitz 1978, 463.

[51] Lefkowitz 1978, 460–2; Dover 1974, 29–30; Gallo 1967, 155.

[52] Hence the notion of what E. M. Forster called Sophocles 'the bishop'; cf. Lloyd-Jones 1971, 193n.13. On poets as priests, Nagy 1979, ch. 18.

[53] Ephorus *FGrHist* 70F1; p. 14 above; Trenkner 1958, 30. Cf. the story that Plato's father was Apollo; Riginos 1976, §1.

not seem to matter which character in which comedy (suppose it was a fanatic?) spoke these lines, or in which context (a trip to Hades?).[54] Philochorus explicitly contended with the distortions of the comic poets by arguing that Euripides' mother was not a vegetable seller but well-born.[55] Satyrus' dialogue also preserves a sense of debate over the application of quotations from plays. One of the characters notes that the comic poets had it in for Euripides.[56] The characters make it clear that it is they, and not the poets themselves, who attribute biographical significance to what they cite ('Aristophanes, as though summoned as a witness'; 'what you say seems to be more subtle than true').[57]

But in the *Vita* all sense of debate has disappeared. Quotations are introduced as evidence without qualification or concern about their provenance. Satyrus in his dialogue has discussions of Socratic notions in Euripides; the *Vita* offers instead a statement about literal collaboration.[58] The *Vita* omits the verbal parallels that Diogenes Laertius cites to 'prove' that Euripides

[54] E.G., Dionysus in Ar.. *Ran.* 66–70. Cf. Callimachus Ep. 23 Pf. about Cleombrotus killing himself because he had read Plato's description of life after death in the *Phaedo*. Cicero, for one, took the joke literally; Riginos 1976, §132. 'If the dead have feeling' is an oratorical commonplace, Dover 1974, 243. Cf. App. 7, p. 173 below and the anecdote, based on Plato's account of Socrates' defence (*Apol.* 41a), that the dying poet Cercidas looked forward to meeting his favourite authors in Hades (Ael., *VH* 13.20, *ap.* Powell p. 202).

[55] His interest in the chronology of Euripides' death may also derive from concern about the use of poetry as evidence (*FGrHist* 328F220; Jacoby 111 B587). Euripides' *Palamedes* had been used as evidence that the Athenians executed Socrates, but Philochorus argued that Euripides had died earlier (*FGrHist* 328F221). Cf. the argument about Pindar's birthplace preserved in *POxy* 2438.ii.4ff.; Gallo 1968, 25–6; Lefkowitz 1975, 75. *POxy* 2506 fr. 98 preserves debate about the timing of Alcaeus' and his brother's deaths.

[56] P. 164 n.5 below.

[57] On the positive qualities of Satyrus' dialogue form; Leo 1912, 274; Arrighetti 1964, 23; Gallo 1967, 158; Momigliano 1971b, 11. The criticisms of S. West 1974, 282–3 do not take into full consideration the differences between literary and non-literary biographies; cf. Leo 1912, 382n.2.

[58] P. 164 n.4 below; p. 132 below. The tendency of biographers to turn inference into fact was noted even in antiquity; Antiphon's biographer observes that Caecilius took Thucydides' praise (8.68) as evidence that Antiphon was Thucydides' teacher (*XOrat* 832e); cf. Fairweather 1974, 258–9.

was Anaxagoras' pupil.[59] Elaborate and appreciative discussion in Satyrus of Euripides' artistic qualities emerges in the short second biography in the *Vita* as a summary negative assessment (126–32).[60] Debate on his attitude toward women survives only in outline; quotation from *Melanippe* is cut to essentials (100–10), and omitted altogether from *Thesmophoriazousae*.[61] Also missing in the *Vita* are Satyrus' quotations of Euripides' views on wealth, demagoguery, family relations and courage; the story of his championing of the poet Timotheus; the anecdote (also in Plu., *Nic.* 29) about how Athenian soldiers won release in Sicily by reciting verses of Euripides.[62] Narrative suffers less attrition than intellectual debate, but even there non-essential detail is pruned away. In Satyrus' account of Euripides' death attention is paid to the role of other characters in the story, Archelaus and the hunters who released the dogs. But the *Vita* concentrates directly on the poet, even to the point of losing the full meaning of Satyrus' punchline.[63]

Excerptors also seem to prefer the negative and the sensational. In Satyrus the story of Euripides and Cephisophon ends with each getting the other's wife; in the *Vita* only Cephisophon wins.[64] Satyrus' account preserved chronological order.[65] But in the *Vita* the anecdote about Euripides' bad breath, originally set in Macedonia, becomes another instance of the Athenians' hatred.[66] In Satyrus Archelaus defends Euripides with the

[59] Euripides' 'golden clod', D.L. 2.10 = fr. 783; Anaxagoras' 'molten mass', D.L. 2.8 = 59A1 DK; Arrighetti 1964, 105–7. On collections of Euripides' sayings, Dihle 1977, 32.

[60] Arrighetti 1964, 101; Delcourt 1933 did not recognise the transformation in her over-schematised account of correspondences.

[61] Leo 1912, 376; Arrighetti 1964, 126–7.

[62] Fr. 39 iii, iv, vi, xix, xxii (Timotheus), cf. the anecdotes about Plato's support of the poet Antimachus, pp. 172–3 below.

[63] P. 165 n.6 below. For the meaning of *esti tis*, 'there is such a thing as', cf. Alcman *PMG* 1.36. The verbal correspondence is not 'almost word-for-word', *pace* Delcourt 1933, 287 and Arrighetti 1964, 145.

[64] The earlier version sounds like the plot of a comedy; Delcourt 1933, 278–9.

[65] Leo 1912, 379; Arrighetti 1964, 21.

[66] P. 167 n.10 below; Leo 1912, 378n.1; Delcourt 1933, 286–7. In a third-century dialogue-biography of Socrates, Xanthippe is shown to be a concerned hostess (*PHib* II 182, p. 27); but the scene emerges in Diogenes Laertius 2.34 as an anecdote critical of Xanthippe. In the papyrus biography

lines about the sweetness of his mouth, but in the *Vita* Euripides speaks the lines himself. By relating anecdotes out of context and after the poet's death, the narrative in the *Vita* preserves primarily a record of elemental expressions of love and of hate. The writings of Heraclides Lembos suggest that works like Euripides' *Vita* were being produced as early as the second century B.C.; collections of anecdotes about Socrates were circulating in the first century.[67] Heraclides epitomised Satyrus' *Lives*, Hermippus' *Lives of the Lawgivers*, of the Seven Wise Men, and of Pythagoras.[68] We can get a sense of Heraclides' methodology and of his audience's interests from his excerpts of Aristotle's *Athenian Constitution*. He reduces an extensive discussion about Solon's laws with long citations of Solon's poetry (v–xiii) into two sentences: Solon cancelled debts, but because of criticism of his reforms he left Athens for Egypt.[69] All that remains of Aristotle's account is a general statement of what Solon did and its unpopularity.

Selection of detail in the *Vita* conveys the impression that Euripides was a lonely misfit, hated in his own home and in his own city. Of the several accounts of his death, it picks the one that emphasises his isolation; no reference is made (as in the Suda) to a plot against Euripides by other poets, or to a love affair with Archelaus' housekeeper (Hermesianax 7.66), or to dying of old age (Adaeus *AP* 7.51 = *Garl.Phil.* 3 G-P).[70] His life has been made sufficiently unpleasant that readers can be content that they have not accomplished as much as he. By emphasising that he wrote his dramas in reaction to particular events, the *Vita* represents Euripides' achievement as a process

---

Socrates speaks of agreeable and disagreeable dinner guests; in Diogenes they are 'reasonable' and 'worthless'. But in some cases lack of factual information contributes to the process; Aubrey's notes on Shakespeare (whom he did not know) are malicious; his life of Milton (whose third wife gave him specific information) respectful; Dick 1972, 36off., 437ff.

[67] Gallo 1974, 182.
[68] Gallo 1967, 157; Arrighetti 1964, 14–15; Momigliano 1971, 79.
[69] Heracl. Lemb. 1.5; Dilts 1971, 9.
[70] On the various traditions, Gow-Page 1965, II 5; Arrighetti 1964, 145–50. Adaeus attempts to rationalise the mythology, like the writer of Sophocles' *Vita*, p. 75 above. To the story of jealous poets, cf. the scholiasts' tales about Pindar's rivalry with Bacchylides, Lefkowitz 1975, 79–85.

requiring no special talent other than emotions like anger or
fear. His gifts become at once accessible and comprehensible.
Centuries later an Arab biographer portrayed Plato as a
Muslim ascetic who loved to be alone in the wilderness and
wept so loud one could hear him crying two miles away.[71]

In Aristophanes' *Frogs* the poet was regarded as a teacher;
Alcidamas' *On Homer* offers the poet's life, and minor works as
'education' for 'lovers of the noble and good'; Satyrus provides
examples of Euripides' moral teachings.[72] But clearly Euripides' poetry served no such ethical purpose for the readers of
his *Vita*. The portrait of the poet suggests that drama is tan-
gential to their lives and perhaps even morally dangerous.
Unfortunately this attitude gives no indication of date or
religious ambience. In the third century B.C. Antigonus of
Carystus reduced the sceptic Pyrrho's style of life to a parody
of his philosophy, attributing no value to physical dangers,
surviving only through the efforts of his friends (D.L. 9.62).
One suspects that his audience was not interested in the complexities of philosophical inquiry, and only patient enough to
grasp a general outline of essentials. Whether school children
or masters or civil servants, they were better entertained by the
actions than by the words of drama; like Trimalchio they might
best enjoy their Homer in live performances of epic battle scenes
(Petron., *Sat.* 59. 3–7; Artem. 4.2). When they visited Salamis,
tourist guides could point out to them Euripides' cave.[73]

The Euripides *Vita* is made up of anecdotes created in or
soon after the poet's lifetime, which derive from his own works
or comic poetry about him. Stories of his early recognition and
versatility, the magnitude of his accomplishments, his isolation,
exile and death suggest that in the fourth century at least he
was regarded as something of a hero. But by the time the *Vita*
was compiled the process of condensation and excerpting made
his stature comfortably unenviable. Though precise dating is
impossible, the basic format of the *Vita* could have been set as

---

[71] Rosenthal 1969, 28–9; Riginos 1976, §107; Dillon 1978, 483–4.
[72] Lefkowitz 1978, 468.
[73] P. 91 above; Aulus Gellius had seen it; see p. 166 n.7 below.

early as the second century B.C. In its present form it would seem best to serve the interests of an audience with some ambition but without the leisure or persistence seriously to acquire culture, and which accordingly would have derived reassurance from the condescending tone of the *Vita*.

It is unlikely that historically accurate information will ever be found to replace the attractive fictions that we must resolutely discard. Turning back to the plays can offer no sure remedy. Euripides' use of sophistic arguments provides evidence of his audience's interests as well as of his own.[74] Psychoanalytic methods, like ancient anecdotes, will tend to reproduce their authors' preoccupations rather than Euripides', e.g. the discovery in dreams from his tragedies of concern with the primal scene.[75] That Euripides won fewer victories than Sophocles says only that audiences liked Sophocles' plays better at the moment; the Athenians still never denied Euripides a chorus.[76]

Great care must also be taken in trying to trace the development of Euripides' interests, or in seeing in his dramas direct reflection of contemporary events. Any dating based on the biography must be questioned: according to the scholia on Aristophanes' *Frogs* 67, the *Bacchae* was produced after Euripides' death along with *Iphigenia at Aulis* and *Alcmeon*. References in the play to Pieria (409–11) and the Lydias valley (568–75) might suggest that he wrote the play while he was in Macedonia.[77] But it is equally possible that the notion of his exile in Macedonia was created to explain the presence of these unusual references in the play, as the scholium to *Nubes* 272 says Aristophanes was born in Naucratis, to explain a single reference to the river Nile.[78] The *Bacchae* is the source also of

---

[74] Finley 1967, 94–101.
[75] Cf. Devereux 1976, 311; on the limitations of the methodology, Lefkowitz 1977, 305–7.
[76] Stevens 1956, 92.
[77] Dodds 1960, xxxix.
[78] Heliodorus *FGrHist* 373F4; cf. Gelzer 1970, 1398. On scholiastic methodology, Slater 1971, 150–2.

the story about the poet's violent death in Macedonia.[79] Thus Greek tragedy may in fact not end where it began, with Dionysus.[80] The actual date of Aeschylus' *Suppliants* indicates that the course of literary history is less easily charted than scholars or their pupils would like.[81]

---

[79] P. 90 above. The story about Sophocles' and Iophon's quarrel (p. 83 above) is taken as proof that Sophocles composed the *OC* toward the end of his life (it was produced by his grandson in 401); yet the anecdote appears to be based on comedy. But the story of Sophocles dying as a result of winning first prize with *Antigone* (p. 82 above) is not used as evidence for dating that play to 406/5, because Aristophanes' suggestion of *c.* 441 seems more plausible.

[80] Lesky 1966, 400.

[81] Lloyd-Jones 1964, 256–84.

# CHAPTER TEN

# Comic Poets

Old comedy, because it is not based on inherited myth and uses a variety of metrical forms, contains relatively less mythical material than other types of ancient poetry,[1] and consequently provides a more precise sense of its historical content. But even though biographies of Aristophanes draw their anecdotes directly from the texts of his plays, they do not attempt to recreate in any detail the chronology or circumstances that he describes. Instead the biographies designate his place in the history of Greek literature, and claim for him a role as champion of Athenian democracy and freedom of speech.

Aristophanes' *Vita* begins by emphasising his ethical achievements: 'It was he who first decided to transform comedy—which was still wandering around in the old style—into something more constructive and serious. Comedy had previously been nastier and more shameless because the poets Cratinus and Eupolis had uttered more slander than was appropriate' (2-5).[2] No sources for this information are specified, but the notion of reforming art in the guise of a wayward and shameless woman sounds as if it came from comedy. Euripides in the *Frogs* says to Aeschylus: 'When I first took over Tragic Art from you, swollen from your bombast and heavy words, I first slimmed her down and took off weight' (939-41). Aristophanes in the parabasis of the *Clouds* speaks of his play as 'basically chaste' (537; cf. Pherecrates fr. 145).[3] The idea that Aristophanes was not only a better poet, but more elegant and less

---

[1] The same distinction applies to middle comedy, cf. Antiphanes ii.90 Kock *ap*. Ath. vi.222b.

[2] See Appendix 6.

[3] Comedy is a character also in Cratinus' *Pytine*, fr. 180 = schol. Ar., *Eq.* 400.

crude than his predecessors and contemporaries comes from Aristophanes' own *parabaseis* (*Ach.* 629ff., *Eq.* 507ff., *Nub.* 518ff., *Vesp.* 1015ff., *Pax* 734ff.; cf. *Ran.* 12, *Vesp.* 64ff.). A contemporary audience would have recognised it as the poet's conventional claim of pre-eminence; but removed from context, stripped of their humour and summarised, these assertions are reported as historical fact.

Aristophanes is then said to have set the model for New Comedy in his *Cocalus* (5–7). Later in the *Vita* (50–5) it is claimed that he gave the *Cocalus* its Menandrian plot and substance because the *chorēgoi* in 387 ruled that no one could be 'ridiculed by name' in any comedy. The notion of the *chorēgoi* appears to be an attempt to give political significance to what had been a natural evolution of comic form. Platonius' treatise on comedy offers a similar explanation for the absence of real names from fourth-century comedy (Kaibel, *CGF*, pp.3–4): free speech was restricted when the oligarchs began to take over; Alcibiades drowned the comic poet Eupolis for saying that he lisped, presumably some time after 415 (Tzetzes in Kaibel, *CGF*, pp.27–8, cf. 3).[4]

Restrictive legislation is cited with suspicious frequency to account for particular references in Aristophanes. Euthymenes is named in the *Acharnians* because he was archon in 439 when an act against comic satire sponsored in the previous year was repealed (schol. *Ach.* 67). Syracosius is mentioned because in 414 he is said to have sponsored a decree forbidding the use of people's names (schol. *Av.* 1297); cf. Eupolis fr. 207). The same legislation is also cited to explain why Phrynichus said in his *Monotropos* that Syracosius 'took away my means of making fun of whom I wanted to' (fr. 26). A similar law was said to have been enacted in 426 because of Aristophanes' attack on Cleon in his *Babylonians* (Ael., *NH* 10.41). If in fact it ever existed, all this legislation appears to have been consistently ineffective; but there appears to be no reference to legal censorship outside commentaries on old comedy.

In the sober context of the *Vita*, not only jokes but practical information takes on political overtones: 'since he was very

<hr>

[4] P. 115 below.

cautious at the start, all the more because he was so gifted, he produced his first plays under the names of Callistratus and Philonides; because of this Aristonymus and Ameipsias made fun of him, saying that (as in the proverb) he was born on the fourth day, to toil for other men' (7–10). It is possible that the source of this information was the *didaskaliai*, if it can be assumed that young poets did not serve as producers of comedies until they gained experience; Philonides was a member of Aristophanes' own *thiasos*.[5] But the notion that poets, like orators, served some sort of apprenticeship may simply derive from literal interpretation of allusions in dramas, e.g. 'since I was a virgin I wasn't able to give birth' (*Nub.* 530, cf. schol. 518). The chorus of the *Knights* claim that Aristophanes hadn't asked for a chorus previously 'because he thought producing a comedy (*kōmōidodidaskein*) was very difficult work' (513ff.) and because he says that a poet, like a pilot, ought to serve first as oarsman and then as officer on the bow before he takes over the helm (541ff.). The analogy of the pilot's training suggests that the production of a comedy was a complex operation that could involve the talents of several poets at a time.[6] Comic poets enjoyed implying that one poet wrote another's plays. Eupolis in his *Baptai* says he helped Aristophanes compose the *Knights* (fr. 78). Aristophanes suggests in the *Clouds* (553ff.) that Eupolis' *Maricas* was a bad reworking of the *Knights*. Dionysus claims in the *Frogs* that Sophocles wrote for his son Iophon (*Ran.* 78–9) and that Cephisophon helped Euripides (*Ran.* 944, fr. 580).[7] Aristophanes' contemporary Teleclides claimed that Socrates and Mnesilochus collaborated with Euripides (fr. 39–40, Eur. *Vit.* 11f.).[8]

As a first illustration of Aristophanes' achievement, his biographer describes his enmity for Cleon the demagogue and his criticism in the *Knights* of Cleon's thefts and tyrannical nature (11–13). Further to exemplify Aristophanes' political courage, the biographer adds that Aristophanes himself acted

[5] Halliwell 1980, 38n.23, 39n.29.
[6] Ibid., 43–4.
[7] Stemplinger 1912, 12–13.
[8] P. 89 n.4 above; cf. charges of borrowing and copying in new comedy, *ap.* Edmonds III B544.

the part of Cleon when none of the costumers would make a mask of him, smearing his face with red dye (13–16). The idea that no one would make a mask of Cleon is based on the lines in the *Knights* that introduce the Paphlagonian stranger (whom the audience knows to be Cleon, 115ff.): 'Don't worry; he doesn't look like himself. The costumers were afraid to make a likeness of him. But he'll be recognisable all the same, because the audience is clever' (230–3).

The story that Aristophanes acted the part himself (the hypothesis adds that he also produced the play) may derive from a literal interpretation of Aristophanes' statement in the parabasis of the *Clouds*: 'I went for Cleon below the belt but I didn't have the nerve to jump on him again when he was down' (549–50; cf. 581). The *Vita* (16–19) claims that Aristophanes' performance was responsible for Cleon's being fined five talents, citing in 'confirmation' Dicaeopolis' lines about Cleon's fine in the *Acharnians* (5ff.).[9] But the *Acharnians* was produced in 425, the year *before* the *Knights*; the biographer's narrative ideas clearly matter more than chronology.

The notion of the poet acting in his own drama conveniently relates his life to his work, as in the anecdote about the picture of Sophocles playing the role of bard in his drama *Thamyris* (*Soph. Vit.* 4).[10] A more natural interpretation of the lines in the *Knights* about Cleon's mask is that the Paphlagonian stranger did not wear a portrait mask, but some sort of grotesque—in the *Wasps* (1031) and *Peace* (751) Cleon is described as the monster Typhoeus.[11] The practice of smearing an actor's face with wine lees is first described in Hellenistic theories about the origins of tragedy; white lead is also mentioned (Suda, s.v. Thespis), but never red dye (*miltos*).[12]

The next anecdote in the *Vita* explains that Cleon had entered a lawsuit against Aristophanes for usurping citizen's rights

---

[9] A standard political accusation of bribery; cf. Plu., *Them.* 21; Timocreon, *PMG* 727.8; Jacoby on Theopompus *FGrHist* 115F94, 86; = Fornara 131B; cf. Hdt. viii.112, and the story that Sophocles made money out of the Samian campaign, p. 83 above.
[10] P. 78 above.
[11] Dover 1967, 22–3; Pickard-Cambridge 1968, 218.
[12] Dover 1967, 18; Pickard-Cambridge 1968, 79–80.

(*graphē xenias*), because the poet had criticised him in the presence of foreigners in his *Babylonians* (20–2). The notion of a trial derives from Dicaeopolis' description in the *Acharnians* of his experiences with an Athenian jury: 'I myself am well aware of what Cleon did to me because of last year's comedy. He dragged me into the Council chamber, accused me, and bad-mouthed me with his lies' (377ff.). The idea that Aristophanes was charged with usurping citizen's rights (i.e. being himself a foreigner) appears to be based on inference from the usual comic accusations about a poet's parentage.[13] Accusing Cleon before foreigners simply represents the central plot of the *Babylonians*, where Cleon was accused of taking bribes from cities subject to Athens.[14] In the *Vita* dramatic context is ignored and Dicaeopolis is assumed to be speaking directly for Aristophanes. A little later in the *Vita* (29–31), Dicaeopolis' lines about Cleon are quoted, but with the clause about 'last year's comedy' removed (they are glossed as 'and so on', 31).[15] That way the lines can be understood to refer to Cleon's enmity for Aristophanes generally, and used to support the notion that Aristophanes had to defend himself against charges that he was not an Athenian citizen.

The 'trial' provides a convenient explanation of the animosity against Cleon in the *Acharnians* and other plays; but it is significant that information about it comes only from commentaries on Aristophanes and that details about the nature of the charges are inconsistent.[16] The scholia to Dicaeopolis' lines in the *Acharnians* claim that Cleon accused Aristophanes also of 'attacking the state' (*adikias eis tous politas egrapsato*) and of committing *hybris* against the *dēmos* and the *boulē* (schol. 378). When the chorus leader in the *parabasis* of the *Wasps* complains about Cleon's harassment, the scholia to the lines suggest that he too might be referring to the same trial (schol. *Vesp.* 1284).

---

[13] Cf. p. 88 above.

[14] Van Daele 1972, 12n.1. Cf. how a comic scene about Cleon and the Athenian assembly turns up as an historical incident in Plutarch: Robertson 1923, 165.

[15] Gelzer 1970, 1398.

[16] Van Daele 1972, 145n.4; cf. Dover 1972, 99–100; Fornara 1977, §131.

Comedy appears to have provided the basis for similar legal incidents in the biographies of other historical figures. A scene in 'a drama' was the source of the story of Sophocles' lawsuit against his son Iophon (*Soph. Vit.* 13).[17] To explain a line in Aristophanes about the Knights hating Cleon, the fourth-century historian Theopompus asserted that Cleon had made attacks on the constitution (schol. *Eq.* 226 = Fornara 131A = *FGrHist* 115F93).[18] Euripides is said to have been tried for impiety by Hygiaenon for advocating perjury in his line 'my tongue swore it but my mind foreswore the oath' (*Hipp.* 612); Euripides replied that there was no need for a law court, since his case had already been tried in the theatre (Ar., *Rhet.* 1416a3). Aristophanes parodies the line twice in the *Frogs* (101, 1471) and once in the *Thesmophoriazousae* (275–6). The story that Hermippus charged Aspasia with impiety (Plu., *Per.* 32) appears simply to replicate the plot of a comedy about her (Edm. 1 285), in the way that the *Thesmophoriazousae* emerges in Satyrus' *Life of Euripides* as a historical plot to kill the poet (39.x; *Vit.* 70–1, 91, 100–4).[19] Diopeithes, accused of being a crazy oracle-monger by Aristophanes and several other comic poets as late as 414 (schol. Ar., *Eq.* 1085, *Vesp.* 380, *Av.* 988; Phrynichus fr. 9, Telecleides fr. 6, Ameipsias fr. 10) is said to have proposed *c.* 430 a law against atheists and philosophers with celestial theories (Plu., *Per.* 32).[20] Satyrus says that Anaxagoras was tried for impiety and medising (Fornara 116c) and that Cleon prosecuted Euripides for impiety (perhaps because at the Dionysia he portrayed Heracles going mad, a situation used as a rhetorical exercise in the third century A.D. (*POxy* 2400).[21] The notion of trials for impiety made particular sense in retrospect because they offered precedents for Socrates' condemnation in 399, especially since Plato has Socrates allege in

[17] Pp. 83–4 above.

[18] Cf. also Theopompus' story about the five talents, p. 108 n.9 above.

[19] Cf. the anecdote that Pericles wept when he spoke in her defence, Fornara §116c; on Euripides and the women, p. 89 above.

[20] Cf. Dover 1976, 39; Phrynichus fr. 9; Stesimbrotus *FGrHist* 107F10a; the trials are treated as historical by Momigliano apud Humphreys 1978, 188. See also Nilsson 1961, 122.

[21] Fairweather 1974, 255; Arrighetti 1964, 125.

his defence that the jurors took seriously the accusations against him in Aristophanes' *Clouds* (*Apol.* 19b–c).[22]

When they draw material from *parabaseis*, where the poet traditionally expressed his own political views, biographers give the poet unwarranted importance by taking his exaggerations literally. The chorus in the parabasis of the *Acharnians* claims that the king of Persia had heard of Aristophanes and had predicted that whichever side he was advising would win the war (647–51)—this to support an even more preposterous claim that the Spartans wanted Aegina not for itself but because they would get Aristophanes along with it. In the *Vita* these absurdities emerge as illustrations of outside recognition: 'the poet's fame was so great that he was known in Persia, and the king wanted to know whose side the comic poet was on' (44–6). The *Vita* asserts: 'He was held in high regard for having got rid of the informers, whom he called Fevers in the *Wasps*' (33–5), citing his attack on informers in the parabasis (1038–9), although a glance at Thucydides would have established that the informers were still effectively at work in 415, seven years after the *Wasps* had been produced. Aristophanes' plea for amnesty in the parabasis of the *Frogs*, according to the *Vita*, is said to have won him public recognition in the form of an olive crown; according to the peripatetic Dicaearchus, his reward was the right of a second performance (fr. 84 W; hypothesis *Ran.* p.82, 39–40).

The stories about the plea for amnesty and the king of Persia are cited as confirmation of a summary assessment: 'People praised and liked him particularly because of his determination to show in his dramas that the government of Athens was free and not enslaved by any tyrant, and that it was a democracy, and that since they were free, the people ruled themselves' (36–9). A final anecdote is appended to suggest that the enduring importance of the comedies is their democratic stance: when Dionysius the tyrant wanted to learn about Athens' government, Plato sent him Aristophanes' poetry and advised him to learn about their government by studying Aristophanes' dramas (46–9). The emphasis in all the anec-

[22] On the actual motives behind the trial, Dover 1976, 46–54.

dotes on the advantages of democracy suggests that they were composed after the middle of the fourth century, like the 'legislation' cited by orators and the forged inscriptions that illustrate to Athenians under Macedonian rule the ideals of their city in the fifth century.[23]

Even comic repartee about Aristophanes' parents emerges in the biographies as serious litigation over his citizenship. In the first *Vita*, the notion that Aristophanes came from Aegina is correctly understood to be an 'assumption based on his having spent a considerable amount of time or on his owning property there' (23–4); the chorus of the *Acharnians* claim that the Spartans wanted the island of Aegina not for its own sake but 'to take away our poet' (654).[24] The same *Vita* reports that Aristophanes defended himself against charges that his father came from Aegina by quoting wittily Telemachus' famous lines about how no one knows his own father (*Od.* 1.215); but the Suda *Life* and the preface to a catalogue of Aristophanes' plays record that 'Aristophanes was a Rhodian or Lindian; some say Egyptian, some from Camirus [in Rhodes]. He was an Athenian by special decree (*thesis*)' (xxxa. 1–2). All these conflicting nationalities sound as if they came from allegations in comedies, like the notion that Sophocles was a Phliasian or Euripides' mother a seller of vegetables.[25] Saying that he was given citizenship looks like a biographer's attempt to resolve the conflict created by his predecessors.

Comic allegations about historical persons are taken seriously in the biographies because they *sound* historical though in fact they may be no less fictitious than Cloud-cuckoo land in the *Birds* or Hades in the *Frogs*. According to his Suda biography, the comic poet Cratinus was a drunk and a pederast; the anonymous treatise on Comedy (Kaibel, *CGF*, p.3) cites Aristophanes as evidence that Cratinus died when the Spartans invaded Attica because 'he fainted; he couldn't bear to see a

---

[23] See esp. Habicht 1961, 35; Woodbury 1973, 10; Dover 1974, 289; Levy 1976, 173–208; Fornara 1977, §55; Murray 1980, 274ff.

[24] Gelzer 1970, 1397.

[25] Pp. 75, 88 above. Cf. the confusion about Antiphanes' origins, Suda s.v.

jar full of wine being broken' (*Pax* 702–3).[26] Phrynichus, Lycis, and Ameipsias, according to the Suda, were 'very frigid comic poets'; this information also is simply a summary of a joke about stock comic routines in Aristophanes' *Frogs*. Ancient scholars apparently did not take into consideration the context of the comic passages that they used as evidence. When Didymus could not find support in Phrynichus' plays for criticisms of Phrynichus, he did not suggest that the criticisms might be false:[27] 'Didymus says ... that Phrynichus was caricatured also for his foreign birth, the poorness of his plays, plagiarising, and metrical irregularities ... but Phrynichus doesn't do this in his surviving plays. A reasonable hypothesis is (*eikos*) that he did something of the sort in his *lost plays*' (schol. Ar., *Ran.* 13). Ancient scholars questioned the tradition that Aristophanes had three sons because of a reference in one of his plays to 'my wife and two innocent children' (fr. 62), without discussing the context or dating of the lines. The third son's name is given either as Nicostratus (xxixa. 4–5) or Philetairus (xxxa. 5); some authorities claimed that his mother was a slave (xxxb. 6).[28]

After historical references disappeared from comedy, biographers inferred what they could from the plots of the plays. Not surprisingly, poets of New Comedy tend to be involved with women. Menander is said to have been in love with a *hetaera* Glycera, a character in his *Perikeiromenē* and other plays (fr. 80, 280) who marries her lover after misunderstanding and separation.[29] According to the Suda (T1 K-Th), Menander was 'absolutely mad for women'; heroes of New Comedy tend to fall in love at first sight (e.g. Sostratus, *Dysc.* 52).[30] Athenaeus preserves an anecdote that suggests that Menander had such

[26] Cratinus portrayed himself as a drunk in his *Pytine* p. 105 n.3 above; cf. Nicaenetus *EG* 3003ff., Gow-Page 1955 on 2711ff. Cf. Aristophanes' jokes about his friends, p. 89 n.3 above.

[27] Cf. also S. West 1970, 295.

[28] Coulon 1972, I iii–iv; Jacoby on *FGrHist* 224F75.

[29] Gomme-Sandbach 1973, 466–9; cf. the story that Antimachus wrote the *Lydē* (p. 119 above) for a Lydian girl Lyde (Hermesianax fr. 2.41ff. = Antimachus T6 Wyss); also the *Lyde* of Lamynthius, and *Leontion* of Hermesianax (Ath. xiii. 597aff.).

[30] Cf. Ovid, *Trist.* ii.369 = Menander T35 K-Th.

difficulties with women that he criticised the comic poet Philemon for calling his beloved *hetaera* (or for that matter, any woman) 'good' in one of his plays (xv. 594d/T12). In the third century A.D. Alciphron composed a correspondence between Menander and Glycera, describing an invitation from Ptolemy to Menander, and a request for Menander to 'make ready the play in which you have introduced me' (iv.19.4/T12). As in the case of Euripides, who is said to have written the *Hippolytus* because he found his wife committing adultery, art is given a direct and tangible connection to the poet's life.[31]

Menander is given a personal appearance that belies his art: 'he was cross-eyed but keen in mind' (Suda, T1), the way the eloquent Sophocles and Plato were said to have had small voices (*Soph.Vit.* 4, D.L. 3.5) and Aristotle is said to have lisped (D.L. 5.1),[32] or the facile Euripides (*Ran.* 96ff./*Vit.* 125ff.) was said to look melancholy, thoughtful and severe (Alex. *Aetol.* 7, *Vit.* 65ff.).[33] Menander's style is accounted for by personal influence. He was said to have been a pupil of Theophrastus, author of the *Characters* (D.L. 5.36/T7)[34] his uncle was Alexis the comic poet (Suda T5), either that, or he studied with Alexis (T2), the way Sophocles is said to have learned about tragedy from Aeschylus (*Vit.* 4), Apollonius to have studied with Callimachus, or Euripides with Anaxagoras and Socrates (*Vit.* 10ff.).[35] Menander's presence in Athens during the regime of Demetrius of Phalerum was taken as indication of his co-operation with tyranny: Demetrius was disgusted by Menander's effeminate dress but praised his beauty when he found out who he was (T9); after Demetrius was exiled, Menander was brought to trial because of their friendship, but Demetrius Poliorcetes' nephew begged him off (T8).

Since nothing is said in any of the biographies about the specific circumstances of Aristophanes' death, presumably his

[31] P. 89 above.
[32] Cf. also Isocrates, *XOrat* 837a; Demosthenes' training program, *XOrat* 844e; Vergil 'was extremely slow in speaking, almost like an uncultivated person', *Vit.Donat.* 16.
[33] Arrighetti 1964, 145; p. 89 n.5.
[34] Lesky 1966, 644.
[35] P. 131 below; Fairweather 1974, 257–9.

choruses (or a character like Dicaeopolis) did not mention it. If they had, a comic threat against Aristophanes' life might have become the basis for an anecdote. Eupolis is said to have been drowned off Sicily or in the Hellespont by Alcibiades, whom he attacked in his play the *Dippers* (Kaibel, *CGF*, pp.27–8, cf. 3). An epitaph about Eupolis suggests that the story of the poet's death was connected with the plot of the comedy: 'Drown me on stage and I'll drown you in the waves of the sea in bitter streams of water' (Cram., *Anec. Par.* 1.540).[36] The story of Eupolis' drowning appealed to Duris of Samos (*FGrHist* 76F73), who apparently enjoyed anecdotes critical of poets;[37] but the scholar-poet Eratosthenes discounted it (*FGrHist* 241F19), on the grounds that Eupolis produced plays after the *Dippers*. Instead Eratosthenes offered a story that showed Eupolis in a favourable light, much as he had redeemed Hesiod's reputation in his *Anterinys*.[38] As in the story of Erigone, a faithful dog is involved: Eupolis' dog Augeas caught and killed his slave Ephialtes as he was stealing Eupolis' plays. When Eupolis died, the dog died of grief, and the site (this time in Aegina) was named 'Dog's Grief'. This story appears to have been invented well after the fact: Pausanias also saw a tomb of Eupolis near the Asopus river in the territory of Sicyon (2.7.3).

In Aristophanes' case biographers appear to have deduced from the *didaskaliai* that the poet died peacefully. An inscription records that his son Araros won the victory, presumably with the *Cocalus* in 387;[39] the *Vita* reports 'in [the *Ploutos*] he introduced his son Araros and so departed from life' (58–9). Sophocles' son Iophon also carried on his father's profession, but according to tradition the two quarrelled before his death (*Vit.* 13). It is interesting that while the tragic poet Sophocles is said to have choked to death while reading the *Antigone* (according to Satyrus, *Vit.* 14),[40] the comic poet Philemon is said to have died more peacefully, after a storm prevented him from reading the third act of a play (Suda). Since apparently

---

[36] Also in Dübner p. xix.61.
[37] P. 127 below.
[38] P. 6 above.
[39] Coulon 1972, iiin.2.
[40] P. 86 above.

no facts were known about Philemon, biographers picked forms of death that seemed to fit the character of his poetry. Plutarch says that Philemon and Alexis died after they were awarded the crown of victory (*Mor.* 785b), much as Sophocles was said to have died of joy after he won with the *Antigone* (*Vit.* 14).[41] According to the Suda, Philemon also died from laughing too much, or after he dreamt that he saw nine young women leaving the room, and was told that they were not permitted to stay.[42] Menander, who wrote plays about separated lovers, and had a tomb in Piraeus, is said to have drowned while swimming off the Piraeus; the story sounds like an incident in a Hellenistic romance—Ovid associates it with Hero and Leander (*Ibis* 591–2).

[41] P. 86 above.
[42] Cf. Archilochus and the Muses, p. 28 above.

# CHAPTER ELEVEN

# Hellenistic Poets

Every assessment of Apollonius' work takes account of his alleged differences with Callimachus,[1] although no surviving text by either poet refers directly to a quarrel. The evidence derives from *interpretation* of Callimachus' statement about poetry and from ancient biographies. Callimachus is said in the Suda to have written 'a poem distinguished for its obscurity and abuse against a certain Ibis who was an enemy of Callimachus—this was Apollonius who wrote the *Argonautica*' (T1.13–15/T39–40). According to the ancient *Lives*, Apollonius was a pupil (*mathētes*) of Callimachus (*Vit.*A 8, B 5 Wendel). Callimachus also is said to have had something to do with the rejection of Apollonius' *Argonautica* and his consequent exile to Rhodes: '[Apollonius] was a pupil of Callimachus in Alexandria, who was a scholar, and he wrote his poems and recited them. Since he was very unlucky and embarrassed he went to Rhodes' (*Vit.*B 5–7). 'First he was closely associated with Callimachus, his own master . . . and turned late in life to composing poetry. And it is said that while still a young man he gave a recitation of the *Argonautica* and was condemned' (*Vit.*A 8–11), left for Rhodes, revised the poem, which was well received. According to *Vita* B, 'some say he went back to Alexandria and recited his poem once again and was held in highest regard, so that he was thought worthy of the libraries and the Mouseion and buried next to Callimachus himself' (11–14). According to a papyrus list of librarians (*POxy* 1241/T13), Apollonius was an Alexandrian who was *called* (*kaloumenos*) a Rhodian, an acquaintance (*gnōrimos*) of Calli-

---

[1] E.g. Pfeiffer 1968, I 140–4; Lesky 1966b, 729–30; Fraser 1972, I 636ff.; Giangrande 1967, 85ff.; 1974, 117ff.; Herter 1973, 196–8.

machus; he was also teacher of the third (or fifth? the ms. reads 'first') king; Eratosthenes succeeded him (*diedexato*), and then Aristophanes of Byzantium. Apollonius' Suda biography (Call. T12) makes him Erastosthenes' successor (*diadochos*) under Ptolemy III Euergetes.

There are significant inconsistencies in this evidence: (1) Apollonius is said to have written the *Argonautica* as a young man *and* turned to writing poetry late in life; (2) he was sent into permanent exile in Rhodes *and* allowed to return and to be buried next to Callimachus; (3) he was teacher of Ptolemy III Euergetes or Ptolemy V Epiphanes, depending upon whether one reads 'third' or 'fifth' where the manuscript reads 'first'. Scholars have tried to work around these inconsistencies because the notion of a literary quarrel seems to be supported by what Callimachus says elsewhere about epic poetry. Vian suggests three possible chronologies of Apollonius' birth (295, 300, 265) and proposes for the composition of the *Argonautica* a date (250–40) that would fit any of them.[2] He links the failure of the *Argonautica* with Callimachus' *Hymn to Apollo*, which he dates to 246. At the end of that hymn Callimachus compares himself to the 'poet who sings as much as the sea', whose work is like the Assyrian river with its mud and trash (106–12). The scholia to the passage state that Callimachus is criticising the people who made fun of him because he could not write a big poem, so as a result he was compelled to write the *Hecalē* (schol. *Hymn* 2.106/T37).

Callimachus also suggests that he has adversaries in the prologue to the *Aetia* (fr. 1): 'Telchines mutter at my song, ignorant men, who are no friends of the Muses, because I didn't complete one uninterrupted song . . . about kings . . . or heroes in thousands of lines but instead like a child roll out a tiny tale' (1–5). A little later he describes how Apollo advised him to keep his Muse thin, and to 'walk on untrodden paths' (23ff.). The scholia to the *Aetia* prologue (1 p.3 Pf) identify the Telchines as two Dionysii, Asclepiades, Posidippus, Praxiphanes and two fragmentary names, but Apollonius is not on the list, and there does not appear to be room for him in the

[2] Vian 1974, x.

papyrus. None the less scholars are inclined to maintain that there is at least a general connection. Vian observes that the lines are directed against the *kind* of poetry that Apollonius wrote.[3] Fraser observes that not only had Apollonius borrowed from Callimachus the notion of Aetia and numerous lines and phrases, but that he had used them in a manner 'changed almost out of recognition'.[4]

The notion of a quarrel with Apollonius gains support from testimonia about other contemporary literary disputes. Callimachus is said to have praised his contemporary Aratus in his *Pros Praxiphanēn* (Call. fr. 460/Prax. fr. 16 Wehrli = T5a Brink; cf. Call. Ep. 27); the scholia list Praxiphanes as one of the Telchines. Somewhere, perhaps even in this same work, Callimachus is said to have criticised Plato for praising the poet Antimachus (fr. 589). Callimachus in an epigram had called Antimachus' poem *Lydē* 'a fat writing [*gramma*] and not incisive' (fr. 398). Then there is the comment 'Callimachus the grammarian said a big book is like a big evil' (fr. 465), which in fact does not refer specifically to the work of Apollonius or any particular poet.

Epigrams by contemporaries of Callimachus reinforce the impression of a literary battle between Callimachus and other poets. An epigram attributed to Apollonius calls Callimachus 'refuse, triviality, wooden-head; the cause of the trouble is Callimachus who wrote the *Causes*' (13 Powell/*EG* 947–8/*AP* 11.275). Asclepiades wrote an epigram in *praise* of the epic *Lydē*: 'Who has not sung of me, who has not read *Lydē*, the joint work (*gramma*) of Antimachus and of the Muses?' (958ff. G-P). His (or Posidippus') epigram describing young men in a brothel as 'colts of the night now snorting' (*hesperinōn pōlōn arti phryasso-menōn*, 977 G-P) is said to be a parody of Callimachus' description in his *Hymn to Athena* of the sacred horses sensing the presence of the approaching goddess (*tān hippōn arti phryasso-menān*, 2).[5] Couat imagines 'a war of epigrams and pamphlets, all of which are now lost, and in which the master's poems and theories had not been spared'. He draws on the story in the

---

[3] Ibid., xviii.
[4] Fraser 1972, I 750.
[5] Ibid., I 558; Bulloch 1981, ad loc.

*Vitae* of Callimachus' early support for Apollonius to explain the intensity of the argument: 'The attacks made by Apollonius knew no bounds; even granted that Callimachus had wronged him, respect and memory of other days ought to have held him back'.[6] Fraser speaks of the 'rather fiery and authoritative temperament of Callimachus'; in addition to the intellectual rift between them, and the break in their 'previously close' relationship, he deduces from the information in the *Vitae* that Apollonius was a native Alexandrian and that Callimachus, an aristocratic Cyrenean (Ep. 21) may have been contemptuous of Apollonius' origins.[7]

All this sounds plausible, especially to Europeans with literary affiliations and sensitivities to the importance of social rank. Scholars have doubted some of the traditions and emphasised the importance of others, but no one, not even Wilamowitz, appears systematically to have investigated the sources of the data about these literary feuds. But if they are like the biographies of other poets, the anecdotes about the quarrel will prove to be based on poetry by and about Callimachus and Apollonius. Not directly, of course, but through that curious process of objectification that characterises ancient scholarship, by which the humorous is taken seriously, and conventional metaphor is interpreted as literal fact.

### Callimachus

Poets' statements about their own poetry, like the end of the *Hymn to Apollo* or the *Aetia* prologue, are particularly susceptible to misunderstanding. Anyone who has read the Pindar scholia will recognise the process: when the poet makes combative references to himself in opposition to others, the others are identified as specific individuals, Bacchylides or Simonides, no matter how generically they are described, whether as athletes, jackdaws, or as 'shrill-voiced birds' or as a 'pair of crows'.[8] But such statements are conventional; all archaic

---

[6] Couat 1931, 517, 531.
[7] Fraser 1972, I 751.
[8] Lefkowitz 1975, 79–82.

poets use them.[9] Their function is to show the essential superiority of the present author. Aristophanes repeatedly claims in *parabaseis* that he is not only a better poet, but more elegant and less crude than his contemporaries (e.g., *Ach.* 629, *Eq.* 507, *Nub.* 518, *Vesp.* 1015, *Pax* 734, cf. *Ran.* 12ff.). In Aristophanes' *Vita* such conventional claims emerge as literary history.[10] The idea of Art as a wayward and shameless female is another comic topos (*Ran.* 939–41, cf. *Nub.* 537; Pherecrates fr. 145 Kock).

At the end of the *Hymn to Apollo* Callimachus makes a declaration of his own excellence along the lines of one of Pindar's first personal statements.[11] 'Envy [*Phthonos*] said secretly in Apollo's ear: "I don't admire the bard whose song is not even as great as the sea." Apollo pushed Envy aside with his foot and said as follows: "The Assyrian river's flow is great, but it carries along much refuse from the land and much filth in its waters. The bees do not bring to Demeter water from every spring, but the water that a clear and undefiled tiny spray sends up from a holy fountain, the very best water"' (105–13). Pindar speaks of envious people, but since he likes to talk about his own achievement in terms of his victor's success, he does not specify whether they are other poets or even what they are envious of (e.g., *Nem.* 4.36ff., *Pyth.* 2.88ff., *Pyth.* 1.81ff.). In *Hymn* 2 Callimachus brings in Envy and Blame, but talks exclusively about poetry: Envy says to the subject of his hymn, Apollo, 'I don't admire the bard whose song is not even as great as the sea' (106). Frederick Williams in his new commentary suggests that the sea signifies Homer; in other words, Envy disapproves of the poet who can't write a *Homeric Hymn*. Apollo responds with a gesture of contempt. He ignores Envy's contention, assuming that no one can match Homer,[12] and answers with a *topos* that for Dionysius of Halicarnassus and Quintilian had come to signify the relationship between Homer and other poets: Homer is the source of all rivers and

---

[9] Lefkowitz 1978, 460–2.
[10] Pp. 105–6 above.
[11] See esp. Williams 1978, 90ff. Cf. Theoc., *Id.* 7.45ff.
[12] Cf. also Pfeiffer 1968, 1 137; Clausen 1964, 184.

springs.[13] When Apollo states that a river like the Euphrates is big but full of mud and refuse, while the small stream retains the purity of its origins, he suggests that ambitious, indiscriminate poems compare less favourably with Homer than a poem on a small scale that retains an essence of the original. Since Pindar refers to his poetry as 'the holy water of Dirce' (*Isthm.* 6.74), it is natural to assume that by the 'pure and undefiled' spring Callimachus means his own *Hymn to Apollo*— I am assuming that like Thucydides (iii.104.4–5) he regarded the *Homeric Hymn* as a unity, by the author of the *Iliad*.[14] In making his comparison between the river and the spring, Callimachus doesn't specify what makes his hymn 'pure' or whom (if anyone) he means by the Assyrian river. He might have had in mind an epic like the *Cypria*, which is big (11 books),[15] and in comparison with Homer, unheroic and diffuse;[16] he might have been thinking of Creophylus,[17] but he does not say. The point is rather that his small hymn, for whatever reason, is closer to the source. Williams suggests that the affinity derives from Callimachus' profound knowledge of Homer, which allows him to apply an unusual word or phrase to a new and unexpected, yet appropriate context.[18] But the scholia to the end of Callimachus' hymn offer a more mechanical interpretation, equating the sea with the 'big stream' of the Euphrates river: 'on account of this [not singing a song as great as the sea], he criticises those who made fun of him for not being able to write a big (*mega*) poem, for which reason he was compelled to write the *Hecalē*' (schol. *Hymn* 2.106/T37). Ancient commentators characteristically sought out particular incidents to 'explain' what poets deliberately left general and metaphorical. When Pindar, in calling attention to the need for due measure in praise, speaks of triumphing over envious 'enemies', the scholia specify: 'this seems to pertain to Simo-

[13] Williams 1978, 87–9; p. 24 above.
[14] P. 15 above.
[15] Cf. also Theodorus' epic *Against the Giants* (24 books), Rhianus' *Heracles* (14 books), or long historical epics like Musaeus' *Perseis* (9), or Philon the Elder's *About Jerusalem* (14). See Ziegler 1966, 15–23.
[16] On the *Cypria*, Griffin 1977, 44ff.; Lloyd-Jones 1973, 121–2.
[17] Clausen 1964, 184.
[18] Williams 1978, 4–5.

nides, since he liked to use digressions' (schol. *Nem.* 4.60b).
When Pindar claims in *Nem.* 7 that he did not 'savage Neo-
ptolemus in ruthless words' by telling the myth about his sacking
Apollo's temple, Aristarchus' pupil Aristodemus specified that
Pindar was apologising to the Aeginetans for what he said about
Neoptolemus in his *Paeans* (schol. *Nem.* 7.150a).[19]

Callimachus tells us more about his poetry in the *Aetia*
prologue, but still in metaphorical terms. He begins negatively,
as Pindar often does, by talking about his 'enemies' the
Telchines. He does not refer directly to any of their established
attributes: they were first inhabitants of Rhodes, wizards,
jealous of teaching their skills to others (Diod. Sic. v.55.1–3),
put to death on Ceos by the gods for their *hybris* (Callim. fr.
75.64–5).[20] Instead he characterises them as 'ignorant, no
friends of the Muses'. Heraclitus, in what has been taken to be
the prologue of his work, speaks of other men as 'unable to
understand' (*axynetoi*, 22B1); Pindar speaks of other poets,
'like a pair of crows talking words not to be fulfilled against
Zeus' sacred bird' (*Ol.* 2.87–8). The Telchines complain that
Callimachus' song (i.e. the present poem, the *Aetia*) is not an
epic (i.e. a continuous story thousands of lines long about kings
and heroes); that he tells 'a tiny tale, like a child' even though
he is an old man. His reply answers all these charges with
ironic exaggeration: someone else can sing epic themes; 'little
nightingales' sing more sweetly (16). The Telchines, the race of
the 'evil eye' (*baskaniē* instead of *phthonos*) should go away;
poetry should be judged by art, not by length; he doesn't
make a big noise, because it is Zeus' job to thunder (17–20).

Callimachus concludes his own defence by saying that he has
been following advice Apollo gave him when he began to write
poetry: 'Fatten sacrificial victims but keep the Muse slender'
(23–4); Euripides speaks of putting tragedy on a diet after she had
been stuffed with Aeschylus' heavy words (*Ran.* 939–41).[21]
Apollo commands Callimachus: 'Don't walk on wagon roads, or
drive your chariot in other's ruts along the wide road, but stay on

[19] Lefkowitz 1980, 39–45; pp. 57–9 above.
[20] Cf. Herter 1975, 45–7.
[21] Clayman 1977, 28.

the narrow path' (25–8); Pindar advises his chorus to 'sing songs of praise, not by going down the worn wagon-road of Homer, but with different horses' (fr. 52b.10–12; cf. *Pyth.* 4.247). Callimachus says (29ff.) that he sings among those who like the shrill voice of cicadas, not the braying of asses; then he wishes that he, through his song, can become a cicada himself, able to shed old age. This claim appears to be another literary allusion, to a biographical tradition of the fifth century, about Hesiod's vigorous old age; according to the epigram attributed to Pindar, Hesiod 'was a young man twice' (*EG* 428, p. 3 above).[22]

By alluding to Aristophanes, Pindar and Hesiod, Callimachus establishes that he is talking as a poet about his claims for his art. The allusions also convey with great economy what he means the *Aetia* to be: as elegant and light as Aristophanes' idea of Euripides' verse, as original as Pindar's, and as immortal (or significant) as Hesiod's. The description of the muttering Telchines makes a dramatic introduction to the prologue; dialogue provides more excitement than a simple narrative about his work. It is important to remember that the Telchines and his reply to them, like Apollo's speech, represent a fictitious situation: the *Aetia* prologue was not intended as a report of an actual historical event any more than the first person statements in Pindar's victory odes. To refer to the *Aetia* prologue as 'Reply to the Telchines' is rather like calling the end of *Pythian* 2 'Reply to the Foxes'.[23]

Where did the scholia to the Aetia prologue get the names for the Telchines: the two Dionysii, Asclepiades, Posidippus, the orator . . . yrippus, and Praxiphanes of Mytilene? We don't know anything about the Dionysii or the orator, but I would suggest that Asclepiades and Posidippus appear on the list because they wrote epigrams praising the *Lydē*. Callimachus in an epigram called the *Lydē* 'fat' (*pachu*, fr. 398); in the *Aetia* prologue he says sacrificial victims should be 'as fat as possible' (*pachiston*), but the Muse should stay thin. The verbal correspondence suggests a link between the general metaphor of the

---

[22] Scodel 1981, 301–20. Callimachus may also have had in mind the notion of the poet as cricket, said to have been used by Archilochus (fr. 167 T = 223 W).

[23] Vian 1974, xv.

*Aetia* prologue and the specific target of Callimachus' epigram; his epigram could be seen to be answering (or answered by) Asclepiades' and Posidippus',[24] the way Chamaeleon represents Sappho as answering Anacreon's poem about the girl from Lesbos (fr. 26 Wehrli). Biographers were eager to establish connections between famous poets.[25] Hermesianax records the chronologically impossible story about Sappho and Anacreon, along with the more plausible story about a love affair between Sappho and Alcaeus (fr. 7.47ff.).

In the literary tradition Callimachus is represented as 'disparaging Antimachus' *Lydē* in his epigram' (fr. 398); but biographers were capable of attributing to an author the words of a participant in a dialogue. Philemon, not a character in his play, is said in the Euripides *Vita* to have wished to hang himself to see Euripides.[26] Other evidence suggests that Callimachus made positive use of Antimachus' poetry: Philodemus says that Callimachus 'took over' (*metalabōn*) Antimachus' version of the story of Apollo's birth, perhaps (since it is the story of a heroine) from the *Lydē* itself.[27] Scholars have assumed that Callimachus resented Asclepiades' (or Posidippus') adaptation into an obscene poem of a phrase from his *Hymn to Athena*; but this is to assume that Callimachus would have regarded the adaptation as parody.[28] Since he did not share our Victorian notions about brothels, he might have regarded it as an amusing compliment, if indeed he did not, with his elegant irony, adapt the line from Asclepiades himself.[29]

It is easier to explain the presence on the scholia list of Praxiphanes of Mytilene. Callimachus was said to have written a work *against* him: 'Callimachus mentioned Aratus not only in his epigrams but in his Against Praxiphanes, praising [Aratus] as a learned man and an excellent poet' (fr. 460/Prax. fr. 16 Wehrli). No other fragment of this work survives, but Pfeiffer suggests that it was a prose monograph

---

[24] Matthews 1979, 47.
[25] Fairweather 1974, 256ff., pp. 64–5 above.
[26] P. 98 above.
[27] Henrichs 1972, 72–7, Text i.971–7.
[28] P. 119.
[29] On questions of dating, Bulloch 1977, 122–3.

like Apollonius' 'Against Zenodotus'.[30] That work appears to have concerned readings in Homer,[31] so by analogy 'Against Praxiphanes' might have involved assessment of other poets like Aratus. Callimachus in his poetry appears to have defended passages obelised by other scholars;[32] even Aristarchus defended Homer against Praxiphanes, who was 'surprised' that Odysseus in *Od.* 11 asked his mother about Telemachus and Penelope 'only at the end of his speech' (fr. 20).

The existence of a work 'Against Praxiphanes' explains Praxiphanes' presence on the scholia list, but there is not any secure evidence that Praxiphanes himself complained about Callimachus. Brink argues that like other members of the 'School of Aristotle' Praxiphanes approved of the long epics Callimachus disdains at the end of the Hymn to Apollo and in the *Aetia* prologue.[33] But the statement in the scholia that the Telchines 'criticised [Callimachus] for the meagreness of his verse and because he did not admire length' (fr. 1.9ff.) is simply a prose gloss of Callimachus' metaphors, the way Pindar's elaborate comments about due measure in *Nem.* 4 are represented in the scholia as 'the law of the encomion prevents me from making long digressions', with his 'enemies' specified as one individual, Simonides, 'since he liked to make digressions' (schol. *Nem.* 4.60b).

It has also been suggested that Callimachus opposed Praxiphanes because they disagreed in their assessment of Plato. Praxiphanes' attitude could be inferred to be favourable because Praxiphanes wrote a dialogue *On Poems* or *On Poets* that featured Plato and Isocrates as characters.[34] Callimachus, on the other hand, is said to have considered Plato a poor judge of poetry (fr. 589). But here again we may be in danger of demanding too much from the kind of evidence provided by summaries and excerpts. Just because Praxiphanes wrote a dialogue about Plato there is no reason to think that his views were any more consistently complimentary than (say) Satyrus'

---

[30] Pfeiffer 1968, 136; Wilamowitz 1924, I 212.
[31] Pfeiffer 1968, I 141, 147–8.
[32] Williams 1978, 88.
[33] Brink 1946, 16ff.; cf. Podlecki 1969, 124–5.
[34] Pfeiffer 1968, 136; Wehrli 1967 on Praxiphanes fr. 15–7.

views of Euripides.[35] Also there is the question of the nature of Praxiphanes' sources for his dialogue 'at a country house with Plato entertaining Isocrates' (fr. 11 Wehrli). In addition to what Plato and Isocrates said about each other in their writings,[36] Praxiphanes had access to characterisations of Plato in comedy: there are twelve references to Plato in fragments of fourth-century plays.[37] Praxiphanes is said to have complained that Plato in the *Timaeus* (27c) first stated the obvious and then put an ordinal after a series of cardinal numbers (1, 2, 3, 4th); Proclus tells the story seriously, but it sounds like the kind of philosophical nitpicking practised by Socrates in Aristophanes' *Clouds* (662–7).[38] So in the end Praxiphanes may have agreed with Callimachus about Plato; Proclus says Duris of Samos shared Callimachus' opinion (*FGrHist* 76F83), and Duris drew his information from peripatetics like Praxiphanes.[39]

At least the conjunction in Proclus' commentary of the names Antimachus, Plato, Callimachus and Duris can show us how originally separate events can be combined and distinct motives conflated.[40] I am inclined to believe that the names Asclepiades, Posidippus and Praxiphanes got into the *Aetia* scholia by a similar process of condensation and association, and that Callimachus' original epigram about Antimachus' *Lydē* need not have been meant more seriously than his witty epigram about Creophylus; there is no reason to think it was written in *response* to Asclepiades' or Posidippus' epigrams on the *Lydē* any more than Xenophon's *Cyropaedia* was written in response to the first two books of Plato's *Republic*, as Aulus Gellius relates (xiv.iii.3).[41]

By the second century the philosophical discussions of the fourth century were characterised as malicious disputes. Plato and Xenophon's different accounts of the education of Cyrus were adduced as evidence of rivalry between them (Herodicus

[35] Pp. 99–101 above.
[36] Riginos 1976, 118.
[37] Düring 1941, 138–9.
[38] Ibid., 125.
[39] Ibid., 146; Jacoby *FGrHist* ad loc.
[40] See pp. 172–3.
[41] Riginos 1976, 60.

*ap.* Ath. xi.504e), even though the passage Herodicus cites from the *Laws* (iii.694c) concerns the education of Cyrus' children.[42] The techniques by which philosophy could be transformed into biography had been well established in Old Comedy: portray doctrines as individuals; describe the creative process as a specific (and hostile) reaction to particular events. In much the same way, I suggest, literary commentary of the third century, originally humorous and allusive, came to be portrayed in the second century as open warfare: Callimachus and Aristarchus are portrayed as pedants (Philip, *Garl.Phil.* 3033ff.; Antiphanes, ibid. 771ff.); by putting them down. a biographer like Herodicus can build up the value of his own scholarly efforts (*EG* 3310ff.).[43] The 'obscurity' and 'abuse' of Callimachus' *Ibis* (T1.13–15) would have made it an appealing source material for biographers, but I do not think that it was originally directed against Apollonius any more than the *Aetia* prologue was directed against Asclepiades, Posidippus, and Praxiphanes; we still don't know who Ovid's *Ibis* is.[44]

### Apollonius

The remaining evidence for the quarrel derives from the two slightly different versions of Apollonius' *Life* that serve as prefaces to the manuscripts of the *Argonautica*. Both *Vitae* are so condensed that they give no indication of their sources, but their narratives follow patterns characteristic of biographical fiction. (1) *Discipleship.* Apollonius is said to have been a pupil of Callimachus (*Vit.A* 3, B5). Fraser sees this discipleship as the key to the bitterness in their relationship, but as Fairweather's data suggest, stories that *x* was *y*'s pupil tend to be narrative metaphors for influence.[45] For example, according to their

---

[42] Düring 1941, 55–6.
[43] Ibid., 7–9. To Philip's epigram cf. Callim. fr. 380; Degani 1973, 83–4. Philetas' elegance (*leptotēs*) was satirised in comedy (Ael., *VH* x.61 = T15a Kuchenmüller). His characterisation later becomes a biographical 'fact': 'they say Philetas had a very light (*leptotaton*) body . . . they say that he had lead weights in his shoes' (Ael., *VH* ix.14 = T15b Kuchenmüller).
[44] Housman 1972, III 1040–2.
[45] Fairweather 1974, 262–3.

*Vitae*, Euripides attended lectures by Anaxagoras, Prodicus and Protagoras; Sophocles studied with Aeschylus. On the basis of Callimachus' epigram about Aratus ('the song and the style are Hesiod's', Ep. 27), Aratus is said to have been an 'emulator' (*zēlōtēs*) of Hesiod (*Vit.* 1 p.p. 10 Martin). (2) *Unpopularity*. According to their *Vitae*, Aeschylus left Athens because he was defeated in a poetic contest by Simonides; Euripides left Athens because audiences preferred Sophocles and because the comic poets 'tore him to pieces in their envy' (*Vit.* 1.120ff. Méridier).[46] Apollonius couldn't endure the 'public disgrace or slander by other poets'; Callimachus is not explicitly connected with his failure in either *Vita*. (3) *Voluntary exile*. Apollonius left Alexandria because of adverse criticism and moved to Rhodes; according to their biographies Homer, Hesiod, Stesichorus, Aeschylus and Euripides were all better received abroad than at home. (4) *Final recognition*. Apollonius is made a Rhodian citizen, his work 'was thought worthy of the Library' and is buried next to Callimachus (*Vit.* B 13ff.). According to the Euripides *Vita*, when Sophocles heard that Euripides had died, he and his actors put on mourning garb and the audience wept (1.46ff.).

Where did this material come from? If Apollonius is like other poets, from poems by him or about him. First of all, there is the uncertainty about his father's name and the appropriateness of his mother's. Two names are proposed for his father; three are given for Pindar's. Two of these occur in Theban *partheneia* (fr. 94b10, *Vit.* 1 p.3 Dr); one is also given as his son's name; a third is also given as his *aulos*-teacher's.[47] The scholia to *Idyll* 7 say that Theocritus' father was Simichus; his *Vita* offers Praxagoras or Simichidas, citing *Idyll* 7.28.[48] The name of Hesiod's father, Dios, derives from Perses' epithet *dion genos* (*Op.* 229).[49] Hesiod's mother has the suitable name Pycimede (Ephorus *FGrHist* 70F1); Pindar's mother is

---

[46] Fairweather 1974, 193.

[47] Lehnus 1977, 78–82. Aratus is said to have mentioned his brothers' names in his letters (*Vit.* i. p.6.5 Martin); but the letters' authenticity was questioned even in antiquity (*Vit.* i. p.10.13ff.).

[48] Gow 1950, II 128.

[49] P. 6 above.

Cleodice, his wife's Megacleia; Apollonius Rhodius' mother is
Rhode. His father's name, Silleus, is a *hapax* (so is Illeus).[50]
If it derives from Silloi ('Lampoons'), it is a patronymic like
*Dionysos huios Stamniou* in Aristophanes' *Frogs* (22) or Archilo-
chus son of Enipo (Critias 88B 44), and its provenance a phrase
like *grammatikoi Mōmou Stygiou tekna* (Philip, *Garl.Phil.* 3033).[51]
I will suggest that the story of Apollonius' voluntary exile in
Rhodes also was occasioned by his origin and his poetry. (1)
The notion that he recited his poems as a young man, but then
recited (or 'published', *epideixasthai*) them later, after revision,
accounts for the existence of the *proekdosis* of the *Argonautica*,
although only six lines of Book I are said to have been affected.
Actually the lines may only have been variants,[52] but the story
of two 'editions' of his work provides a convenient explanation
for the discrepancies. (2) The idea of voluntary exile in Rhodes
explains his epithet 'Rhodian'. Two other aetiologies are
preserved in the *Vitae*: his mother's name Rhode, and the
phrase *erythriasas* ('blushing', B 7). In historical terms, it is a likely
place to have gone to, for practical reasons. Praxiphanes of
Mytilene is also called 'Rhodian', presumably because he
worked there (fr. 2 Wehrli).[53] The 'explanation' that 'he was
highly thought of there, and for this reason put himself down as
Rhodian in his poetry' (*Vit.* A 14f.), is in fact the reason for the
story; one can compare how the discrepancy between
Aristophanes' Athenian citizenship and foreign birthplaces is
accounted for in his Suda biography: 'Aristophanes, a Rhodian
or a Lindian; some say he was Egyptian, others from Camirus; he
was an Athenian by decree (*thesei*), for he was enrolled as a citizen
(*epolitographēthē*) (*Vit.* xxx.1ff. Koster).
     The most natural explanation of why Apollonius called
himself a Rhodian is not proposed by his biographers: that he
came from Rhodes to begin with, as an émigré to Alexandria,

     [50] But cf. Sellius the grammarian, Suda s.v. and *POxy* 1235.
     [51] P. 26 n.6 above. According to schol. Ar. *Av.* 281, the tragic poet Philocles
was called 'son of Halmion' (salty) as an epithet, because of his pungency.
     [52] Haslam 1978b, 67.
     [53] Cf. the Carthaginian general Hannibal the 'Rhodian', Polyb. i.46.4
Walbank. The poet Philetas of Cos was also said to be 'Rhodian' (schol.
Theoc., *Id.* 7.40).

like Callimachus of Cyrene. The sensational stories are preferred by biographers because they bring some discredit to the
poet:[54] Juvenal's references to Egypt in Satire xv are explained
not as examples of his erudition but by the story that he was
sent off to Egypt on military service as an old man because of
implied insults to the court in his comments about the actor
Paris in Satire vii.90–2.[55] For Apollonius at least there was the
historical precedent of Aeschines; a papyrus biography of the
second century A.D. makes even his reasons personal rather
than political (so *XOrat.* 840d): he didn't get the minimum
fifth of the votes in a lawsuit he brought against Demosthenes
(*POxy* 1800.40–74).

The story of Apollonius' unpopularity and voluntary exile
of course supports the notion that he belongs (at least as an
honorary member) among the Telchines; but the *Vitae* and the
papyrus list of librarians preserve another popular notion of
the relation between Callimachus and Apollonius: Apollonius
was the *mathētēs* of Callimachus, or according to the papyrus
list of librarians (Callim. T13), *gnōrimos*, which comes to much
the same thing—Chares a *gnōrimos* of Apollonius, wrote a book
*About Apollonius' Histories* (schol. A.R., 2.1053–7a). Being
called a *mathētēs* does not constitute evidence that Apollonius
literally studied under Callimachus or had a close personal
relationship with him; that Euripides attended lectures by
Anaxagoras, Prodicus, and Protagoras (*Eur.Vit.* 10) means
only that his contemporaries, like Aristophanes, pointed out
similarities in their works.[56] If Apollonius is called a *mathētēs* of
Callimachus, his contemporaries thought his work was influenced by Callimachus. Simichidas, the narrator of Theocritus'
*Idyll* 7, compares himself to Sicelidas (Asclepiades) and
Philetas (40); Theocritus' *Vita* reports that 'he listened to
(*akoustēs gegone*) Philetas and Asclepiades, whom he mentions'.

---

[54] P. 128 above; Düring 1941, 132.
[55] Syme 1979, 1–15; Fairweather 1974, 241–2.
[56] Dover 1976, 51. The terms *mimēsis (imitatio)* or *zēlōsis (aemulatio)* are
applied to distant prececessors; see Russell 1979, 2, 10. E.g., on the basis of
Callimachus' *Epigr.* 27 and a few verbal parallels Aratus is said to have been
a *zēlōtēs* of Hesiod; §19 (1); see also Degani 1973, 86–7. Sophocles is called a
*zēlōtēs* of Homer, schol. *Il.* 16.722.

What these contemporaries meant by 'influence' can be
understood by analogy: in Euripides' case 'studying with'
means taking over ideas from, e.g., Anaxagoras. The third-
century poet Alexander Aetolus calls Euripides 'good old
Anaxagoras' boarding student' (fr. 7 Powell).[57] Saying that
'Socrates and Mnesilochus appear to have collaborated with
him' means that someone, in this case the comic poet Teleclides,
had noted similarities of content: 'that fellow Mnesilochus is
cooking up a new play for Euripides, and Socrates is supplying
him with firewood' (fr. 39, 40/*Eur.Vit.* 12ff.).[58] The scholia to
Apollonius 1 1309 note 'the line is Callimachus'' (*Aet.* 1.12.6);
but they don't say anything about the other verbal similarities
noted by recent scholars, e.g., in Jason's prayer (*Aet.* fr. 18.5–
7/A.R. 1 411 and IV 1701), in the choice of rare words for
blindness (Call. *Hymn.* 5.103/A.R. II 444) or to describe height
(*Hymn* 6.37, A.R. II 360, IV 945) or in references to obscure
geography (*Aet.* 1.19/A.R. IV 1706ff.).[59] So apparently Apollonius' contemporaries were not as sensitive about questions of
imitation as we have become, or they might have suggested that
Callimachus *collaborated* with Apollonius.[60] If by 'discipleship'
they meant 'ideas', Callimachus also told the story of the
Argonauts' return in Book I of the *Aetia* (fr. 7–18); Apollonius
twice refers to Callimachus' account of Jason's prayer. Callimachus wrote a work 'Rivers of the World' (fr. 457–9) which
the scholia to Apollonius cite as 'Rivers of Asia' (1 1165/Call.
fr. 459); Apollonius has Phineus describe in detail the rivers
of Pontus (II 360).[61] Both Callimachus and Apollonius wrote
about foundation legends and aetiologies, like the story about
the Argo's anchor stone at Cyzicus (Call. fr. 108–9/A.R. 1
955ff.). But just because the scholia to Apollonius say that

[57] P. 89 above.
[58] Cf. stories that Plato got 'help' from Epicharmus, with forged letters
(cf. p. 129 n.47) to 'prove' it (D.L. 3.9, 18) or transcribed Protagoras'
*Controversies* into *Resp.* (D.L. 3.37); Riginos 1976, 165–6. For other examples, see
esp. Stemplinger 1912, 12–29.
[59] Bulloch 1977, 116ff.; Eichgrün 1961, 111ff.; Fraser 1970, nn.162, 169.
[60] Cf. how Plato is said first to have brought Sophron's mimes to Athens
and then to have modelled his characters on them: he slept with a copy of
Sophron under his pillow (D.L. 3.18); Riginos 1976, §128.
[61] Williams 1978, 91.

'Callimachus also mentions [the anchor stone]' means only that they know he wrote a poem about it; they also cite Alcaeus (fr. 440). Fraser may well be right in thinking that 'Apollonius had Callimachus in mind when he wrote the *Argonautica*'; but the many correspondences of topic and vocabulary he cites are not 'enough to deprive him of the title of an independent poet'.[62] By the same standards Callimachus could be considered unoriginal because of his frequent allusions to Homer and the *Homeric Hymns*, or because he drew on Antimachus' *Lydē* for his version of the story of Apollo's birth.[63]

Whoever may or may not be found behind the masks of the characters in Theocritus' *Idyll* 7, Simichidas describes a world where poets try to measure up to the standards set by their predecessors (Sicelidas-Asclepiades and Philetas, 40). They applaud what other poets sing, and exchange tokens of *xenia* when they part (129); competition is friendly; friends who start together remain together and drink with one another at the end of the day. Callimachus at the end of *Hymn* 2 and at the beginning of the *Aetia* describes himself as isolated and combative, like an archaic poet; but in epigram 56 he praises Aratus. Poems that *compliment* other poets, whether contemporaries or predecessors, like Asclepiades (958ff. G-P) and Posidippus (3086ff. G-P), are no less representative of the literary climate of the day.

## Conclusion

If being a *mathētēs* of Callimachus can be interpreted as a compliment, and if Callimachus is talking about someone else when he complains about cyclic poems, how should we begin to talk about Apollonius? I would suggest that we should begin by judging him by the same standards as Callimachus, by expecting learned allusions and significant variations in Homeric phrases. For example, the opening lines of the *Argonautica*: 'I begin with you, Phoebus, and recall the famous deeds of men born long ago, who drove the well-benched Argo

[62] Fraser 1972, i 628, 640; cf. Wilamowitz 1924, ii 167ff.
[63] See p. 125.

at Pelias' command down through the mouth of the Black Sea and through the Cyanean rocks after the Golden Fleece' (1–4). The first words, 'I begin with you Phoebus', suggest the format of a *Homeric Hymn* (e.g. 2.1); but putting 'I begin' first gives prominence to the poet, and then the subject of the poem turns out to be not the god, but the famous deeds of 'men born long ago'. 'Born long ago' (*palaigenēs*) in Homer is the epithet of old men, but Apollonius substitutes 'men' (*phōtōn*). These changes establish that, like the poet of a hymn, he needs no intermediary to address his subject matter but controls it himself; his language derives from Homer, not in formulae, but word by word. Interestingly, too, the subject is not one man, but the famous deeds of many. He starts right in with a description of their mission; Fraser comments that the *Argonautica* 'plunges immediately *in medias res*; almost no explanation is given of the task placed on Jason by Pelias . . .' 'Telchines murmur against me'[64] is an even more abrupt beginning, and the *Aeneid* is not much better. Vergil mirrors Apollonius' syntax, with a plural subject for his song followed by a relative clause, and reference to a violent journey under compulsion.

The *Eclogues* and *Georgics* show that Vergil studied Callimachus;[65] but there is much in the *Aeneid* that indicates that he knew Apollonius well, besides the reminiscences in his characterisation of Dido of Apollonius' Hypsipyle or Medea. When in Callimachus' *Aetia* Jason prays to Apollo on his voyage home he is 'grieving at heart' (fr. 18.5); Apollonius in Book IV makes the situation even more painful: the heroes do not know where they are, 'the tears flowed down his face in his distress' (1072). The first time Jason prays to Apollo in the *Argonautica*, again with Callimachus' geographical references in mind (1 419/ Callim. fr. 18.7), he confidently offers a sacrifice. Aeneas in Book I is a combination of Odysseus and Jason. His words paraphrase Odysseus' speech to his men as they approach Scylla and Charybdis (*Od.* 12.200), but the setting also draws on the description of *both* of Jason's prayers in the *Argonautica*, the sacrifice in the first book that predicts the success of the

[64] Fraser 1972, I 640.
[65] Clausen 1964, 192–6.

voyage, and the despair of Jason when they do not know where they are or where they are going, like Odysseus' men when they first arrive on Circe's island (10.189ff.). Vergil explains the cause of Aeneas' *dolor* at the beginning of Book II; he speaks again of Scylla's cliffs and rocks in Book III, where his men are described as *ignari viae* before they come to the Cyclops (557ff.). Jason's men in Book IV 'did not know at all, and they entrusted their return to the sea' (1700–1).

Vergil could have learned from either Callimachus or Apollonius how to evoke a Homeric context,[66] and to call attention to the inner feelings of his characters; but it was in Apollonius' narrative that he could observe how to indicate by reminiscence the relation between events. For example, he could see how Apollonius' repeated references to crimson in the description of Jason's cloak (*ereuthos, ereuthēessa*, 1 726–7) foreshadows the 'crimson' (*ereuthomenos*) light of the shining star to which Jason is compared, which enchants but disappoints the eyes of brides (1 778); Hypsipyle's cheeks blush crimson (*erythēne*, 791); Hylas 'crimson' (*ereuthomenos*) in his beauty and grace catches the attention of the Nymph who drowns him (1230). Not that Apollonius' diction can match Callimachus' memorable precision of word choice and placement, or that Vergil did not add new emotional depth; but I think one can see that Vergil at least thought that Callimachus and Apollonius were fighting on the same side in the Battle of the Books.

---

[66] Wilamowitz 1924, II 164.

# Conclusion

He had brought a large map representing the sea,
    Without the least vestige of land:
And the crew were much pleased when they found it to be
    A map they could all understand.

Lewis Carroll, *The Hunting of the Snark*, Fit ii.

The poverty of the information preserved about the Hellenistic poets points up how little the Lives tell us about what we most want to know: why poets wrote and how they worked. The notions of discipleship and emulation only bear witness to the most obvious correspondences: nothing is said about intellectual influence, training, or what they read. Humour is represented as serious criticism; it is as if a modern account of Bloomsbury were to be written on the basis of caricatures in weekly magazines, with no reference to the documents and letters that record what was actually done and said. The vast resources available to biographers of poets living in the last two centuries have raised our expectations. In particular we miss the presence of a shaping intelligence in most ancient biographies of poets. In a few of the *Lives*, an occasional voice is heard in protest: 'Homer did not die in Ios, as some people think'; 'One ought not to believe Ister when he says Sophocles was an Athenian and not a Phliasian.' There are occasional expressions of approval: 'Pindar was not only a fine poet, but he was a man beloved by the gods' (*Vit.* 4); 'If one wanted to compare [Aeschylus'] work to his predecessors, one would be amazed at the poet's intelligence and inventiveness' (*Vit.* ii.15ff.). But nowhere is there the involvement or judgment on the biographers' part that gives serious biography its value.

Instead the *Lives* seem to have been created by an unconscious process, always unperceived but none the less informing. Anecdotes based on comic verse or misquotation show the poet to be exceptional; signs of favour are balanced by incidents of failure and hatred; eventually a physical representation, a tomb or some memento like Pindar's chair or Euripides' writing stylus, provide mute testimony to the power of verses now only infrequently heard or read. Archilochus was worshipped on Paros as a hero, but increasingly for the power behind his words rather than the words themselves. First Demeas in the second century provided a prose gloss to some of his war poetry; then Mnesiepes in the first century offers a narrative emphasising early signs of the young Archilochus' greatness, without any direct reference to the poet's own words. Homer, inexorably, becomes removed from his greatest works, the *Iliad* and the *Odyssey*; the Herodotean *Life* concentrates on his physical suffering, his epigrams and his minor poems.

It may seem the cruellest irony that incomparable intellectual achievement comes to be represented in such childish and trivial ways; but at least it is a form of tribute, a sign that even when archaic language is no longer understood, dramas are not enacted, and little is ever read, that everyone in a community remains aware that a great poet had been there. In the village of Pityos today, on the island of Chios, men and children remember that Homer had stayed there on his way from the port city to Volissos on the west coast. Few if any will have read Homer in the ancient Greek, but most will have heard some verses in translation. For them a marble slab commemorates his visit; like the tombstone dearly paid for over time for a dead parent, it provides a tangible and immediate tribute of what so few people have the power to express in words. Homer himself (at least as we prefer to think of him) might have preferred a recitation of his own poetry.

For ordinary men the *Lives* in their way preserved a distant sense of the critical judgments passed on by the experts. Homer's travels explained that certain works and verses were indeed authentic; stories of discipleship acknowledged signs of influence or development. Anecdotes preserve an impression of how well a poet was known and appreciated, like the story of the Athenian soldiers reciting Euripides in Sicily (Plu., *Nic.*

29). The anecdotes about Aristophanes' battles with Cleon offer tribute to the intellectual freedom of the fifth century as well as to Aristophanes' own courage. The epigrammists' distorted reminiscences of literary disputes in Alexandria at least suggest how important scholarship was to the poets of Callimachus' day.

We might have retained a clearer sense of the original value of the *Lives* and anecdotes had more biographers been like Plutarch than Herodicus. But a derisive tendency predominates; much of the biographers' material is drawn from comedy. Inevitably and consistently the biographies in their final form offer simple and demeaning portraits of the poets; they make many of their achievements appear miraculous and represent others as mere reflexes, so that even a Homer or a Pindar need not be too greatly envied. Callimachus complains in the *Aetia* prologue of the Telchines who mutter at his song, the 'race of the evil eye'. Since he is talking about poetry, ancient scholars inferred that the Telchines were other poets. But Callimachus, like Pindar, was aware that envy is not the sole provenance of one's colleagues or rivals; audiences and patrons seek to be pleased and flattered; the gods themselves were thought to resent consistent success. If the poets had been able to predict their future, they would have realised that their biographers would have posed an even greater threat to their achievement. Who else managed for so long to misconstrue the poets' explicit intentions, and to convince audiences to begin with *them* rather than with the poets' own works?

# Appendixes

## I. THE LIFE OF HOMER[1]

[1] Herodotus of Halicarnassus wrote the following history of Homer's background, upbringing and life, and sought to make his account complete and absolutely reliable:

After Cyme (the old Aeolian one) was founded, there came together various Hellenic families in that city, including some from Magnesia. Among them was Melanopus the son of Ithagenes, himself the son of Crethon. Melanopus was not a rich man; in fact, he had only limited means. This Melanopus married in Cyme the daughter of Omyres. She bore him a female child, to whom he gave the name Cretheis. Both Melanopus and his wife then died, but Melanopus had made his daughter the ward of a close friend, Cleanax of Argos.

[2] But after some time had gone by it turned out that the girl had had sexual relations with a man and had secretly become pregnant. At first she kept it a secret, but when Cleanax realised it, he was distressed by what had happened, and he called Cretheis aside and took her to task, because he was concerned about the disgrace especially among his fellow citizens. So he made the following provision for her: the Cymeans happened at that time to be building a town in a corner of the valley of the Hermus river. Theseus gave the settlers the town's name, Smyrna, because he wanted to have a memorial to his wife's name, which was Smyrne. Theseus was one of the founders of Cyme, among the foremost Thessalians, descended from Eumelus the son of Admetus. He was a very wealthy man. It was there that Cleanax sent Cretheis, to

[1] Ed. Wilamowitz 1929.

Ismenias of Boeotia. He had been assigned to the colonists by lot, and happened to be a particularly good friend of his.

[3] After some time had gone by Cretheis went with the other women to a festival on the banks of the river called Meles, and since her time was already near, she bore Homer; he was not blind, but could see. She gave her son the name Melesigenes, calling him after the river. For a while Cretheis stayed in Ismenias' house. But after some time she left and undertook to support herself and her son by working with her hands. She took on odd jobs with various people, and educated her son as best she could.

[4] There was in Smyrna at that time a man by the name of Phemius, who taught boys their letters and all their poetry. He paid Cretheis—since he lived alone—to work some wool for him; he took fleeces from his boys for pay. Since she did the work for him in good order and behaved herself properly, she pleased Phemius greatly. Finally he proposed that she live with him. He persuaded her by various arguments, the sort of thing that he thought would appeal to her, particularly about her son, that he would adopt him, and that if the boy were brought up and educated by him he would be a noteworthy man. He had seen that the child was clever and particularly good-looking. So he persuaded her to do as he said.

[5] The boy had natural talent, and as soon as his drill and education began, he surpassed all the others by far. After some time, when he had reached maturity, he proved to be in no way inferior to Phemius in his teaching. And so when Phemius died he left everything to the boy. Not long afterwards, Cretheis died too. Melesigenes established himself in the teaching profession, and because he was now by himself, he was noticed by more people, and both the locals and new arrivals from abroad became admirers of his. For Smyrna was a market town, and quantities of grain were brought there, much of it grain brought into the city from the surrounding countryside. Visitors, as soon as they finished their work, stopped and rested at Melesigenes' school.

[6] Among the visitors to his school was a merchant, Mentes, who came from the region near Leucas. He had sailed to

Smyrna to buy produce, an educated man, at least by the standards of that time, and very knowledgeable. He persuaded Melesigenes to sail with him and to disband the school: he would receive a salary and all expenses. The idea was that he ought to see foreign lands and cities while he was still young. I think particularly that the notion of travel was very appealing to him, since possibly even then he was thinking of becoming a poet. So Melesigenes disbanded his school and went off in the ship with Mentes, and wherever he went he saw all the countryside and learned by asking questions. It is probable that even then he was writing down a record of it all.

[7] After they had travelled back from Tyrsenia and Iberia they came to Ithaca. And it happened that Melesigenes, who already had suffered from eye disease, became much worse. Because he needed treatment Mentes left him in Ithaca when he was ready to sail to Leucas, at the house of a man who was an especially good friend of his, Mentor of Ithaca the son of Alcimus, and he asked him to take great care of Melesigenes. Mentor nursed him assiduously—he was comfortably off and enjoyed by far the greatest reputation for justice and hospitality among the Ithacans. It was there that Melesigenes happened to make inquiries and learn about Odysseus. Now the Ithacans say that Melesigenes became blind when he was on their island, but I say that he regained his health then, and later became blind in Colophon. And the Colophonians agree with me about this.

[8] Mentes on his way back from Leucas sailed to Ithaca and collected Melesigenes. He sailed about with Mentes for a long time, but when he got to Colophon it turned out that he developed eye trouble again and could no longer resist the disease, and so it was in Colophon that he became blind. From Colophon then, now blind, Melesigenes came back to Smyrna, and so took up composing poetry.

[9] After some time, since he had no means of support in Smyrna he decided to go to Cyme. He journeyed through the plain of Hermus and went to Neon Teichos, a colony of Cyme. The settlement had established eight years after the founding of Cyme. There the story is told that he went and stood at an armourer's shop and recited these first verses:

Respect a man who needs hospitality and a home.
you who dwell in the steep city that is the fair daughter of Cyme,
lowest foothill of high-wooded Saedene,
you who drink the ambrosial water of a divine river,
whirling Hermus, whom immortal Zeus begot.

[Epigram 1]

Saedene is a mountain that lies above the Hermus river and Neon
Teichos. The armourer's name was Tychius. When he heard the
verses he thought he should take the man in, especially since he
took pity on him and his request because of his blindness. So he
told him to come into his workroom and invited him to share
what he had. Melesigenes went in, and as he sat in the armourer's
shop recited his poetry also to others who were there, the poems
*Amphiaraus' Expedition to Thebes*, and the *Hymns* to the gods which
he had written, and when he produced aphorisms out of what the
people sitting in the leather-worker's shop said in general
conversation, Melesigenes seemed remarkable to all who heard
him.

[10] For a time, then, Melesigenes was able to make a living
from his poetry in the area around Neon Teichos. The people of
Neon Teichos showed me the spot where Homer sat and
recited his verses, and they had great reverence for the place.
A black poplar tree also grows there, which they say has been
growing there since the time when Melesigenes came to their
city.

[11] After some time, when he found himself idle and helpless
and with barely enough to eat, Melesigenes decided to go to
Cyme to see if he could do any better. As he was about to start
off he spoke these verses:

May my feet bring me straight to a city of righteous men;
their hearts are generous and their intentions best.

[Epigram 2]

He journeyed from Neon Teichos and came to Cyme, making
his way through Larisse, since this was the easiest route for him.
So, as the people of Cyme tell it, the story is that he wrote the
following epigram for Midas son of Gordios, the king of

Phrygia, at the request of Midas' inlaws. The epigram is still inscribed on the stele of the tomb, in four verses:

> As long as water flows and the tall trees bloom,
> and the rising sun shines and the bright moon,
> I shall remain here on this tomb of great lamentation
> and tell passers-by that Midas is buried here.

[Epigram 3]

[12] Melesigenes sat down and joined the old men's discussions in the town square of Cyme, and recited the verses he had composed. He brought pleasure to all who heard him, who then became admirers of his. When he realised that the Cymeans liked his poetry and found that they enjoyed listening to him, he made the following proposals to them: he said that if they wanted to feed him at public expense, he would make their city very famous. The people who listened to him were eager to do this, and they advised him to go to the town senate and ask the senators, and they said that they would come and help him. He took their advice and when the senate met came into the senate house and asked the man who was appointed to that office to lead him into the meeting. He promised that he would and at the appropriate moment he led him in. Melesigenes stood in front of the meeting and made the argument about public support that he had made in his conversations. After he had spoken, he went out and sat down.

[13] They deliberated about what they ought to say in reply to him. The man who brought him in and other senators who had been in his audiences at the conversations were eager to support him. But the story is that one of the magistrates opposed his request, using among his arguments that if they thought it right to feed hostages [*homēroi*], they would acquire a large and useless crowd of hangers-on. It was as a result of this event that the name Homer replaced Melesigenes, since the Cymeans call blind men *homēroi*. And so the man who was previously called Melesigenes acquired the name Homer. And strangers have continued to do so, when they tell stories about him.

[14] In the end the argument was won by the magistrate, not

to support Homer, and the rest of the senate also agreed. The officer came out and sat down next to Homer. He went over the arguments on both sides about his request and what the senate had decided. Homer, when he had heard this, lamented his fate and recited the following verses:

> To such a fate Zeus gave me as prey
> When as a child I played at the knee of my dear mother.
> Her by the will of Zeus the people of Phricon
> once sheltered, riders of wild horses,
> they waged war faster than raging fire
> against Aeolian Smyrna, the sea's neighbour, sea-shaken.
> The glorious water of the holy Meles runs through it
> from that source the Muses rose up, the glorious children of Zeus
> and were willing to praise its rich land
> and the city of its people.
> But they scorned the holy voice, the renown of song
> in their folly. This one of them shall recall when he is in trouble,
> the man who decided my fate, with his taunts to them.
> The destiny Zeus gave me when I was born
> I shall endure, bearing what is yet to come with patient heart.
> No longer do my limbs strive to remain in the holy streets
> of Cyme, but my strong heart urges me
> to go to other men's cities, weak as I am.

[Epigram 4]

[15] After that he moved from Cyme to Phocaea, after placing a curse on the Cymeans that no famous poet would be born in their country who would bring the Cymeans glory. When he arrived in Phocaea he lived in the same way as before, reciting his poetry as he sat in on the men's discussions. In Phocaea at that time there lived a certain Thestorides who taught boys their letters—not an honourable man. When he learned of Homer's poetry he made proposals to him of this sort: he said that he was prepared to take Homer in and look after him and feed him, provided that he could write down what Homer had composed and could take down whatever new poetry Homer composed.

[16] Homer listened and decided that he would agree, since he was in need of the necessities of life and to be taken care of.

While he stayed with Thestorides he composed the *Little Iliad*, the epic that begins:

I sing of Ilion and Dardania with its good horses
the city for which the Danaans suffered greatly, servants of Ares.
[*Il. Par.* 1 Allen]

He also wrote the epic called *Phocais*, which the Phocaeans say he composed while he was in their city. When Thestorides had written down the *Phocais* and everything else Homer composed, he decided to move away from Phocaea, because he wanted to represent Homer's poetry as his own. Also, he no longer took care of Homer as he had before. Homer then composed the following verses:

Thestorides, of the many things that make no sense to mortals, none is more incomprehensible than the human mind.
[Epigram 5]

Thestorides then moved from Phocaea to Chios and set up a school and recited Homer's epics as his own. He won much praise and profit from them. Homer meanwhile went back to his old way of life in Phocaea and made a living from his poetry.

[17] Not long after some Chian merchants arrived in Phocaea, and heard poetry by Homer that they had first heard many times in Chios from Thestorides. They told Homer that there was someone in Chios who recited the same verses, a teacher of letters, who had indeed won great praise for his recitations. Homer realised that this teacher might be Thestorides and wanted with all his heart to go to Chios. But when he went down to the harbour he could not catch any boats sailing to Chios, though some men were getting ready to sail to Erythraea for lumber. Homer was happy to make the voyage to Erythraea, and he went up to the sailors and asked them to take him on as a passenger. He recited persuasive verses with which he was bound to convince them. They decided to take him, and told him to get into the boat. Homer praised them greatly and got in the boat. After he was seated, he recited these verses:

Hear me, Poseidon with your great strength, earthshaker,
you who protect [?] with its broad dancing places and
   holy Helicon,
grant us a fair wind and that there be a voyage home without
   pain
for these sailors who are the ship's escorts and captains.
Grant that when I come to the foothills of Mimas
with its high cliffs, that I find men who respect me, pious men,
and may I be avenged on the man who deceived me
and angered Zeus god of guests and a guest's table.

[Epigram 6]

[18] When they got to Erythraea after a calm voyage, Homer then spent the night on the boat. The next day he asked one of the sailors to bring him to the city. And they sent some-one with him. Homer travelled until he came to Erythraea, a place which is steep and mountainous, and he spoke these verses:

Queen earth giver of all, giver of honeysweet happiness,
I see how to some men you appear arable
but to others infertile and harsh, when you are angry at them.

[Epigram 7]

When he got to the city of Erythraea, he asked about the voyage to Chios. A man greeted him who had seen him in Phocaea, and embraced him. Homer asked him to find a boat, so he could make the crossing to Chios.

[19] Since no vessel was going out from the harbour, the man took him to where the fisherman's boats set out. And somehow it happened that there were some fishermen who were getting ready to sail to Chios. The man who led Homer there asked them to take Homer on board. But they took no account of him and set sail without him. So Homer spoke these verses:

Sailors who travel by sea, ill-fated
like trembling diver-birds you lead an unenviable life;
respect the honour of Zeus god of guests and his high power,
for dreadful is the judgment of Zeus god of guests, when his law
   is broken

[Epigram 8]

When they set sail it happened that an adverse wind sprang up. So they turned back and returned to the place from where they had set out, and they found Homer still sitting on the beach. When he discovered that they had come back he said: 'Strangers. An adverse wind sprang up and caught you. But now take me along with you and you will be able to make your voyage.' The fishermen now were sorry that they hadn't taken Homer on at first. They said that they wouldn't leave him behind, if he wanted to sail with them, and they told him to get on board. And so once they took him with them they set sail and beached the ship on a promontory.

[20] The fishermen set about their work; Homer spent the night on the beach. But during the day he journeyed forth and after wandering around came to the place that is called Pitys. And while he stopped there for the night a fruit from a pine tree fell on him, the kind some call *strobiloi* (spinning tops) and others cones. And Homer spoke these verses:

> Another pine tree drops better fruit than you
> a tree in the hills of windy Ida with its many glens,
> there men will acquire the iron for war, at the time
> when the Cebrenians rule the country.
>
> [Epigram 9]

At that time the Cymeans were getting ready to found Cebrenia on Mt. Ida, and from there came a great supply of iron.

[21] Homer got up from under the pine tree and set out after the sound of goats being herded. When their dogs barked at him, he cried out. When he heard Homer's voice, Glaucus—for that was the name of the man herding the goats—ran quickly and called off the dogs and frightened them away from Homer. For a long time he was in a state of amazement about how a blind man could have come by himself to such a remote place and what he wanted. He went up and asked him who he was and how he had come to this uninhabited spot and places without paths, and what he needed. Homer related all that he had suffered, and led him to pity him. Glaucus, as it seems, was not an ignorant man. He took Homer along and led him to his hut and kindled a fire and prepared dinner. And as he

put the food beside him [22] he told Homer to eat. But since his dogs stood round and barked at them as they ate, as was their habit, Homer spoke these verses to Glaucus:

Glaucus, guardian of pastures, I shall put some verses in your heart:
give dinner first to your dogs by the gates
of your courtyard. For that is best. Your dog first hears
a stranger approaching and the wild animal nearing your fence.

[Epigram 11]

When Glaucus heard this he was pleased by the advice and held Homer in high regard. After they ate dinner they feasted on conversation. When Homer described in detail his wanderings and the cities to which he had come, Glaucus was amazed at what he heard. And then when it was time to go to bed, they broke off their conversation. [23] The next day Glaucus decided to make a trip to his master to tell him the story on Homer's behalf. He ordered a fellow slave to herd his goats and he left Homer inside after telling him: 'I shall be back soon.' He went to Bolissos—it is near Pitys. And when he was able to see his master he told him the whole truth about Homer and about his arrival, since he considered it astonishing, and he asked his master what he should do about him. His master didn't take much account of what he said. He considered Glaucus a fool to take in cripples and feed them. But none the less he told Glaucus to bring the stranger to him. [24] Glaucus went to Homer and described what had happened and told Homer to make the journey to his master, since he would prosper there. Homer was willing to make the journey. So Glaucus took him along and brought him to his master. When the Chian spoke with Homer he found him to be clever and widely experienced. He urged Homer to remain and take charge of his children. The Chian had young children, and it was these whom he appointed Homer to educate. Homer did this. While he was with the Chian in Bolissos he composed the *Cercopes* and the *Battle of the Frogs and Mice* and the *Battle of the Starlings* and the *Heptapacticē* and the *Epicichlidēs* and all the other children's works attributed to Homer. As a result he became famous also in the city of Chios because of his poetry. When Thestorides heard that Homer was on the island, he went and sailed away from Chios. [25] After some time Homer asked the Chian to send him to the city of Chios; he set up a school there and taught boys his poetry. He seemed particularly clever to the Chians, and many were impressed by him. Since he made a good living, he took a wife, who bore two daughters to him. One of these died without marrying, but the other set up house with a man from Chios.

[26] He tried through his poetry to pay back the thanks which he owed; first to Mentor of Ithaca in the *Odyssey*, because he had nursed him assiduously, when he was suffering from eye disease on Ithaca, by putting his name into the poetry and saying that he was a comrade of Odysseus. He composed the story that when Odysseus sailed off to Troy, he appointed Mentor to take charge of his household, because he was the best and most honoured of all the Ithacans. Often elsewhere in his poetry he paid tribute to him by making Athena look like Mentor whenever she engaged in conversation with someone. He repaid his own teacher Phemius for his upbringing and education in the *Odyssey*, particularly in these verses:

> A herald put a beautiful lyre into the hands
> of Phemius, who far surpassed others in singing
> [*Od.* 1.153–4]

and also:

> but he played the lyre and began to sing a beautiful song
> [*Od.* 1.155]

He also remembered the ship owner with whom he had sailed round and had seen many cities and countries—the man whose name was Mentes—in these verses:

> I, Mentes, say that I am the son of warlike
> Anchialus, and I rule over the Taphians who love rowing.
> [*Od.* 1.180–1]

He also paid thanks to Tychius the armourer, who took him in when he came to his armourer's shop in Neon Teichos, in these verses in the Iliad:

Ajax came near carrying a shield like a tower,
bronze, seven hides thick, that Tychius had laboured to make,
the armourer, who made his house in Hyle.

[*Il.* 6.219–21]

[27] Because of this poetry Homer became famous throughout
Ionia, and word about him also spread to mainland Greece,
and since many people had come to him the Chians advised
him to go to Greece. He welcomed the suggestion and was very
eager to make the journey. [28] Since he knew that he had
written many fine tributes to Argos, but none to Athens, he
inserted into his poetry in the greater *Iliad* the verses glorifying
Erechtheus in the *Catalogue of Ships*:

The people of great hearted Erechtheus, whom Athena raised,
daughter of Zeus, and the grain giving earth bore.

[*Il.* 2.2547–8]

He also praised their general Menestheus as best of all at
deploying infantry and cavalry in these verses:

These then Menestheus son of Peteos led, no man was like him
on earth in arranging in battle horses and soldiers with their
shields.

[*Il.* 2.552–4]

He put Ajax son of Telamon and the men from Salamis with the
Athenians in the *Catalogue of Ships* in these verses:

Ajax brought twelve ships from Salamis;
He stood when he brought them where the Athenian troops
were stationed.

[*Il.* 2.557–8]

He also wrote in the *Odyssey* that when Athena came to speak to
Odysseus she went back to the city of Athens, thus honouring that
city far beyond others in these verses:

She came to Marathon and to the wide streets of Athens
and went into the well-built house of Erechtheus.

[*Od.* 7.80–1]

[29] When he had inserted these verses in his poetry and finished his preparations to go to Greece, he made the voyage to Samos. The people there happened to be deliberating at that moment the festival of Apaturia. One of the Samians saw Homer coming, who had seen him previously in Chios, and went to his kinsmen and told them about him in detail, since he held him in the highest esteem. His kinsmen told him to bring Homer along, and he met Homer and said: 'Stranger, since the city is celebrating the Apaturia my kinsmen wish you to celebrate with them.' Homer said that he would come and went with the man who invited him. [30] As he made his journey he encountered women sacrificing to the protectress of children in the crossroads. The priestess said to him in anger, at the sight of him: 'Man, get away from our rites.' Homer took what she said to heart and asked the man who was leading him who was the person who spoke and to what god was he sacrificing. The man told him that it was a woman sacrificing to the protectress of children. When Homer heard his answer he uttered these verses:

Hear me, as I pray, Protectress of Children, grant that this woman
reject love and sex with young men, but let her delight in old
men with grey brows whose strength has been blighted, but whose
hearts still feel desire.

[Epigram 12]

[31] When he came to the man's kinsmen and stood on the threshold of the house where they were having their banquet, some of them said that there was a fire burning in the house, others say that they kindled one then, because Homer uttered the following verses:

A man's crown is his children, a city its towers;
Horses are an ornament to a field, and ships to a sea,
Possessions bring a house glory, and honourable kings
Seated in the marketplace are an ornament for their subjects to see;
but a house is more honourable to look on when a fire is burning.

[Epigram 13]

Homer went inside and sat down and ate with the kinsmen, and they honoured him and held him in high regard.

And then after Homer had spent the night there, [32] the next day as he was leaving some potters saw him as they were lighting their kiln to make a pot, they called out to him because they had heard that he was a poet, and asked him to sing for them. They said that they would give him the pot and whatever else they had. Homer sang this song for them; it is known as the *Kiln*.

If you will pay me for my song, o potters,
come then Athena and hold your hand over their kiln.
May their cups turn a good black and all their bowls.
[I pray] that they be well fired and win profit by their price,
that many, sold in the market, and many [sold] in the streets,
that many bring gain, for me and for them to realise.
But if you [potters] turn shameless and tell me lies,
then I shall invoke the destroyers of kilns,
Smasher and Scatter and Sooty and Crasher
and Rawcrusher, who brings great problems to your craft.
Hear me; [ruin] the fire-porch and the chambers, let the whole kiln
be shaken, while the potters weep loudly.
As a horse's jaw grinds, may the kiln grind
   all things inside it and turn them to sherds.
  Come, daughter of the Sun, Circe with your many spells,
  cast your cruel spells on them, harm the potters and their
    handiwork.
  Come, Chiron and bring many Centaurs,
  both those who escaped Heracles' hands and those who perished;
  May they hit these pots hard, may the kiln collapse,
  and may the potters weep as they look at their ruined handiwork.
  I will rejoice as I look on their unlucky craftsmanship.
And if anyone peers in [the spy-hole], may his whole face be burned
over, so that all men may know that they should be honest.

                   [Epigram 14/Hesiod, fr. 302 MW]

[33] Homer spent the winter in Samos. He went out at the time of the new moon festival to the houses of rich people and made some money by singing these verses, the song called *Eiresione*. Some children from the countryside took him around and kept him company.

   We find ourselves at the home of a man with great power,
   A man with great power who thunders loudly in his prosperity.

Doors, open by yourselves. For vast Wealth goes inside.
and with Wealth flourishing Happiness
and kindly Peace. Let all his grain bins be full.
Let the pile of barley flow from the kneading trough.
Now may the smiling barley with sesame . . .
. . .
Your son's wife will come out from a chair to you.
Swift-footed mules will bring her to your house.
Let her weave her cloth as she walks on *electrum*.
I come, I come each year like the swallow;
I stand before your door barefoot, so bring something quickly.
We ask you for Apollo's sake, lady, give us something.
If you do, give us something good. If you don't, we won't stay.
For we did not come here to live in your household.

[Epigrams 15 and 16]

These verses were sung in Samos for a long time by children,
when they would go begging at the festival of Apollo.

[34] When the spring came Homer tried to sail to Athens
from Samos. He set sail along with some Samians and was
taken to Ios. They put ashore not at the city but on the beach.
It happened that when Homer got on board he began to feel
sick. When he got off the boat he slept on the beach because he
was weak. Since they were kept on shore for several days
because of lack of winds, people kept coming out from the
town and spent time with him. When they heard him they had
high regard for him. [35] While the sailors and some people
from the town were sitting with Homer some fisher boys sailed
to the place and got out of their boat and came over to them.
They said the following: 'Come, strangers, listen to us, and see
if you can understand what we say to you.' One of the people
there told them to speak. And they said: 'We are the ones who
caught what we left behind. We didn't catch what we bring.'
Some say they spoke in verse:

All we caught we left behind; what we didn't catch we bring.

[Epigram 17]

When the people there weren't able to understand what they
said, the boys explained that when they went fishing they
couldn't catch anything. But when they sat on the land they

looked for lice, and the lice they caught they left behind and the lice they couldn't catch they brought away with them. When Homer heard that, he uttered these verses:

> From the blood of fathers like yourselves you are descended;
> Not from those with ancient inheritance or with boundless
>   herds of sheep.
>
> [Epigram 18]

[36] It happened that Homer died from this sickness in Ios, not because he couldn't understand what the boys said, as some think, but from weakness. When he died he was buried in Ios there on the beach by the sailors and the citizens who had been present during the conversation with him on the beach. And at a much later time the people of Ios wrote this epitaph, since his poetry had become famous throughout the world and was admired by all. The verses are not Homer's—

> Here the earth covers the sacred head
> of the poet who gave heroes glory, divine Homer.

[37] That Homer was an Aeolian and not from Ios or a Dorian I have made clear by what I have said, and one can also provide the following evidence. It is likely that such a great poet when he was composing his poetry would find for his poetry the best practices among men or choose those of his own native country. You will be able to judge yourself when you listen to the following verses. For either he discovered the best form of sacrifice or he composed poetry about sacrifice in his own country. He speaks as follows:

> First they drew back their heads and slaughtered and flayed
> And cut off the thigh pieces and covered them with fats
> making a double fold and set the raw meat on them.
>
> [*Il.* 1.459–61]

In these lines nothing is said about the loins that they use in sacrifice. Among all Greeks the Aeolian race alone does not roast the loin. One can be certain also from the following verses that since he is an Aeolian he naturally observes these customs:

The old man roasted it on the split wood and poured out the
  bright wine
and in their hands the young men held out to him the
  five-pronged forks.

[*Il.* 1.462–3]

Only the Aeolians roast entrails on the five-pronged forks,
the other Greeks use three. The Aeolians also call the number
five [*pente*] *pempe*. [38] This is what I know about Homer's
background and death and life. One might also assess Homer's
death accurately and correctly by making the following
calculation:

From the time of the expedition to Troy which Agamemnon
and Menelaus organised, it was one hundred and thirty years
before Lesbos was colonised by towns; previously Lesbos had
no towns. Twenty years after Lesbos was settled, Aeolian
Cyme and the town called Phriconis were settled. Eighteen
years after Cyme Smyrna was colonised by Cymaeans and at
that time Homer was born. From the time Homer was born,
there were 622 years until Xerxes' crossing—in his campaign
against the Greeks, when he bridged the Hellespont and
crossed from Asia into Europe. From this point it is easy to
measure the time if one wishes by referring to the Archons in
Athens. Homer was born 168 years after the Trojan war.


## 2. THE LIFE OF PINDAR[1]

[1] The poet Pindar was a Theban from Cynoscephalae, which
is a village in the territory of Thebes. He was the son of Daiphantus, or according to other authorities, of Pagondas. Still
others trace his genealogy to Scopelinus. Some say that Scopelinus was his uncle and that, since he played the *aulos*, he taught
his skill to Pindar. His mother was Cleodice. Other authorities
spell it Cledice.

[2] When Pindar was a boy, according to Chamaeleon and
Ister, he went hunting near Mt. Helicon and fell asleep from

[1] Ed. Drachmann 1903.

exhaustion. As he slept a bee landed on his mouth and built a honeycomb there. Others say that he had a dream in which his mouth was full of honey and wax, and that he then decided to write poetry.

[3] Some authorities say that at Athens his teacher was Agathocles, others say Apollodorus. Apollodorus also, when he was in charge of the dithyrambic choruses and had to be out of town, entrusted their direction to Pindar even though he was still a boy. Pindar directed them so well that he became famous.

[4] When he said that Athens was the bulwark of Hellas [fr. 76] he was fined one thousand drachmas by the Thebans, and the Athenians paid the fine on his behalf.

[5] He was not only a beautiful poet, but he was a man dear to the gods. For example, the god Pan was seen between Cithaeron and Helicon singing a paean of Pindar. Accordingly Pindar wrote a song to the god in which he offers his gratitude for the honour, the poem that begins 'O Pan, Pan protector of Arcadia and guard of sacred shrines' [fr. 95]. And Demeter also appeared in a dream and blamed him, because for her alone of all the gods he had written no hymn. So he wrote her the poem that begins 'Queen, lawgiver [?] with golden headband' [fr. 37]. And he also built an altar to both gods outside his house.

[6] When Pausanias the king of the Lacedaemonians was razing Thebes, someone wrote on Pindar's house: 'Don't set fire to the home of the poet Pindar.' As a result his was the only house that remained unburned, and it is now the magistrate's hall in Thebes.

[7] At Delphi also when the priest is getting ready to close the temple he announces each day: 'let Pindar the poet come to join the god at dinner.' For the poet was born during the Pythian festival, as he himself says 'the quadrennial festival with its procession of oxen, in which I first was put to bed in swaddling clothes' [fr. 193].

[8] There is a story that pilgrims went to the temple of Ammon to ask for Pindar what was best for men, and the poet died on that very day.

[9] He lived at the time of Simonides, though he was younger, Simonides older. In fact both of them celebrated the same

events. Simonides wrote about the naval battle at Salamis [fr. 536] and Pindar celebrated the kingdom of [?] [fr. 272]. Both of them were together at the court of Hieron the tyrant of Syracuse.

[10] He married Megacleia the daughter of Lysitheus and Calline and had a son Daiphantus, for whom he wrote a song for the Daphnephoria. He had two daughters, Protomache and Eumetis.

[11] He wrote seventeen books: hymns, paeans, dithyrambs (2), prosodia (2), partheneia (2) and allegedly a third book which has the title of separate partheneia, hyporchemes (2), encomia, lamentations, victory odes (4).

[12] There exists an epigram with the following conclusion:

How Protomache and Eumetis weep for you in shrill voices, your wise daughters, when they came from Argos bringing home in an urn your remains which had been gathered from a foreign funeral pyre.

## 3. THE LIFE OF AESCHYLUS[1]

[p.1] Aeschylus the tragic poet's nationality was Athenian; his deme Eleusis. He was the son of Euphorion, the brother of Cynegirus. His family was aristocratic. He began writing tragedies when he was a young man and he raised standards far above his predecessors, in writing and in staging, [5] in the splendour of his choral productions, in his actors' costumes and in the serious content of his choral songs. As Aristophanes says:

Oh you who first piled up serious speeches and crowned tragic talk. [*Ran.* 1004]

He was a contemporary of Pindar's, having been born in the sixty-fourth Olympiad. They say that he was heroic and that he fought in the battle of Marathon [10] along with his brother Cynegirus, and in the naval battle at Salamis along with his

[1] Ed. Page 1972.

younger brother Ameinias, and also in the infantry battle at Plataea.

In the composition of his poetry he strove for a grand style, by using compound words and epithets, [15] and also metaphors and every other device that could lend weight to his diction. The plots of his plays do not abound in reversals and complexities like those of later poets, for he aimed solely at investing his characters with dignity. He thought that heroic grandeur struck the proper archaic note, [20] but that cunning ingenuity and sententiousness were foreign to tragedy. It was for this reason that Aristophanes made fun of him in his comedies, because of his stress on the excessive dignity of his characters. For example, in the *Niobe*, Niobe sits silent by her children's tomb for three scenes with her head covered, and does not utter a word; and in the *Ransom of Hector* [25] Achilles with his head covered similarly does not utter anything except a few words [p.2] at the beginning, in conversation with Hermes. For this reason one could find many outstanding illustrations of his striking dramatic contrivances but few aphorisms or pathetic scenes or other effects calculated to produce tears. He used visual effects and plots [5] more to frighten and amaze than to trick his audience.

He went off to stay with Hieron, according to some authorities, because he was criticised by the Athenians and defeated by Sophocles when the latter was a young man, but according to others because he was defeated by Simonides in an elegy for those who died at Marathon. Elegy in particular needs to have the conciseness necessary to arouse emotion, [10] and Aeschylus' poem (as the story goes) was not suitable. Some say that during the performance of the *Eumenides*, when he brought the chorus on one by one, he so frightened the audience that children fainted and unborn infants were aborted.

Then he went to Sicily at the time that Hieron was founding the city Aetna and put on the *Women of Aetna*, [15] as a favourable portent for a good life for the people living in the city. He was also greatly honoured both by Hieron and by the people of Gela, and after living there for two years he died, an old man, in the following way: an eagle had caught a tortoise, and because it did not have the strength to get control of its prey threw it down on some rocks in order to break its shell. But the tortoise fell instead [20] on the poet and killed him. For he had received an oracle: 'Something thrown from the sky will kill you.' After his death the people of Gela buried him richly in the city's cemetery and honoured him extravagantly by writing the following epigram:

This tomb in grainbearing Gela covers an Athenian, Aeschylus son of Euphorion, who died here. [25] The famous grove of Marathon could tell of his courage and the longhaired Mede knew it well.

All who made their living in the tragic theatre went to his tomb to offer sacrifices and recited their plays there.

The Athenians [p.3] liked Aeschylus so much that they voted after his death to award a golden crown to whoever was willing to put on one of his dramas. He lived sixty-three years, during which time he wrote seventy dramas and in addition about five satyr plays. [5] He won quite a few victories after his death.

Aeschylus was first to enhance tragedy with highly heroic effects and to decorate the stage and to astound his audience's eyes with splendour, through pictures and devices, with altars and tombs, trumpets, images and Furies. He equipped the actors with gloves and dignified them with long robes and [10] elevated their stance with higher buskins. He used Cleander as first actor; then with him as second actor Mynniscus of Chalcis. It was he who invented the third actor, though Dicaearchus of Messene says it was Sophocles.

If one wanted to compare the simplicity of his dramatic art [15] to dramatists after him, one might think it insignificant and unsophisticated. But if one compared his work to his predecessors, one would be amazed at the poet's intelligence and inventiveness. Anyone who thinks that the most perfect writer of tragedy is Sophocles is correct, but he should remember that it was much harder to bring tragedy to such a height after Thespis, Phrynichus [20] and Choerilus, than it was by speaking after Aeschylus to come to Sophocles' perfection.

There is an inscription on his tomb:

I died, struck on the forehead by a missile from an eagle's claws.

They say that he put on [25] the *Persians* in Sicily at Hieron's request and was highly praised for it.

## 4. THE LIFE OF SOPHOCLES[1]

[1] Sophocles was an Athenian by birth. He was the son of Sophillus who was not a carpenter in spite of what Aristoxenus tells us [fr. 115 Wehrli] nor a bronze-smith, nor a sword-maker by trade in spite of what Ister tells us [*FGrHist* 334F33]. As it happened, his father owned *slaves* who were bronze-smiths and carpenters. For it is not logical that a man descended from a tradesman would be considered worthy of a generalship along with Pericles and Thucydides, who were the most important men in the city. Indeed, if his father had been a tradesman, he would not have got off without abuse from the comic poets. Nor ought one to believe Ister [*FGrHist* 334F34] when he says Sophocles was not an Athenian but rather a Phliasian. Even if Sophocles' family originally came from Phlious, still one cannot find this information in any author other than Ister. In fact Sophocles was an Athenian by birth. His deme was Colonus. He was distinguished both because of his life and his poetry. He was well-educated and raised in comfortable circumstances, and he was involved in government and in embassies abroad.

[2] They say that he was born in the second year of the seventy-first Olympiad, when Philip was archon in Athens [495/4 B.C.]. He was seven years younger than Aeschylus, and twenty-four years older than Euripides.

[3] He trained with other boys both in wrestling and in music, and won crowns for both, as Ister says [*FGrHist* 334F35]. He studied music with Lamprus, and after the naval battle at Salamis, when the Athenians were standing round the victory monument, Sophocles with his lyre, naked and anointed with oil, led the chorus which sang the paean at the victory sacrifice.

---

[1] Ed. Radt 1977.

[4] He learned about tragedy from Aeschylus. He also was responsible for innovations in the dramatic competitions. He was the first to break the tradition of the poet's acting because his own voice was weak. For in the old days the poet himself served as one of the actors. He changed the number of chorus members from twelve to fifteen and invented the third actor.

[5] They say that he also took up the lyre and that only in the *Thamyris* did he ever sing; on account of this there is a picture of him playing a lyre in the Painted Stoa.

[6] Satyrus says [*FHG* 3.161ff.] that Sophocles invented the crooked staff himself. Ister also says [*FGrHist* 334F36] that he discovered the white half-boots that actors and chorus members wear, and that he wrote his dramas to suit their characters, and that he organised a *thiasos* to the Muses of cultivated people.

[7] In a word, his character was so charming that he was loved everywhere and by everyone.

[8] He won twenty victories, according to Carystius [*FHG* 4.359]. He often won second prize, but never third.

[9] The Athenians elected him general when he was sixty-five years old, seven years before the Peloponnesian war began, in the war against the Anaioi.

[10] He was so loyal to Athens that when many kings sent for him he did not want to leave his country.

[11] He held the priesthood of Halon, who was a hero under Chiron's tutelage along with Asclepius. After Sophocles' death Halon's shrine was maintained by his son Iophon.

[12] Sophocles was more pious than anyone else, according to what Hieronymus says [fr. 31 Wehrli] . . . about his golden crown. When this crown was stolen from the Acropolis, Heracles came to Sophocles in a dream and told him to go into the house on the right and it would be hidden there. Sophocles brought this information to the citizens and received a reward of a talent, as had been announced in advance. He used the talent to establish a shrine of Heracles Informer.

[13] The story is told by many authorities that at some point he brought a lawsuit against his son Iophon. Iophon was his son by Nicostrate, but he had a son Ariston by Theoris of Sicyon, and he was especially fond of this son's child, whose name was Sophocles. Once in a drama he portrayed Iophon

. . . as being envious of him and as making accusations to his
clansmen that his father had lost his mind in his old age. They
censured Iophon. Satyrus [*FHG* 3.162] says the poet said: 'If I
am Sophocles I'm not out of my mind; if I am out of my mind,
I'm not Sophocles', and then he produced the *Oedipus*.

[14] Ister [*FGrHist* 334F37] and Neanthes [*FGrHist* 84F18]
say he died in the following way. When Callippides the actor
came from the workshop in Opus and around the time of the
festival of the Choes sent Sophocles a bunch of grapes, and
when Sophocles put a grape that was still unripe into his
mouth, he choked because of his advanced age and died.
Satyrus says [*FHG* 3.162] that when Sophocles was reciting
the *Antigone* and came to a passage toward the end of the play
that did not have a break or mark for a pause, he strained his
voice too much and gave up his life along with his voice. Some
say that after he recited the drama, and he was proclaimed
winner, he was overcome by joy and died.

[15] His body was placed on top of his ancestral tomb near
the road to Deceleia, eleven stades from the city wall. Some
say that they put up a statue of a siren in his memory; others, a
bronze Cheledon. Since the Spartans were building a wall at
this spot against the Athenians, Dionysus appeared to Lysander
in a dream and ordered that the man should be buried. When
Lysander ignored the dream Dionysus appeared to him a
second time with the same message. Lysander then asked some
fugitives who had died, and learned that it was Sophocles. So
he sent a herald and allowed the Athenians to bury the body.

[16] Lobon says that this epitaph was written on his tomb:

In this tomb I hide Sophocles who won first prize with his tragic
art, a most holy figure.

[17] Ister says [*FGrHist* 334F38] the Athenians voted to
sacrifice to him each year because of his excellence.

[18] He wrote one hundred and thirty dramas, as Aristophanes says [p. 249, fr. iv N] of which seventeen are spurious.

[19] He competed against Aeschylus, Euripides, Choerilus,
Aristias and many others, including his son Iophon.

[20] In general he used Homeric vocabulary. He took his

plots from the direction set by the epic poet and drew on the *Odyssey* for many of his dramas. He gives the etymology of Odysseus' name [*Od.* 19.406ff.] the way Homer did:

> I am Odysseus, named correctly for my troubles. For many impious people have been angry [*odysanto*] at me [fr. 965].

He delineated character, elaborated and used contrivances skilfully, reproducing Homer's charm. For this reason a certain Ionian says only Sophocles is a pupil of Homer. Certainly many poets have imitated one of their predecessors or contemporaries, but Sophocles alone culled the best from each. For this reason he was also called 'the bee'. He brought everything together: timing, sweetness, courage, variety.

[21] He knew how to match timing and events, so that he could delineate a whole character from a fraction of a line or from a single speech. This is the greatest mark of poetic skill, to delineate character or effect.

[22] Aristophanes says [fr. 580A Edmonds] that 'a honeycomb sat on him', and elsewhere (T108 Radt) that Sophocles' mouth is smeared with honey.

[23] Aristoxenus says [fr. 79 Wehrli] that he was the first of the Athenian poets to put Phrygian music into his own songs and to mix in the dithyrambic style.

## 5. THE LIFE OF EURIPIDES[1]

Euripides the poet was the son of Mnesarchides, a storekeeper, and of Cleito, a vegetable-seller.[2] He was an Athenian. He was born in Salamis while Calliades was archon in the seventy-

---

[1] Ed. Méridier 1929. In the translation of the *Vita* I have followed Méridier's text: a chronological account (1–49), a set of anecdotes (50–113); then a second short biography with comments on the poet's style (114–35). For the reader's convenience footnotes mark correspondences with earlier sources.

[2] Text of Satyrus from *POxy.* IX 1176, on the advice of S. West 1966, 546–50, though with some modifications to Hunt's translations. For *Vita* 1–44,

fifth Olympiad, the year when the Greeks fought the naval battle against the Persians.[3]

[5] At first he practised for the pancration or boxing, because his father had understood an oracle to mean that he would win at contests in which crowns were awarded. And they say that he won a victory in games at Athens. Once he understood the oracle's meaning he turned to writing tragedy; he introduced many innovations, prologues, philosophical discourses, displays of rhetoric and recognition scenes, [10] because he attended lectures by Anaxagoras, Prodicus and Protagoras. Socrates [the philosopher] and Mnesilochus appear to have collaborated with him in some of his writings;[4] as Teleclides says: 'that fellow Mnesilochus is cooking up a new play [15] for Euripides, and Socrates is supplying him with firewood' [fr. 39, 40]. Some authorities say that Iophon or Timocrates of Argos wrote his lyrics.[5]

They say that he was also a painter and that pictures of his are shown at Megara, that he was a torchbearer in the rites of Apollo Zosterius and that he was born on the same day as Hellanicus, [20] which was the day that the Greeks won the naval battle at Salamis, and that he began to compete in dramatic contests at the age of twenty-six. He emigrated to Magnesia and was awarded the privileges of a *proxenos* there and freedom from taxation. From there he went to Macedonia and stayed at the court of Archelaus. [25] As a favour to him he wrote a drama named for him, and he made out very well there because he was also appointed to an administrative post. It is said that he wore a long beard and had moles on his face; that

---

cf. also the translation of F. A. Paley, *Euripides* I[2] (Cambridge 1872) lx–lxii.

Cf. *FGrHist* 328F218: 'It isn't true that his mother was a vegetable-seller, for it happens that both his parents were well-born, as Philochorus demonstrates.'

[3] Cf. Jacoby on *FGrHist* 239A50, 63; 244F35.

[4] Cf. Satyr. fr. 39 col. ii 8–22, citing two lines of dialogue from a drama: ' "When this is done in secret, whom do you fear?" "The gods, who see more than men." Such a conception of the gods will be Socratic; for in truth what is invisible to mortals is to the immortal gods easily seen . . .'

[5] Cf. Satyr. fr. 39 col. xvi 17–29: 'The verses have the appearance of being by one of his competitors, as you say. But here too the comic poet's attack on Euripides is mischievous.'

his first wife was Melito, his second Choirile. He left three sons: the oldest [30] Mnesarchides, a merchant; the second, Mnesilochus, an actor; the youngest, Euripides, who produced some of his father's dramas.

He began to produce dramas when Callias was archon in the first year of the eighty-first Olympiad [456 B.C.]. First he put on the *Peliades*, with which he won third prize. He wrote a total of ninety-two dramas, [35] of which seventy-eight are extant. Of these three are spurious: *Tennes*, *Rhadamanthys* and *Perithous*. He died, according to Philochorus, when he was over seventy years old [*FGrHist* 328F220], according to Eratosthenes, seventy-five [*FGrHist* 241F12], and he was buried in Macedonia. He has a cenotaph in Athens, with an inscription on it either by Thucydides the historian or by the lyric poet Timotheus: [40] 'All Hellas is Euripides' memorial, but the land of Macedonia holds his bones, for it took in the end of his life. His fatherland was the Greece of Greece, Athens. Having brought great pleasure with his poetry he also won many men's praise' [*EG* 500ff. = *AP* 7.45]. [45] They say that both monuments were struck by lightning. They say that Sophocles, when he heard that Euripides had died, went before the public in a dark cloak and brought his chorus and actors on stage without crowns on their heads in the ceremonial parade preceding the dramatic competition, and that the citizens wept.

Euripides died in the following manner.[6] [50] There was a

---

[6] Cf. Satyr. fr. 39 col. xx 22–35: '(A) Well, these were the events of Euripides' life. The death he met was very violent and peculiar, according to the version of the oldest Macedonian story-tellers. (Diodor.) What was their account? (A) There is in Macedonia . . .'; fr. 39 col. xxi: '. . . and he begged them off. Some time afterwards Euripides happened to be alone by himself in a grove at a distance from the city, while Archelaus went out to the chase. When they were outside the gates the huntsmen loosed the hounds and sent them on in front, while they themselves were left behind. The dogs fell in with Euripides unprotected and killed him, the huntsmen arriving on the scene later. Hence they say the proverb is still in use among the Macedonians, "There is such a thing as a dog's justice".' Cf. Hermesianax 7.61–68 Powell: 'I say that that ever-watchful man, who from all . . . developed a hatred of all women from the depth of his soul, struck by Eros' bent bow could not get rid of nocturnal agonies but wandered down the back alleys of Macedonia pursuing Archelaus' housekeeper, until Fate found a death for Euripides when he encoun-

town in Macedonia called the village of the Thracians because Thracians had once settled there. At some point a female Molossian hound belonging to Archelaus had strayed into the village. This dog the Thracians, as is their custom, sacrificed and ate. Accordingly Archelaus fined them one talent. Since they did not have the money, they asked Euripides to get them released from their debt to the king. [55] Some time later, when Euripides was resting by himself in a grove near the city and Archelaus came out to hunt, his dogs were released by their keepers and fell on Euripides. The poet was torn to shreds and eaten. [60] These dogs were the descendants of the dog that was killed by the Thracians. This is the origin of the Macedonian proverb, 'a dog's justice'.

The story is that in Salamis he furnished a cave that had an opening on the sea and that he spent his days there in order to avoid the public. Because of this he drew most of his comparisons from the sea.[7] [65] His looks were melancholy, thoughtful and severe; he hated laughter and he hated women.[8] On that account Aristophanes found fault with him: 'to me [Euripides] seems sour to speak to.'

They say that after he married Mnesilochus' daughter Choirile and realised that she was unfaithful [70] he first wrote the play *Hippolytus*, in which he exposes women's immorality, and then he divorced her. When her next husband said: 'she is chaste in my household,' Euripides replied: 'you're a fool if you think the same woman will be chaste in one man's house

---

tered Arrhibus' hateful dogs' (reading *ex onychōu* at 62 with Jacobs; see A. Cameron, '*Tener Unguis*', *CQ* N.S. 15 [1965] 83). Also the Suda, s.v. Eur.: 'He died as a result of a plot by Arrhibius of Macedon and Crateuas of Thessaly, who were poets and envied him and persuaded Lysimachus, who was bought for ten minas, to release on Euripides the royal dogs which he had raised.'

[7] Cf. *FGrHist* 328F219: 'Philochorus says that he had on the island of Salamis a foul and wretched cave (which we have seen) in which Euripides wrote his tragedies.' Satyr. fr. 39 col. ix: 'He was the owner of a large cave there with the mouth towards the sea, and here he passed the day by himself engaged in constant thought or writing, despising everything that was not great and elevated. Aristophanes at least says, as though summoned as a witness for this very purpose, "He is like what he makes his characters say". But once when witnessing a comedy he is said . . .'

[8] Cf. n.10 below.

but not in another's.' [75] He took a second wife, but when he found she tended to be unchaste, he was more readily encouraged to slander women. The women planned to kill him and to come to his cave, where he spent his time writing.[9]

He was accused (enviously) of having Cephisophon as co-author of his tragedies. [80] Hermippus [fr. 94 Wehrli] also says that after Euripides' death Dionysius the tyrant of Sicily sent a talent to his heirs and got his harp, his tablet and his stylus; and when he saw them, he ordered the people who brought them to dedicate them as offerings in the temple of the Muses, and he had his own and Euripides' names inscribed on them. [85] For this reason he said he was considered a great friend of foreigners since foreigners particularly liked him, while he was hated by the Athenians. When a boorish youth said enviously that Euripides had bad breath, Euripides said: 'don't criticise me; my mouth is sweeter than honey and the Sirens.'[10]

[90] Euripides made fun of women in his poetry for the following reason. He had a home-bred slave named Cephisophon.[11] He discovered his own wife misbehaving with this boy.

[9] Cf. n.12 below.

[10] Cf. Arist. *Pol.* 1311b30f. (tr. Jowett): 'In the conspiracy against Archelaus, Dechamnichus stimulated the fury of the assassins and led the attack; he was enraged because Archelaus had delivered him to Euripides to be scourged; for the poet had been irritated at some remark made by Dechamnichus on the foulness of his breath.' Cf. Satyr. fr. 39 col. xx 1–15: ' "... his mouth is ... and extremely malodorous". "Hush boy", he interrupted, "what mouth has there been such or could be sweeter than that from which issue songs and words like his?" ' Also Alex.Aetol. 7 Powell: 'Good old Anaxagoras' boarding student looks sour to me and as if he hates laughter, and he hasn't learned to joke even in his cups; but whatever he might write had been made of honey and of the Sirens.'

[11] Cf. Satyr. fr. 39 col. xii 16–35: 'You have clearly comprehended my meaning and absolved me from developing it. He was embittered against the sex for this reason. He had, it seems, in his house a homebred slave named Cephisophon; and he detected his wife in misconduct with this person'; fr. 39 col. xiii: '... bearing the outrage [calmly], as is related, directed the woman to live with the young man. When he was asked "What is the meaning of this?", he said, "In order that my wife may not be his, but his mine—for that is just—if I wish". And he continued to oppose the whole sex in his poetry. (Di.) Quite absurdly! For why is it more reasonable to blame women because of a seduced woman than men because of the man who seduced her? As Socrates said, the same vices and virtues are to be found in both.'

At first he tried to dissuade her, and when he couldn't convince her, he left his wife to Cephisophon. [95] Aristophanes too refers to this: 'O best and darkest Cephisophon, you lived with Euripides in a lot of ways, and you wrote his poetry (so they say) along with him' [fr. 580]. [100] They also say that women lay in ambush for him at the Thesmophoria because of his criticisms of them in his poetry.[12] They wanted to destroy him, but they spared him first because of the Muses and then because he promised never again to say anything bad about them. For example, [105] this is what he said about women in the *Melanippe*: 'In vain men shoot their criticism at women. The bow twangs and misses. Women—I say—are better than men!' [fr. 499 N] and so on. Philemon was so devoted to Euripides that he dared to say the following of him: [110] 'If it's true the dead have feeling, as some men say, then I would hang myself so I could see Euripides' [fr. 130 Kock].

Euripides was the son of Mnesarchides. He was an Athenian. The writers of Old Comedy made fun of him in their plays by calling him the son of a woman who sold vegetables. [115] Some say that at first he was a painter but that after he had studied with Archelaus the natural philosopher and with Anaxagoras he started to write tragedies. For this reason presumably he was also somewhat arrogant and kept away from ordinary people and had no interest in appealing to his audiences. [120] This practice hurt him as much as it helped Sophocles. The comic poets too attacked him and tore him to pieces in their envy.

He disregarded all this and went away to Macedonia to the

---

[12] Cf. Satyr. fr. 39 col. x: 'Everyone disliked him, the men because of his unsociableness, the women because of the censures in his poems. And he incurred great danger from both sexes, for he was prosecuted by Cleon the demagogue in the action for impiety mentioned above, while the women combined against him at the Thesmophoria and collected in a body at the place where he happened to be resting. But notwithstanding their anger they spared the man, partly out of respect for the Muses . . .'; fr. 39 col. xi: (a long quotation about women from Euripides' *Melanippe*; the lines quoted in the *Vita* are not included in the surviving papyrus); fr. 39 col. xii: (several lines quoted from Ar. *Thesm.* 374–75, 335–37, parodying the style of a decree) '". . . Lysilla was the secretary, Sostrate proposed it". "If there be a man who is plotting against the womenfolk or who, to injure them, is proposing peace to Euripides and to the Medes . . .".'

court of King Archelaus,[13] and when he was returning there late one evening he was killed by the king's dogs. He began to produce dramas around the eighty-first Olympiad, when Calliades was archon.

[125] Because he used the middle style he excelled in expression and used reasoning perfectly on either side. In his lyric poetry he was inimitable, and he elbowed virtually all the other lyric poets aside.[14] But in dialogue he was wordy and vulgar and [130] irritating in his prologues, most rhetorical in his elaboration and clever in his phrasing and capable of demolishing previous arguments.

He wrote a total of ninety-two dramas, of which sixty-seven are extant and three in addition that are falsely attributed to him; also eight satyr plays, among these one that is falsely attributed to him. He won five victories.

## 6. THE LIFE OF ARISTOPHANES[1]

Aristophanes the comic poet's father was Philippus. His nationality was Athenian, from the deme of Kydathenaion, and from the tribe of Pandionis. It was he who first is thought to have transformed comedy—which was still wandering around in the old style—into something more useful and more respect-

---

[13] Cf. Satyr. fr. 39 col. xvii: 'These then, as I said, in their expression of views sought popular favour. He however, after putting in, so to speak, an obstructive plea, renounced Athens. (Di.) What was the plea? (A) It was entered in the following choral ode: "I have put wings of gold on my back, and the Sirens' winged sandals; lifted high into the wide upper air, I shall go to Zeus . . ."' [fr. 911 N]; fr. 39 col. xviii: '. . . began the songs. Or do you not know that it is this that he says? (Di.) How then? (A) In saying "to mingle my flight with Zeus" he metaphorically designates the monarch and also magnifies the man's power. (Di.) What you say seems to me to be more subtle than true. (A) Take it as you like. Anyhow, he migrated and spent his old age in Macedonia, being held in much honour by the sovereign; and in particular the story is told that . . .'

[14] Cf. Satyr. fr. 8: '. . . in emulation of the beauties of Ion, he developed and perfected [tragedy] so as to leave no room for improvement to his successors. Such were the man's artistic qualities. Hence Aristophanes wishes to measure his tongue "by which such fine expressions were polished".'

[1] Ed. Koster, 1975.

able. Comedy had previously been spiteful and more shameful, because the poets Cratinus and Eupolis uttered more slander than was appropriate. Aristophanes was first also to demonstrate the manner of New Comedy in his *Cocalus*, a play Menander and Philemon took as starting point for their dramatic compositions.

Since he was very cautious at the start, all the more because he was gifted, he produced his first plays under the names of Callistratus and Philonides. Because of this Aristonymus [fr. 4] and Ameipsias [fr. 28] made fun of him, saying that (as in the proverb) he was born on the fourth day, to toil for other men. [11] Later on he entered the contests for himself.

He was in particular an enemy of Cleon the demagogue and wrote the *Knights* as an attack on him. In that comedy he exposes Cleon's thefts and his tyrannical nature, and since none of the costumers had the courage to make a mask of Cleon's face because they were too frightened, since Cleon acted like a tyrant, Aristophanes acted the part of Cleon, smearing his face with red dye, and was responsible for Cleon's being fined five talents by the *Knights*, as he says in the *Acharnians*:

> But one thing really made me happy: when I saw
> those five talents that Cleon vomited up. [5ff.]

[20] Aristophanes had become Cleon's enemy because Cleon had entered a lawsuit against him because of his being foreign, and because in his play the *Babylonians* Aristophanes criticised the elected magistrates while foreigners were present.

Some say that he was a foreigner himself, inasmuch as some say he was a Rhodian from Lindos, others that he was an Aeginetan, an assumption based on his having spent a considerable amount of time there or on his owning property there. According to other authorities it was that his father Philippus was an Aeginetan. Aristophanes absolved himself from these charges by wittily quoting Homer's lines:

> My mother says I'm his son, but I don't know myself.
> For no one knows his own father. [*Od.* 1.215f.]

When he was informed against a second and third time he also got off, [30] and now that his citizenship was established he won out over Cleon. As he says, 'I myself know how I was treated by Cleon' [*Ach.* 377], etc. He was held in high regard because he got rid of the informers, whom he called Fevers in the *Wasps*, where he says 'they strangle their [?] fathers at night and choke their grandfathers' [1038–9].

People praised and liked him particularly because of his determination to show in his dramas that the government of Athens was free and not enslaved by any tyrant, and that it was a democracy and that since they were free, the people ruled themselves. [40] For this reason he won praise and a crown of sacred olive, which was considered equal in worth to a golden crown, when he spoke in the *Frogs* about the men who had been deprived of their rights:

> it is just that the sacred chorus give the city
> much good advice. [686ff.]

The metre called Aristophanean was named after him, since he was well known. The poet's fame was so great that it was known in Persia, and the king of the Persians asked whose side the comic poet was on. There is also the story that when Dionysius the tyrant wanted to learn about Athens' government, Plato sent Aristophanes' poetry and advised him to learn about their government by studying Aristophanes' dramas. [50] He was imitated by the writers of New Comedy, I mean Philemon and Menander. When the decree about *chorēgoi* was passed that no one could be ridiculed by name and the *chorēgoi* were no longer rich enough to provide subsidies to train choruses, and because of these measures the substance of comedy had been completely removed (the purpose of comedy being to ridicule people), Aristophanes wrote the *Cocalus* in which he introduces seduction and recognition and other such events, which Menander especially likes. When once again the subsidies for training choruses were taken away, Aristophanes, when he wrote the *Ploutos*, in order to give the actors in the scenes time to rest and to change, wrote 'for the chorus' in the directions, in the places where we see the poets of New Comedy writing in 'for the chorus' in emulation of Aristophanes.

In that drama he introduced his son Araros and so departed from life, [60] leaving three sons, Philippus (named after his grandfather), Nicostratus, and Araros. He mentions his children in these lines: 'I am ashamed before my wife and my helpless children' [fr. 588], perhaps meaning them. He wrote forty-four plays, of which it is alleged that four are spurious. These are *Poetry, The Shipwrecked Man, Islands,* [?] *Niobus*—which some authorities say are by Archippus.

### 7. PLATO AND ANTIMACHUS

Proclus mentions Callimachus' (fr. 589) and Duris' (*FGrHist* 76F83) approval of Plato's judgment of poetry in connection with an anecdote (once again) about Antimachus. Heraclides Ponticus (fr. 6 Wehrli) says he was sent by Plato to collect Antimachus' poetry (T1 Wyss), even though most people at the time preferred the work of Choerilus; Riginos 1976, 124. The poem Antimachus recited does not appear to have been the *Lydē*, because according to another anecdote, perhaps from the same original source, he obliterated the text after the recital, and was comforted by Plato; Riginos 1976, 125; Matthews 1979, 44–5.

Riginos suggests that Heraclides' story is probably true, since Heraclides was Plato's own pupil; 1976, 127. But statements that Heraclides was a *gnōrimos* of Plato (Suda = fr. 2 Wehrli) or Plato's *zēlōtēs* (D.L. v.86 = fr. 3 Wehrli) may (as in the case of Apollonius and Callimachus) only represent intellectual influence. In any case, being a contemporary or even a friend is no guarantee of accuracy; Ion of Chios' stories about Aeschylus and Sophocles are only meant to be representative of the poets' characters (pp. 67, 81 above).

Heraclides' anecdotes about poets also seem meant to represent characteristics; in order to make a general point he reports information not recorded elsewhere. e.g., that Socrates' mistreatment by the Athenians had precedents in Homer's being fined fifty drachmae for insanity, or Tyrtaeus being considered mad, and of their honouring Aeschylus' friend Astydamas (rather than Aeschylus) with a golden statue (fr.

169). He cites a lamentation about the death of Palamedes from Euripides' drama (fr. 588 N) in 'confirmation', much as a character in Satyrus' dialogue uses lines from a choral ode about flying on golden wings to show that Euripides was thinking of going to Macedonia (39 xvii; p. 169 n.13 above). Heraclides (fr. 170) also tells a story about Aeschylus being accused of profaning the Eleusinian mysteries, but being acquitted because his brother Cynegirus' hands were cut off and he himself had been wounded at Marathon. In 'confirmation' he cites an epitaph that mentions Aeschylus' courage but not his injuries or Cynegirus' at Marathon (*EG* 454ff.); he does not add that Cynegirus (at least according to Herodotus 6.114) was killed (p. 69 above). Like the story of Sophocles' quarrel with Iophon (pp. 84–5 above), the anecdote about Aeschylus and the mysteries appears to be based on a scene of comedy that made fun of the poet's interest in the cult of his home town (p. 68 above). Heraclides also wrote forgeries of Thespis' dramas; Gudeman 1894, 58–9.

Heraclides' story about Plato's championing of Antimachus (fr. 6) shows that the philosopher already as a young man had an interest in the narrative poetry that he later both employs and condemns in his writings (e.g., *Resp.* 10.607b). Like Homer, who is said to have visited Ithaca as a young man, Plato began his career by practising what he preached. Condensed and excerpted, the story could also be used *against* him; even the most persuasively articulated of Plato's doctrines were heavily satirised in antiquity. For example, there is Callimachus' epigram about how Cleombrotus was encouraged to commit suicide because of Plato's doctrine in the *Phaedo* of the immortality of the soul (*Epigr.* 23; Riginos 1976, 132; p. 99 n.54 above). Cf. the epigram for the atheist Hippon, finding immortality in death, 38B2 DK). Anecdotes of this sort offer the most insubstantial evidence about a writer's views of other writers. Since Proclus speaks only in general terms about Callimachus' disapproval of Plato's views on poetry, it is possible to *assume* that he considered them no more extensively than in an epigram or epigrams; his epigram for Aratus (27) is the source of the statement in Aratus' Vita that Aratus was a *zēlōtēs* of Hesiod (p. 131 n.56 above).

# Bibliography

The abbreviations used in the text appear in square brackets.

Allen, T. W. (ed.). 1912. *Homeri Opera*, v. Oxford. [Allen]

Allen, T. W. 1924. *Homer: the Origins and the Transmission*. Oxford.

Andrewes, A. 1938. 'Eunomia', *Classical Quarterly* 32: 89–102.

Arrighetti, G. 1964. *Satiro, Vita di Euripide* (Studi Classici e Orientali 13). Pisa.

Austin, C. (ed.). 1968. *Nova Fragmenta Euripidea*. Berlin. [Austin]

Austin, N. 1967. 'Idyll 16: Theocritus and Simonides', *Transactions of the American Philological Society* 98: 1–21.

Barlow, S. A. 1971. *The Imagery of Euripides*. London.

Bell, J. 1978. 'Simonides in the anecdotal tradition', *Quaderni Urbinati di Cultura Classica* 28: 29–86.

Benton, S. 1969. 'Pet weasels: Theocritus xv.28', *Classical Review* 19: 260–2.

Bieler, L. 1935. *Theios Aner: das Bild des göttlichen Menschen in Spätantike und Frühchristentum*. Vienna.

Boardman, J. 1975. *Athenian Red Figure Vases*. London.

Brecht, R. 1931. *Motiv und Typengeschichte des griechischen Spottepigrams* (Philologus Suppl. 22).

Brelich, A. 1958. *Gli eroi greci*. Rome.

Brink, K. O. 1946. 'Callimachus and Aristotle', *Classical Quarterly* 40: 1–26. [Brink]

Buck, C. D. 1933. *Comparative Grammar of Greek and Latin*. Chicago.

Bulloch, A. W. 1977. 'Callimachus' Erysichthon, Homer, and Apollonius Rhodius', *American Journal of Philology* 98: 97–123.

Bulloch, A. W. 1981. *Callimachus' Hymn to Athena*. Cambridge.

Bundy, E. L. 1962. *Studia Pindarica* (University of California Publications in Classical Philology 1, 2: 1–92).

Burkert, W. 1969. 'Das Prooimium des Parmenides', *Phronesis* 14: 1–30.

Burkert, W. 1972. *Homo Necans*. Berlin.

Burkert, W. 1972b. 'Die Leistung eines Kreophylus', *Museum Helveticum* 29: 74–85.

Burkert, W. 1977. *Griechische Religion der archaischen und klassischen Epoche*. Stuttgart.

Burkert, W. 1979. 'Kynaithos, Polycrates, and the Homeric Hymn to Apollo', *Arktouros* (Festschrift B.M.W. Knox), 53–61. Berlin.

Cadoux, T. J. 1948. 'The Athenian Archons from Kreon to Hypsichides', *Journal of Hellenic Studies* 68: 70–123.

Calame, C. 1977. *Les Choeurs de jeunes filles en Grèce archaique.* Urbino.

Calder, W. M. 1974. 'Kalamis Atheniensis', *Greek, Roman, and Byzantine Studies* 15: 274.

Calder, W. M. and Kopff, E. C. 'The student-teacher topos in biographical fiction', *Classical Philology* 72: 53–4.

Chroust, A.-H. 1973. *Aristotle: New Light on his Life and Some of his Lost Works.* London.

Clausen, W. 1964. 'Callimachus and Latin poetry', *Greek, Roman, and Byzantine Studies* 5: 181–96.

Clayman, D. L. 1977. 'The origins of Greek literary criticism and the Aetia prologue', *Wiener Studien* 11: 27–34.

Coldstream, J. N. 1976. 'Hero-cults in the age of Homer', *Journal of Hellenic Studies* 96: 8–17.

Cook, J. M. 1951. 'Archaeology in Greece', *Journal of Hellenic Studies* 71: 245–6.

Couat, A. 1931. *Alexandrian Poetry*, tr. J. Loeb. London.

Coulon, V. and Van Daele, H. 1972–3. *Aristophane* (ed. Budé). Paris.

Crow, M. M. and Olson, C. C. (eds). 1966. *Chaucer Life Records.* Austin/Oxford.

Davies, J. K. 1971. *Athenian Propertied Families.* Oxford.

Davison, J. A. 1968. *From Archilochus to Pindar.* London: 196–225.

Degani, E. 1973. 'Note sulla fortuna di Archiloco in epoca ellenistica', *Quaderni Urbinati di Cultura Classica* 16: 79–104.

Delcourt, M. 1933. 'Les Biographies anciennes d'Euripide', *Antiquité Classique* 2: 271–290.

den Boer, W. 1968. 'Graeco-roman historiography', *History and Theory* 7: 60–75.

den Boer, W. 1969. 'Theseus: the growth of a myth in history', *Greece and Rome* 16: 1–13.

Detienne, M. and Vernant, J.-P. 1978. *Cunning Intelligence in Greek Culture and Society.* London.

Devereux, G. 1976. *Dreams in Greek Tragedy.* Berkeley.

Dick, O. L. 1972. *Aubrey's Brief Lives.* Harmondsworth.

Dickie, M. 1978. 'The argument and form of Simonides 542 *PMG*', *Harvard Studies in Classical Philology* 82: 21–33.

Diels, H. and Kranz, W. (eds). 1954. *Die Fragmente der Vorsokratiker.* Berlin. [DK]

Dihle, A. 1977. 'Die Satyrspiele "Sisyphos" ', *Hermes* 105: 28–42.

Dihle, A. 1956. *Studien zur griechischen Biographie* (Abhandlungen der Akademie der Wissenschaften in Göttingen, Phil.-Hist. Klasse III.37).

Dillon, J. 1978. Review of Rosenthal 1969 in *Journal of the American Oriental Society* 98: 483–4.

Dilts, M. R. (ed.). 1971. *Heraclidis Lembi Excerpti Politiarum* (*Greek, Roman, and Byzantine Monograph* 5) Durham.

Dodds, E. R. 1960. *Euripides, Bacchae* (2nd ed.). Oxford.

Dodds, E. R. 1965. *Pagan and Christian in an Age of Anxiety*. Cambridge.

Dover, K. J. 1957. 'The political aspect of Aeschylus' *Eumenides*', *Journal of Hellenic Studies* 77: 233–5.

Dover, K. J. 1967. 'Portrait masks in Aristophanes', *Komoidotragemata* (Studia Aristophanea . . . W.J.W. Koster in honorem): 16–28.

Dover, K. J. 1972. *Aristophanic Comedy*. Berkeley.

Dover, K. J. 1973. *Thucydides* (*Greece and Rome* Survey 7). Oxford.

Dover, K. J. 1974. *Greek Popular Morality in the Time of Plato and Aristotle*. Oxford.

Dover, K. J. 1976. 'The freedom of the intellectual in Greek society', *Talanta* 7: 24–54.

Dover, K. J. 1977. 'Ancient interpolations in Aristophanes', *Illinois Classical Studies* 2: 136–62.

Dover, K. J. 1978. *Greek Homosexuality*. London.

Dover, K. J. 1980. *Plato, Symposium*. Cambridge.

Dow, S. 1969. 'Some Athenians in Aristophanes', *American Journal of Archaeology* 73: 234–5.

Drachmann, A. B. 1964 [1903]. *Scholia Vetera in Pindari Carmina*. Leipzig. [Dr]

Düring, I. 1941. *Herodicus the Cratetean: A Study in the Anti-Platonic Tradition* (Kungliga Vitterhets Historie och Antikvitets Akademiens Handlingar, Del. 51–2) Stockholm.

Düring, I. 1957. *Aristotle in the Biographical Tradition* (Studia Graeca et Latina Gothoburgensia 5). Göteborg.

Easterling, P. E. 1978. 'The Second Stasimon of the Antigone', *Dionysiaca: Nine Studies in Greek Poetry* (Festschrift D. Page) Cambridge: 141–58.

Edelstein, L. 1966. *Plato's Seventh Letter*. Leiden.

Eichgrün, E. 1961. *Kallimachos und Apollonios Rhodios*. Berlin.

Eisenhut, W. 1958. *Dictyis Cretensis Ephimeridos Belli Troiani Libri*. Leipzig. [Eisenhut]

Evelyn-White, H. G. 1914. *Hesiod, The Homeric Hymns and Homerica*. London.

Fairweather, J. 1973. 'The Death of Heraclitus', *Greek, Roman, and Byzantine Studies* 14: 233–9.

Fairweather, J. 1974. 'Fiction in the biographies of Ancient Writers', *Ancient Society* 5: 234–55.

Farnell, L. R. 1896–1909. *The Cults of the Greek States*. Oxford.

Farnell, L. R. 1921. *Greek Hero Cults*. Oxford.

Fehling, D. 1971. *Die Quellenangaben bei Herodot: Studien zur Erzählkunst Herodots* (Untersuchungen zur antiken Literatur und Geschichte 9) Berlin.

Fehling, D. 1979. 'Zwei Lehrstücke über Pseudo-Nachrichten (1. Die Homeriden)', *Rheinisches Museum* 122: 193–9.

Finley, J. H. 1967. *Three Essays on Thucydides*. Cambridge, Mass.

Finley, M. I. 1965. 'Myth, memory, and history', *History and Theory* 4: 281–302.

Finley, M. I. 1975. 'The Ancestral constitution', *The Use and Abuse of History*, 34–59. London.

Fontenrose, J. 1978. *The Delphic Oracle*. Berkeley.

Fornara, C. W. 1971. *Herodotus: an Interpretive Essay*. Oxford.

Fornara, C. W. 1977. *Archaic Times to the End of the Peloponnesian War*. Baltimore.

Fraenkel, E. 1950. *Aeschylus, Agamemnon*. Oxford.

Fraenkel, E. 1957. *Horace*. Oxford.

Fränkel, H. 1975. *Early Greek Poetry and Philosophy*. New York.

Fraser, P. 1972. *Ptolemaic Alexandria*. Oxford.

Freeman, K. (tr.) 1957. *Ancilla to the Presocratic Philosophers*. Cambridge, Mass.

Friedel, O. 1879. *Die Sage vom Tode Hesiods* (Jahrbüch für cl. Philol. Suppl. 10). 236–78. Leipzig.

Friedländer, P. 1969. *Studien zur antiken Literatur und Kunst*. Berlin: 237–9.

Friis Johansen, H. 1962. 'Sophocles 1939–1959', *Lustrum* 7: 109–12.

Gabathuler, M. 1937. *Hellenistische Epigramme auf Dichter*. Basel.

Gallo, I. 1968. *Una nuova biografia di Pindaro*. Salerno.

Gallo, I. 1967. 'La *vita di Euripide* di Satiro e gli studi sulla biografia antica', *La Parola del Passato* 113: 134–60.

Gallo, I. 1974. 'L'origine e lo sviluppo della biografia greca', *Quaderni Urbinati di Cultura Classica* 18: 173–86.

Gallo, I. 1976. 'Solone a Soli', *Quaderni Urbinati di Cultura Classica* 21: 29–36.

Gay, P. 1974. *Style in History*. New York.

Gelzer, T. 1970. 'Aristophanes', Nachträge zu *Real-Encyclopaedie* Suppl. xii: 1395–402.

Gentili, B. and Prato, C. 1979. *Poetarum Elegiacorum Testimonia et Fragmenta*. Leipzig. [GPr]

Giangrande, G. 1967. '"Arte Allusiva" and Alexandrian Epic Poetry', *Classical Quarterly* 17: 85–97.

Giangrande, G. 1974. 'Kallimachos und Antimachos', *Hermes* 92: 117–19.

Gill, C. 1973. 'The death of Socrates', *Classical Quarterly* 23: 25–8.

Gomme, A. W. and Sandbach, F. H. 1973. *Menander, A Commentary*. Oxford.

Gow, A. S. F. 1950. *Theocritus*. Cambridge.

Gow, A. S. F. and Page, D. L. 1965. *The Greek Anthology: Hellenistic Epigrams*. Cambridge. [GP]

Gow, A. S. F. 1967. 'Mousers in Egypt', *Classical Quarterly* 17: 195–7.

Gow, A. S. F. and Page, D. 1968. *The Garland of Philip*. Cambridge.

Graham, A. J. 1978. 'The Foundation of Thasos', *British School Annual* 73: 61–98.

Greene, W. C. 1938. *Scholia Platonica* (American Philological Assoc. Monographs 8). Haverford. [Greene]

Greenewalt, C. H. 1978. *Ritual Dinners in Early Historic Sardis* (California Publications in Classical Studies 17). Berkeley.

Griffin, J. 1977. 'The Epic Cycle and the uniqueness of Homer', *Journal of Hellenic Studies* 97: 39–53.

Griffith, M. 1977. *The Authenticity of 'Prometheus Bound'*. Cambridge.

Grilli, A. 1978. 'Ennius Podager', *Rivista di Filologia e di Istruzione Classica* 106: 34–8.

Gronewald, M. 1974. 'Fragmente aus einem Sapphokommentar: Pap. Colon. inv. 5860', *Zeitschrift für Papyrologie und Epigraphik* 14: 114–16.

Gudeman, A. 1894. 'Literary frauds among the Greeks', *Classical Studies in Honor of H. Drisler*. New York: 52–74.

Habicht, C. 1961. 'Falsche Urkunden zur Geschichte Athens im Zeitalter der Perser Kriege', *Hermes* 89: 1–35.

Halliwell, S. 1980. 'Aristophanes' apprenticeship', *Classical Quarterly* 30: 33–45.

Hammond, N. G. L. 1959. *A History of Greece*. Oxford.

Harding, P. 1976. 'Androtion's political career', *Historia* 25: 186–200.

Hartmann, A. 1917. *Untersuchungen über die Sagen vom Tod des Odysseus*. Munich.

Haslam, M. 1978. 'The versification of the new Stesichorus', *Greek, Roman, and Byzantine Studies* 19: 29–57.

Haslam, M. 1978b. 'Apollonius of Rhodes and the Papyri', *Illinois Classical Studies* 3: 47–73.

Heiserman, A. 1977. *The Novel before the Novel*. Chicago.

Henrichs, A. 1972. 'Toward a new edition of Philodemus "On Piety"'. *Greek, Roman, and Byzantine Studies* 13: 72–6.

Henrichs, A. 1979. 'Callimachus *Epigram* 28: a fastidious priamel', *Harvard Studies in Classical Philology* 83: 207–12.

Hercher, R. 1873. *Epistolographi graeci*. Leipzig.

Herter, H. 1973. 'Kallimachos', *Real-Encyclopaedie* Suppl. xiii: 184–226.

Herter, H. 1975. 'Böse Dämonen im frühgriechischen Volksglauben', *Kleine Schriften*, 45–7. Munich.

Hess, K. 1960. *Der Agon zwischen Homer und Hesiod* (diss. Zürich) Winterthur.

Hignett, C. 1952. *A History of the Athenian Constitution*. Oxford.

Hiller, E. 1872. *Eratosthenis Carminum Reliquiae*. Leipzig.

Homeyer, H. 1962. 'Zu den Anfängen der griechischen Biographie', *Philologus* 106: 75–85.

Housman, A. E. 1972. *Classical Papers*. Cambridge.

How, W. W. and Wells, J. 1912. *A Commentary on Herodotus*. Oxford.

Humphreys, S. C. 1978. *Anthropology and the Greeks*. London.

Huxley, G. 1974. 'Aristotle's interest in biography', *Greek, Roman, and Byzantine Studies* 15: 203–13.

Jacoby, F. 1912. 'Hellanikos', *RE* viii 104–53 = *Griechische Historiker* 263–87.

Jacoby, F. 1933. 'Homerisches', *Hermes* 68: 1–50. ( = *Kleine Philologische Schriften* 11–53).

Jacoby, F. 1949. *Atthis*. Oxford.

Jacoby, F. 1959. 'Diagoras *ho atheos*', *Abhandlungen der deutschen Akademie der Wissenschaften zu Berlin*, Sprach., Lit., Kunst Klasse 3.

Jaeger, W. 1934. *Aristotle: Fundamentals of the History of his Development*. Oxford.

Jaeger, W. 1965. *Paideia*, tr. G. Highet. New York.

Jameson, M. 1971. 'Sophocles and the Four Hundred', *Historia* 22: 533–41.

Kambylis, A. 1965. *Die Dichterweihe und ihre Symbolik*. Heidelberg.

Kassel, R. 1966. 'Kritische und exegetische Kleinigkeiten §15'. *Rheinisches Museum* 109: 8–10.

Kassel, R. 1979. 'Ein neues Philemonfragment', *Zeitschrift für Papyrologie und Epigraphik* 36: 15–21.

Kirk, G. S. and Raven, J. E. 1957. *The Presocratic Philosophers*. Cambridge.
Kirk, G. S. 1973. 'Methodological reflexions on the myths of Heracles', *Il Mito Greco*. Urbino: 285–97.
Knox, B. M. W. 1964. *The Heroic Temper: Studies in Sophoclean Tragedy*. Berkeley.
Knox, B. M. W. 1979. 'Aeschylus and the third actor', *Word and Action*. Baltimore.
Kock, T. 1976 [1880]. *Comicorum Atticorum Fragmenta*. Leipzig. [Kock]
Koerte, A. and Thierfelder, A. 1952. *Menandri quae supersunt*[2], vol. II. Leipzig. [K-Th]
Koster, W. J. W. 1975. Scholia in Aristophanem I. 1a. Groningen. [Koster]
Kuchenmüller, G. 1928. *Philetae Coi Reliquiae*. Baden. [Kuchenmüller]
Kumaniecki, C. F. 1929. *De Satyro Peripatetico*. Krakow.
Kurtz, D. and Boardman, J. 1971. *Greek Burial Customs*. London.
Lattimore, R. 1939. 'The Wise Advisor in Herodotus', *Classical Philology* 34: 24–35.
Leach, E. 1970. *Claude Lévi-Strauss*. New York.
Lefkowitz, M. R. 1973. 'Critical stereotypes and the poetry of Sappho', *Greek, Roman, and Byzantine Studies* 14: 113–23.
Lefkowitz, M. R. 1975. 'Pindar's Lives', *Classica et Iberica* (Festschrift Marique) Worcester, Mass.: 71–93.
Lefkowitz, M. R. 1975b. 'The influential fictions in the scholia to Pindar's *Pythian 8*', *Classical Philology* 70: 173–85.
Lefkowitz, M. R. 1976. *The Victory Ode: An Introduction*. Park Ridge.
Lefkowitz, M. R. 1976b. 'Fictions in literary biography: the new poem and the Archilochus legend', *Arethusa* 9: 181–9.
Lefkowitz, M. R. 1977. Review of Devereux 1976 in *American Journal of Philology* 98: 305–7.
Lefkowitz, M. R. 1978. 'The poet as hero: fifth-century autobiography and subsequent biographical fiction', *Classical Quarterly* 28: 1–11.
Lefkowitz, M. R. 1979. 'The Euripides *Vita*', *Greek, Roman, and Byzantine Studies* 20: 187–210. Reprinted here as Chapter 9.
Lefkowitz, M. R. 1980. 'Autobiographical fiction in Pindar'. *Harvard Studies in Classical Philology* 84: 29–49.
Lefkowitz, M. R. 1980b. 'The quarrel between Callimachus and Apollonius', *Zeitschrift für Papyrologie und Epigraphik*. Reprinted here as Chapter 11.
Lehnus, L. 1977. 'Scopelino "Padre" di Pindaro'. *Rendiconti del Istituto Lombardo*, Classe di Lettere 3: 78–82.
Lehnus, L. 1979. *L'inno a Pan di Pindaro*. (*Testi d Documenti per lo Studio dell' Antichità*). Milan.
Leo, F. 1901. *Die Griechisch-Römische Biographie*. Leipzig.
Leo, F. 1912. 'Satyros, *Bios Euripidou*', *Ausgewählte Kleine Schriften* Rome (1960): II 365–82.
Lesky, A. 1966. 'Die Maske des Thamyris', *Gesammelte Schriften*. Bern.
Lesky, A. 1966b. *A History of Greek Literature*. New York.
Lesky, A. 1972. *Die Tragische Dichtung der Hellenen* (3rd ed.). Göttingen.
Lévi-Strauss, C. 1968. 'The structural study of myth', *Myth: A Symposium*, ed. T. Sebeok. Bloomington.

Levy, E. 1976. *Athènes devant la défaite de 404* (Bibl. des Écoles françaises d'Athènes et de Rome 225). Paris.

Livrea, E. 1973. *Argonauticon Liber IV*. Florence.

Lloyd-Jones, H. 1964. 'The "Supplices" of Aeschylus: the new date and old problems', *Antiquité Classique* 33: 356–74.

Lloyd-Jones, H. 1966. 'Problems of early Greek tragedy: Pratinas, Phrynichus, and the Gyges fragment', *Estudios sobre la tragedia griega*. Madrid: 11–33.

Lloyd-Jones, H. 1971. *The Justice of Zeus*. Berkeley.

Lloyd-Jones, H. 1973. 'Stasinus and the Cypria', *Stasinos* 4: 115–22.

Lloyd-Jones, H. 1973b. 'Modern interpretation of Pindar: the Second Pythian and Seventh Nemean Odes', *Journal of Hellenic Studies* 93: 109–37.

Loeffler, I. 1963. *Die Melampodie*. Meisenheim.

Macleod, C. W. 1976. 'Callimachus, Virgil, Propertius, and Lollius', *Zeitschrift für Papyrologie und Epigraphik* 23: 41–2.

Macleod, C. W. 1979. 'Horatian imitatio and *Ode* 2.5', *Creative Imitation in Latin Literature*, ed. D. West and T. Woodman. Cambridge.

Martin, J. 1974. *Scholia in Aratum Vetera*. Leipzig. [Martin]

Martina, A. 1968. *Solon: testimonia veterum*. Rome. [M]

Matthews, V. J. 1979. 'Antimachean anecdotes', *Eranos* 77: 43–50.

McKay, K. J. 1959. 'Hesiod's rejuvenation', *Classical Quarterly* 9: 1–5.

Mehmel, F. 1940. *Virgil und Apollonios Rhodios* (Hamburger Arbeit zur Altertumswissenschaft 1).

Mejer, J. 1978. *Diogenes Laertius and his Hellenistic Background* (Hermes Einzelschriften 40). Wiesbaden.

Méridier, L. 1925. *Euripide*, vol. 1. Paris. [Méridier]

Merkelbach, R. and West, M. L. (eds). 1967. *Fragmenta Hesiodea*. Oxford. [MW]

Milobenski, E. 1964. *Der Neid in der griechischen Philosophie* (Klass.-philo. Studien 29). Wiesbaden.

Misch, G. 1951. *A History of Autobiography*. Cambridge, Mass.

Momigliano, A. 1971. *The Development of Greek Biography*. Cambridge, Mass.

Momigliano, A. 1971b. 'Second thoughts on Greek biography', *Meded. d. Kon. Ned. Akad. v. Wet. Afd. Lett.*, *Nieuwe Reeks* 34: 245–56.

Momigliano, A. 1972. 'Tradition and the Classical historian', *History and Theory* 11: 282–6.

Murray, O. 1980. *Early Greece*. London.

Nägelsbach, K. F. V. 1884. *Homerische Theologie* (3rd ed.). Nuremberg.

Nagy, G. 1973. 'Phaethon, Sappho's Phaon, and the white rock of Leucas', *Harvard Studies in Classical Philology* 77: 141–3.

Nagy, G. 1979. *The Best of the Achaeans*. Baltimore.

Nauck, A. 1889, *Tragicorum Graecorum Fragmenta*. Leipzig. [N]

Nestle, W. 1898. 'Die Legende vom Tode des Euripides', *Philologus* 57: 134–49.

Nilsson, M. P. 1906. *Griechische Feste*. Leipzig.

Nilsson, M. P. 1961. *Greek Folk Religion*. New York.

Nilsson, M. P. 1967. *Geschichte der griechischen Religion* (3rd ed.). Munich.

Nisbet, R. G. M. 1961. *Cicero In Pisonem*. Oxford.

Nisbet, R. G. M. and Hubbard, M. 1978. *A Commentary on Horace, Odes Book II.* Oxford.

Nisetich, F. J. 1977. 'The leaves of triumph and mortality', *Transactions of the American Philological Association* 107: 235–64.

Noble, J. V. 1965. *The Techniques of Attic Painted Pottery.* New York.

Ostwald, M. 1969. *Nomos and the Beginnings of Athenian Democracy.* Oxford.

Owen, A. S. 1936. 'The date of Sophocles' Electra', *Greek Poetry and Life.* Oxford: 148–9.

Padel, R. 1974. 'The Imagery of the Elsewhere', *Classical Quarterly* 24: 227–41.

Page, D. L. 1953. *Corinna* (Society for Promotion of Hellenic Studies, Suppl. Paper 6).

Page, D. L. 1955. *Sappho and Alcaeus.* Oxford.

Page, D. L. 1962. *Poetae Melici Graeci.* Oxford. [*PMG*]

Page, D. L. 1972. *Aeschyli Tragoediae.* Oxford. [Page]

Page, D. L. 1974. *Supplementum Lyricis Graecis.* Oxford. [*SLG*]

Page, D. L. 1975. *Epigrammata Graeca.* Oxford. [*EG*]

Parnell, T. 1715. 'An essay on the life, writings, and learning of Homer', *The Iliad of Homer*, tr. A. Pope, 1–55. London.

Parsons, P. 1977. 'Callimachus: Victoria Berenices', *Zeitschrift für Papyrologie und Epigraphik* 25: 1–50.

Pascal, R. 1960. *Design and Truth in Autobiography.* Cambridge, Mass.

Passow, F. 1912. *Handwörterbuch der griechischen Sprache*, rev. W. Crönert. Leipzig.

Pearson, A. C. 1928. *Sophoclis Fabulae.* Oxford. [Pearson]

Perry, B. E. 1952. *Aesopica* Urbana. [Perry]

Perry, B. E. 1967. *The Ancient Romances.* Berkeley.

Pfeiffer, R. 1949–53. *Callimachus.* Oxford. [Pf]

Pfeiffer, R. 1960 [1928]. 'Ein neues Altersgedicht des Kallimachos', *Ausgewählte Schriften.* Munich. 98–132.

Pfeiffer, R. 1968. *A History of Classical Scholarship*, 1. Oxford.

Pickard-Cambridge, A. W. 1968. *The Dramatic Festivals of Athens* (2nd ed., eds J. Gould and D. M. Lewis). Oxford.

Podlecki, A. J. 1969. 'The Peripatetics as literary critics', *Phoenix* 23: 114–37.

Podlecki, A. J. 1979. 'Simonides in Sicily', *La Parola del Passato* 34: 5–16.

Powell, J. U. 1925. *Collectanea Alexandrina.* Oxford. [Powell]

Radt, S. 1977. *Tragicorum Graecorum Fragmenta*, vol. IV: *Sophocles.* Göttingen. [Radt]

Rankin, H. D. 1977. *Archilochus of Paros.* Park Ridge.

Rankin, H. D. 1978. 'The New Archilochus', *Quaderni Urbinati di Cultura Classica* 28: 7–27.

Renehan, R. 1971. 'The Michigan Alcidamas Papyrus', *Harvard Studies in Classical Philology* 75: 85–105.

Richardson, N. J. 1975. 'Homeric professors in the age of the Sophists', *Proceedings of the Cambridge Philological Society* 21: 63–81.

Richardson, N. J. 1979. Review of West 1978 in *Journal of Hellenic Studies* 99: 171.

Richardson, N. J. 1981. 'The Contest of Homer and Hesiod and Alcidamas' Mouseion', *Classical Quarterly* 31: 1–10.

Riginos, Alice Swift. 1976. *Platonica: The Anecdotes concerning the Life and Writings of Plato* (Columbia Studies in the Classical Tradition 3). Leiden.

Roberts, W. R. (ed.). 1901. *Dionysius of Halicarnassus: the Three Literary Letters.* Cambridge.

Robertson, D. S. 1923. 'Cleon and the Assembly', *Classical Review* 37: 165.

Rose, H. J. 1931. 'The Epigram on Pindar's death', *Classical Quarterly* 25: 121–2.

Rose, V. 1886. *Aristotelis Fragmenta.* Leipzig. [Rose]

Rosenthal, F. 1969. *The Classical Heritage in Islam.* Berkeley.

Rossi, L. E. 1968. 'La Fine Alessandrina dell' Odissea e lo *Zelos Homerikos* di Apollonio Rodio', *Rivista italiani di filologica classica* 98: 151–63.

Ruck, C. P. 1976. 'Euripides' Mother: Vegetables and the Phallos in Aristophanes', *Arion* NS 2: 13–57.

Ruschenbusch, E. 1966. *Solonos Nomoi* (Historia Einzelschrift 9). Wiesbaden.

Russell, D. A. 1973. *Plutarch.* London.

Russell, D. A. 1979. 'De imitatione', *Creative Imitation in Latin Literature*, ed. D. West and T. Woodman. Cambridge.

Saller, R. 1980. 'Anecdotes as historical evidence for the Principate', *Greece and Rome* 27: 69–83.

Sanctis, G. de. 1898. *Atthis.* Florence (1975).

Sandbach, F. H. 1967. *Plutarchi Fragmenta.* Leipzig. [Sandbach]

Schadewaldt, W. 1959. *Legende von Homer dem Fahrenden Singer.* Zürich.

Schoeck, H. 1970. *Envy.* New York.

Schoenbaum, S. 1970. *Shakespeare's Lives.* Oxford.

Scodel, R. 1981. 'Hesiod Redivivus', *Greek, Roman and Byzantine Studies* 21: 301–20.

Skiadas, A. D. 1965. *Homer im Griechischen Epigramm.* Athens.

Slater, W. J. 1971. 'Pindar's House', *Greek, Roman, and Byzantine Studies* 12: 141–52.

Slater, W. J. 1972. 'Simonides' house', *Phoenix* 26: 232–40.

Snell, B. 1938. *Leben und Meinungen der Sieben Weisen.* Munich.

Snell, B. 1966. 'Zur Geschichte vom Gastmahl der Sieben Weisen', *Gesammelte Schriften.* Göttingen: 115–18.

Snyder, J. M. 1974. 'Aristophanes' Agathon as Anacreon', *Hermes* 102: 243–6.

Speyer, W. H. 1971. *Die literarische Fälschung im heidnischen und christlichen Altertum* (Handbuch der Altertumswissenschaft I. 2).

Stanford, W. B. 1963. *Aristophanes, The Frogs.* London.

Stemplinger, E. 1912. *Das Plagiat in der griechischen Literatur.* Berlin.

Stevens, P. T. 1956. 'Euripides and the Athenians', *Journal of Hellenic Studies* 76: 87–94.

Stillwell, R., MacDonald, W. L., and McAllister, M. H. (eds). 1976. *The Princeton Encyclopedia of Classical Sites.* Princeton.

Stroud, R. 1979. *The Axones and Kyrbeis of Drakon and Solon* (California Publications in Classical Studies 19). Berkeley.

Suerbaum, W. 1968. *Untersuchungen zu Selbstdarstellung älterer römischer Dichter*.
Svenbro, J. 1976. *La Parole et le marbre*. Lund.
Syme, R. 1968. *Ammianus and the Historia Augusta*. Oxford.
Syme, R. 1971. *Emperors and Biography: Studies in the Historia Augusta*. Oxford.
Syme, R. 1972. 'Fraud and Imposture', *Pseudepigrapha* I, *Entretiens Hardt* 18: 3–21.
Syme, R. 1979. 'The Patria of Juvenal', *Classical Philology* 74: 1–15.
Szegedy-Maszak, A. 1978. 'Legends of the Greek Lawgivers', *Greek, Roman, and Byzantine Studies* 19: 199–209.
Taplin, O. 1972. 'Aeschylean silences and silences in Aeschylus', *Harvard Studies in Classical Philology* 76: 57–97.
Taplin, O. 1977. *The Stagecraft of Aeschylus*. Oxford.
Tarán, L. 1965. *Parmenides*. Princeton.
Tarditi, G. 1968. *Archilochus: Fragmenta*. Rome. [T]
Trenkner, S. 1958. *The Greek Novella in the Classical Period*. Cambridge.
Vahlen, J. 1928. *Ennianae Paesis Reliquiae*. Leipzig [Vahlen]
Van Daele, *see* Coulon.
Vernant, J.-P. 1974. *Mythe et pensée chez les grecs*. Paris.
Vian, F. 1974. *Apollonius de Rhodes, Argonautiques* I–II. Paris.
Von der Mühll, P. 1975. 'Antiker Historismus in Plutarchs Biographie des Solon', *Kleine Schriften*. Basel: 328–43.
Walbank, F. 1957. *A Historical Commentary on Polybius*, vol. I. Oxford.
Webster, T. B. L. 1936. *An Introduction to Sophocles*. Oxford.
Webster, T. B. L. 1964. *Hellenistic Poetry and Art*. New York.
Webster, T. B. L. 1967. *The Tragedies of Euripides*. London.
Wehrli, F. 1967–9. *Die Schule des Aristoteles* (2nd ed.). Basel. [Wehrli]
Wehrli, F. 1973. 'Gnome, Anekdote, und Biographie', *Museum Helveticum* 30: 193–208.
Wehrli, F. 1974. *Hermippus der Kallimacheer* (*Die Schule des Aristoteles*, Suppl. 1) Basel.
Wendel, C. 1958 [1935]. *Scholia in Apollonium Rhodium Vetera*. Berlin. [Wendel]
West, M. L. 1964. 'The Muses buy a cow', *Classical Review* 14: 141–2.
West, M. L. 1966. *Hesiod, Theogony*. Oxford.
West, M. L. 1967. 'The Contest of Homer and Hesiod', *Classical Quarterly* 17: 433–50.
West, M. L. 1971. 'Stesichorus', *Classical Quarterly* 21: 302–14.
West, M. L. 1971b. *Iambi et Elegi Graeci*. Oxford. [W]
West, M. L. 1974. *Studies in Greek Elegy and Iambus*. Berlin.
West, M. L. 1978. *Hesiod, Works and Days*. Oxford.
West, S. 1966. Review of Arrighetti 1964. *Gnomon* 38: 546–50.
West, S. 1970. 'Chalcenteric negligence', *Classical Quarterly* 20: 288–96.
West, S. 1974. 'Satyrus: Peripatetic or Alexandrian', *Greek, Roman, and Byzantine Studies* 15 (1974) 279–86.
Wilamowitz-Moellendorff, U. von. 1895 [1969]. *Euripides Herakles* (2nd ed.). Darmstadt.

Wilamowitz-Moellendorff, U. von. 1914. *Aischylos, Interpretationen.* Berlin. [Wil; in Ch. 14]

Wilamowitz-Moellendorff, U. von. 1916. *Die Ilias und Homer.* Berlin.

Wilamowitz-Moellendorff, U. von. 1924. *Hellenistische Dichtung.* Berlin.

Wilamowitz-Moellendorff, U. von. 1929. *Vitae Homeri et Hesiodi.* Berlin. [Wil; in Chs 1 & 2]

Willcock, M. M. 1977. 'Ad hoc invention in the Iliad', *Harvard Studies in Classical Philology* 81: 41–53.

Williams, F. 1978. *Callimachus' Hymn to Apollo: A Commentary.* Oxford.

Winter, J. G. 1933. *Life and Letters in the Papyri.* Ann Arbor.

Woodbury, L. 1968. 'Pindar and the Mercenary Muse: *Isthm.* 2. 1–13', *Transactions of the American Philological Association* 99: 527–42.

Woodbury, L. 1970. 'Sophocles among the Generals', *Phoenix* 24: 209–24.

Woodbury, L. 1973. 'Socrates and Aristides' daughter', *Phoenix* 27: 7–25.

Wyss, B. 1936. *Antimachi Colophonii Reliquiae.* Berlin. [Wyss]

Ziegler, K. 1966. *Das Hellenistische Epos.* Leipzig.

Ziegler, K. 1950. 'Plagiat', *Real-Encyclopaedie* 20.2: 1956–97.

# Index